THE GOOD PARTY GUIDE

BY
HAZEL SHESTOPAL

Edited by Barry M Gallafent
Designed by Marwain Print Services Ltd
Cover design and colour illustrations by James Kessall
Original drawings by Keely Marie Blake

ISBN 0 905377 48 6

Printed and bound in England by
Grillford Ltd - Granby - Milton Keynes

Contents

Preface _____

The information shown in this book is the latest available at the time of compilation and may have altered before publication. Whilst every effort has been made to ensure accuracy, the author and publishers do not accept any liability for errors or omissions.

For future editions, I would be grateful to receive suggestions for possible entries in any of the categories, especially of any new venues that you may have discovered. I would like to hear from party givers as well as party services that would like to be considered for inclusion.

Please write to:

> The Good Party Guide
> Marwain House
> Clarke Road
> Mount Farm
> Milton Keynes
> MK1 1LG

I would like to extend my thanks to all the party experts who have submitted words of professional advice for the introductions to various sections of this book and to all the establishments, companies and individuals listed within, all of whom have contributed invaluably to it's compilation.

The success of any party depends on careful planning and scrupulous organization. The aim of The Good Party Guide is to take the headache out of the arrangements by guiding you through the minefield of party services available.

Every facet of party planning has been taken into consideration while compiling this book. The Good Party Guide is packed with ideas and inspiration, and is an indispensable source of information. It lists the names, addresses and details of people and establishments involved in one way or another with the party industry, all of whom offer a top class service. Although I have personally visited all the venues listed in the book (as well as several that are not), the descriptions of entries in the other categories were compiled mostly from information sent in by the companies concerned and not always from personal experience. However, all the entries have been recommended to me by a variety of sources, most commonly by venues where they have worked and left an impression. Where appropriate, I have included invaluable advice from the experts, written in their own words.

So, where should you start? Having decided loosely on the type of party you want, how many guests there will be and how much you are prepared to spend, there are several ways to start the 'ball' rolling. You could firstly choose the venue and let them either handle all the arrangements for the function or point you in the right direction to do it yourself. Or you could start with the caterer who will be able to suggest venues and again might be able to plan the entire event. Alternatively, you can go directly to professional party planners and allow them to stage manage every aspect from beginning to end, or just some of it. Occasionally, entertainment agencies, marquee companies, decorators and other services will also offer a party planning service. In fact, you can personally organise as much or as little as you like, as long as you remain involved to oversee that your party it exactly what you want and not just what the party planner thinks you should have.

Always insist on a written confirmation of all the relevant details of each booking. This ensures that there are no misunderstandings and provides a useful prompt if you subsequently amend any of your plans. Be certain to advise everyone concerned if you do make any changes. The Check List at the back of the book will help you to keep a record of your arrangements and make sure that no element has been overlooked.

Where possible, arrange for invoices to be sent after the event. If this is agreed beforehand, it will prevent you being called away from your guests abruptly at the end of your party to pay the caterer, staff, band and so on. If they insist on payment on the night, they should be prepared to wait until a suitable time for you to discreetly slip away, or perhaps your toastmaster will deal with the matter for you. But receiving an invoice a few days later will give you time to reflect on the event and add an appropriate gratuity if you were impressed with the service.

Ultimately though, it is the people that make the party - and that includes you. The professionals that you employ will be working to ensure that your guests enjoy themselves, but they will only feel comfortable if they see that you are too. If you are confident about the arrangements you've made and that you haven't overlooked anything vital - RELAX. It's too late once the party has begun to worry about what might go wrong. You have experts on hand to sort out any last minute hitches. If they can't, it is unlikely that you could do any better and more than likely no-one but you will ever notice that anything is other than perfect. So put any problems out of your mind and prepare to accept a barrage of compliments.

VENUES

Venues

The number of places that are available to hire for parties in London is enormous. In theory, you can hire almost anywhere, providing you have the resources. But good venues get booked up well in advance, sometimes as much as three years! So you will need to start thinking about where to have your party as early as possible, or risk disappointment. To find the most suitable venue for your particular needs, you should first ask yourself several questions:

How many guests will there be? Check the capacities of the venue according to the type of function it will be. I have included the maximum capacities for a banquet (sit-down dinner or luncheon), dinner dance (this often decreases the number in order to keep the dance floor free, though sometimes tables can moved after the meal), and reception (cocktail reception or finger/ fork buffet when guests will generally be standing throughout). The figures quoted are the recommended comfortable maximums. At some venues it is possible to increase these by using adjoining rooms or adding a marquee, but avoid the temptation to squeeze in more than the banqueting manager advises. Equally, you do not want to choose a venue that is so big that your guests will be looking for each other. Many venues can be made smaller using screens or room dividers.

What type of party will it be? A formal party might be better held in an elegant traditional or period setting, such as a livery hall or a stately home, while a theme party might require a specific style or even no style at all so that you could decorate it accordingly without any influence from the room's features. Some of the museums and tourist attractions are ideal settings for theme parties, requiring only the minimum of decorations or props. For a summer party, you might want to choose a venue which has a garden or terrace where your guests can enjoy a pre-dinner drink or cool down when the dancing gets hot. If you're planning a lively disco party, you might be looking for a more modern venue or a nightclub where the most up-to-date sound and lighting systems and special effects are already at hand.

Does it have to be in a specific area? If most of the guests will be coming from one side of London, it would seem a bit inconsiderate to choose a venue on the other. For weddings, you will proba- bly be looking for a venue not too far away from the church. Also, consider any parking difficulties that your guests might have attending a party in central London. Obviously mid-week, daytime parties will pose more of a problem than evenings and week-ends. Many venues have their own car parks or nearby NCPs and I have indicated this.

Do you want to be able to choose your own caterer? There are plenty of venues that will leave the choice of caterer entirely up to you, though they will be happy to offer suggestions. Otherwise, they might insist that you choose from a list of recommended caterers that have successfully worked at that venue in the past and so understand any difficulties or restrictions that there might be. Other venues might allow you to bring in outside caterers only for special dietary reasons, such as for kosher functions. In such cases, they might insist that you hire a kosher caterer with whom they have an exclusive arrangement. Sometimes, outside caterers are allowed to use the venue only on Sundays when the facilities would otherwise tend to be under-used. Some of the venues listed will occasionally allow in outside caterers in special circumstances, but do not advertise the fact, so it's always worth asking the banqueting manager. Be prepared, though, for hefty room charges.

Is having the party at home a possibility? If your home is suitable, or can be made suitable with the addition of a marquee, a party given at home will have an informal, warm and happy atmosphere, especially for family occasions. However it will need some thought beforehand to minimise wear and tear on both your home and your nerves. If the thought of hordes of people stampeding through your bedroom looking for the loo worries you, perhaps you should think again. Similarly, if you are tempted to ask your guests to wear slippers to protect your parquet floors from stilettos, then a party at home is not for you.

Having narrowed down the options, make appointments to visit several venues that are possibilities and compare them. If at all possible, visit when the room is set up for a function, or even while a function is in progress. You might want to take some photos while you are there, they will help you to recall the venue when you come to make your final decision.

8

Hotel banqueting suites come in all shapes, styles and sizes. You will be able to leave all the arrangements to the banqueting manager who will organise the food, drinks, cake and decorations, and quite often the entire event including the entertainment, toastmaster and photography. Holding the party in a hotel might be the answer if there are many out-of-town guests. Quite often the host and hostess and their guests will be offered preferential room rates. Look out for hidden charges though, such as room hire, corkage if you are taking in your own drinks, and possibly staff overtime if the party over-runs.

BASIL STREET HOTEL Knightsbridge, SW3 1AH
Tel: 071-581 3311 Fax: 071-581 3693

Banquet: 120, Dinner Dance: 100, Reception: 300
Built in 1910, the Basil Street Hotel - located close to Harrods - has a charming country house ambience. The Parrot Club is a large drawing room with pale pink panelled walls, tinted Art Deco mirrors and choice antiques. It is available every evening and all day on Saturdays. The highly experienced catering team provide an excellent standard of traditional cuisine and claim that every wish can be catered for. There is parking for 500 cars opposite the hotel.

THE BERKELEY Wilton Place, SW1X 7RL
Tel: 071-235 6000 Fax: 071-235 4330

The banqueting suites at The Berkeley are all on the ground floor and share a separate street entrance in Wilton Place which leads through a tented corridor. As well as the suites listed here, there are three smaller suites and a 68 seat exclusive cinema. Classical French haute cuisine is served at The Berkeley, each menu individually discussed with the client. There is a car park under the hotel.

The Ballroom Banquet: 216, Dinner Dance: 180, Reception: 450
The mirrored ceiling and modern crystal chandeliers give this glittering ballroom an added sparkle. The decor is pink and grey with a swirling patterned carpet and white marble and mirror columns. There is plenty of natural daylight, a central dance floor and a white piano. The adjacent Crystal Room can be used for the reception.

Crystal Room Banquet: 60, Dinner Dance: 60, Reception: 120
Another unusual room, the Crystal Room has illuminated walls, grey carpet and drapes, and white leather padded doors. Guests can be received in the smaller, 19th century style Waterloo Room.

BROWN'S HOTEL Albermarle and Dover Street, W1A 4SW
Tel: 071-493 6020 Fax: 071-493 9381

Clarendon Room Banquet: 70, Reception: 100
Since James Brown first opened his hotel in 1837, it has gradually expanded to incorporate 14 elegant town houses. The stylish Clarendon Room retains some of the fine Victorian mouldings. The red moire walls are adorned with pencil sketches of past members of the Grillions Club who still dine here fortnightly while parliament is in session. The room has plenty of natural light with crystal chandeliers supplying the evening lighting. Dancing is not permitted but the hotel can organise some light background music. Brown's also has six smaller suites for private entertaining. The highly experienced catering team provides first class traditional cuisine and fine wines.

CANNIZARO HOUSE West Side, Wimbledon Common, SW19 4UP
Tel: 081-879 1464 Fax: 081-879 7338

Viscount Melville Suite Banquet: 76, Reception: 100
Cannizaro House, said to be London's first country house hotel, is a stylish Georgian mansion backing onto Cannizaro Park. The Viscount Melville Suite is a newly designed suite of three interconnecting rooms on the ground floor, overlooking Wimbledon Common. The suite is attractively decorated in shades of green and pink. Pre-dinner drinks could either be served in the

cocktail bar or, in summer, on the terrace overlooking the park. The menu selector offers a wide and interesting choice of traditional and modern English cuisine and French wines.

CHESTERFIELD HOTEL   35 Charles Street, Mayfair, W1X 8LX
Tel: 071-491 2622 Fax: 071-409 1726

Royal Suite (Charles/Queens) Banquet: 100, Dinner Dance: 80, Reception: 150
Just off Berkeley Square, The Chesterfield has a quiet, secluded atmosphere. The Royal Suite can be divided into The Charles Suite and The Queen's Suite for smaller functions. These first floor suites benefit from of natural daylight and air-conditioning, have a smart blue and gold decor and chandeliered lighting. There is a varied range of menus to select. The wood panelled Library and the glass domed Terrace Room are also available for private parties.

CLARIDGE'S Brook Street, W1A 2JQ
Tel: 071-629 8860 Fax: 071-499 2210

All the banqueting suites at Claridge's are on the ground floor and interconnect so can be used in any combination. Using all the rooms, it would be possible to hold a reception for up to 900 people. Claridge's have a reputation for serving fine French and international food and wine and offer a very personal and complete party planning service.

The Ballroom Banquet: 200, Dinner Dance: 180, Reception: 350
Designed by Oswald Milne in the early 1930's, the Ballroom has its own street entrance with a marbled rotunda and reception area. It is decorated in subtle yellow and grey with etched mirrors and elegant chandeliers. Like all the banqueting rooms at Claridge's, the Ballroom benefits from natural daylight.

Mirror Room Banquet: 40, Reception: 120
Adjoining the Ballroom is the Mirror Room, classically decorated with mirrored walls and a delicate grey and yellow colour scheme with details picked out in gold leaf. It is often used together with the Ballroom with access through three large doors.

French Salon Banquet: 86, Reception: 120
The French Salon lies between the Mirror Room and the Drawing Room and can be used with either, both or on it's own. It is sumptuously decorated in soft pinks in the style of Louis XV. The unique mouldings and cornices are particularly impressive, as are the silver based chandeliers, marble fireplace and mural.

Drawing Room Banquet: 96, Reception: 120
The 18th century style Drawing Room features two fine Adam fireplaces, elaborately moulded ceiling and beautiful antique crystal chandeliers, set off by the elegant blue and cream decor.

CLIVE HOTEL AT HAMPSTEAD Primrose Hill Road, NW3 3NA
Tel: 071-586 2233 Fax: 071-586 1659

Kenwood Suite Banquet: 250-300, Dinner Dance: 250, Reception: 300
The Kenwood Suite benefits from natural daylight from large windows at either end. The room, which can be divided in two, is decorated with an attractive pink and rust colour scheme. Facilities include a permanent bar and moveable stage and dance floor. The private street entrance, cloakroom and toilet facilities are all on a lower level with stair or lift access to the suite. A pre-dinner reception can be held in the Marcus Bohn Suite on the lower level. Also available for private hire is the Ladbroke Suite which can take up to 100 guests. The in-house catering offers a wide range of three and four course dinners together with an exhaustive buffet menu. The Clive Hotel has a separate kosher kitchen adjacent to the Kenwood Suite for use by outside kosher caterers. The hotel car park has only 15 spaces but street parking is unlimited.

CROYDON PARK HOTEL 7 Altyre Road, Croydon, Surrey CR9 5AA
Tel: 081-680 9200 Fax: 081-760 0426

Centennial Suite Banquet: 200, Dinner Dance: 180, Reception: 220
This modern, versatile suite, on the ground floor of the hotel, is very popular for weddings and other celebrations. It has an adjoining reception room, loading bay, air-conditioning and a portable dance floor and can be divided into three sections. It is simply decorated with gold trimmed cream walls and dark red doors, carpet and chairs. Three large rectangular chandeliers are inset into the ceiling. The hotel restaurant is sometimes used for weddings when the Centennial Suite is not available. The in-house caterers provide general banqueting cuisine. The hotel has a car park with 118 spaces.

CUMBERLAND HOTEL   Marble Arch, W1A 4RF
Tel: 071-262 1234 Fax: 071-724 4621

Carlisle Suite and Gloucester Suite Banquet: 375, Dinner Dance: 325, Reception: 500
Entered from the foyer of the hotel, a few steps lead down to the traditionally styled Carlisle Suite, with its blue and red carpet and beige walls. A small area can be partitioned off for pre-dinner drinks when the room is used for functions of less than 100 guests. For more than 100, the adjoining Gloucester Suite is used for the reception. This is lined in faded oak panelling with three recesses and is lit by chandeliers. The in-house catering is of a high standard and the choice is flexible. There are four NCP car parks nearby.

Production Box Banquet: 600, Dinner Dance: 550, Reception: 800
The Production Box is 750 square meters of blank space. This state-of-the-art venue was especially designed for maximum flexibility and is ideal for lavishly set theme parties. The black walls and pillars are a perfect base on which to start the transformation, the high tech ceiling can take a full lighting rig and several tons of ancillary equipment. Access for huge props is from street level with a seven and a half ton hoist to assist.

THE DORCHESTER   Park Lane, W1A 2HJ
Tel: 071-629 8888 Fax: 071-409 0114

The Dorchester, one of the world's most renowned grand hotels, opened its doors again in November 1990 after nearly two years of extensive refurbishment. Executive Chef Willi Elsener has prepared a wide variety of luncheon and dinner menus to delight banqueting clients, combining the finest foods with outstanding wines. The service and attention to detail are exceptional. The Dorchester has three public car parks in close proximity.

Ballroom Banquet: 550, Dinner Dance: 450, Reception: 1000
The sumptuous, mirrored Ballroom has classic blue, pink and white furnishings and decor. Wall chandeliers compliment the decorative ceiling over a large dance floor which is carpeted when not required. Three inter-connected anterooms, the Crush Hall, the Silver Room and the Gold Room - each one more lavish than the last - lead to the Ballroom and are used for receptions.

Orchid Room Banquet: 160, Dinner Dance: 120, Reception: 250
Oliver Ford designed the graceful Orchid Room in Wedgwood-style pale blue and white with a glittering chandelier hanging over the central dance floor. Not surprisingly, this room is very popular for weddings. It has its own anteroom and adjoins the dignified pine-panelled Holford Room which can be used for receptions. The Orchid Room and the Holford Room can be accessed from the hotel foyer. Smaller suites are available.

Hotels

DUKES HOTEL 35 St James's Place, SW1A 1NY
Tel: 071-491 4840 Fax: 071-493 1264

Marlborough Room Banquet: 50, Dinner Dance: 40, Reception: 120
Tucked away in a secluded, gas-lit courtyard, this Edwardian building has an air of tranquil dignity about it. The Marlborough Suite is small, intimate and charmingly decorated in subtle shades of pinks, golds and ivory. Being self-contained, it has its own bar, cloakrooms and kitchen. The predominantly English cuisine is the same as for the restaurant which, along with the service and presentation, is of the highest standard. There is also a small Roof Garden adjacent to the Penthouse which can cater for elegant summer cocktail parties for up to 100 guests.

EDWARDIAN INTERNATIONAL Bath Road, Hayes, Middx UB3 5AW
Tel: 081 759 6311 Fax: 081-759 4559

County Suite Banquet: 360, Dinner Dance: 300, Reception: 550
Situated on the outskirts of Heathrow Airport, the luxurious Edwardian International opened in January 1991 after a multi-million pound refurbishment. The County Suite divides into four unequal quarters - the Surrey, Sussex, Norfolk and Suffolk Suites. The suite is stylishly decorated with pale grey silk and yew panelled walls, hand-made rust patterned carpet and enormous rectangular chandeliers. The portable dance floor and stage provide complete flexibility. There is a separate lobby with two entrances and a loading bay large enough to get a vehicle through. High class traditional cuisine and fine wines are offered, though the catering is extremely flexible and will occasionally allow in outside caterers. There is parking for up to 300 cars.

EXCELSIOR HEATHROW Bath Road, West Drayton, Middx UB7 0DU
Tel: 081-759 6611 Fax: 081-759 3421

Forte Suite Banquet: 650, Dinner Dance: 550, Reception: 900
The Forte Suite is a self-contained complex which has a private entrance from its own car park and a reception area with two bars and cloakrooms. It is an extremely flexible modern suite which can be divided into three equal areas. In-house catering offers a wide choice of imaginative and exciting menus.

Ambassador/Concorde Suites
Banquet: 260 (Ambassador 150, Concorde 90), Dinner Dance: 180 (Ambassador 100),
Reception: 350 (Ambassador 180, Concorde 120)
The two suites join together as one or can be divided by a wooden partition and used separately, the dance floor being in the Ambassador section. Full height windows open onto a small garden which can be used for drinks if the weather permits.

Viscount Suite Banquet: 140, Dinner Dance: 90, Reception: 175
The Viscount Suite has natural light and a low ceiling supported by three pillars. There is a central dance floor which can be carpeted if not required. Other suites, including the Draitone Manor Library, are available for smaller functions.

FORTE CREST ST.JAME'S Jermyn Street, St James's, SW1Y 6JF
Tel: 071-930 2111 Fax: 071-839 2125

Park Room Banquet: 75, Dinner Dance: 70, Reception: 125
This is a bright, airy room benefitting from natural daylight through windows at both ends. The walls are half mahogany panelled and there is a recess housing a fixed bar. The room is air-conditioned and peacefully quiet being located between the car park on one side and a courtyard on the other. There is a good selection of interesting menus to choose from, including finger buffets and fork buffets. Parking is available for up to 80 cars on request.

Gallery Lounge Reception: 70
Suitable for an elegant cocktail party overlooking St James's and Jermyn Street, the lounge is decorated in reds, blues and golds and supported by mahogany-clad pillars. Plants and gorgeous flower displays are dotted around. There is even a piano.

Millers Restaurant Banquet: 70, Reception: 100
This long, rectangular room has a mahogany-panelled alcove at one end which may be used separately seating twelve people around an oval table. Windows provide natural light. There is a small area set aside for pre-dinner drinks. This first-class restaurant serves traditional cuisine complimented by a fine selection of wines.

FORUM HOTEL 97 Cromwell Road, SW7 4DN
Tel: 071-370 5757 Fax: 071-373 1448

London Suite Banquet: 250, Dinner Dance: 200, Reception: 600
The banqueting suites at this modern hotel, the tallest in London, are situated on the first floor. The London Suite can be divided by soundproofed screens into the Brompton, Barnes and Chelsea Rooms for smaller parties. Decorated in soft tones of peach and grey, the suite is bright and airy with natural daylight. For evening functions, the atmosphere is transformed by subdued down-lighting concealed in the low ceiling. The suite can be used in conjunction with the adjoining Mayfair Suite, which can accommodate 140 for a reception or 80 for a dinner. There is a variety of menus to select from, or personal menus can be suggested. The hotel has its own underground car park.

GLOUCESTER HOTEL 4-18 Harrington Gardens, SW7 4LH
Tel: 071-373 6030 Fax: 071-373 0409

Cotswold Suite Banquet: 350, Dinner Dance: 280, Reception: 500
The modern, flexible, suite on the ground floor has its own street entrance from Ashburn Place, at the side of the hotel. This leads to a separate reception area then through to the Cotswold Suite via an attractive double staircase with chrome banisters. Alternatively, access can be via the hotel lobby, using the adjacent Courtfield Suite as a reception area. The air-conditioned Cotswold Suite is decorated in pastel shades of green and lilac and is lit by four rectangular chandeliers. Banqueting offers an exciting selection of French cuisine. There is an underground car park. with 120 spaces.

Hotels

Gloucester Hotel Continued....

Ashburn Suite Banquet: 200, Dinner Dance: 150, Reception: 350
Set away, on the first floor of the hotel, is the Ashburn Suite, a light, airy room with natural daylight and soft aqua-blue furnishings. The ceiling is low with small flush crystal chandeliers. The suite, which is air-conditioned, can be divided into two, the Collingham and Hereford Rooms.

**GORING HOTEL Beeston Place, Grosvenor Gardens, SW1W 0JW
Tel: 071-834 8211 Fax: 071-834 4393**

Ebury Room Banquet: 50, Dinner Dance: 50, Buffet: 75, Reception: 100
The Ebury Room has been stylishly designed with light wood panelled walls and a separate bar area attractively decorated with bare bricks, plants and a waterfall. A wide range of menus is available, ranging from finger buffets through to five or six course banquets. The style of food is generally classic French and English.

**GREAT FOSTERS Stroude Road, Egham, Surrey TW20 9UR
Tel: 0784 433822 Fax: 0784 472455**

400 years ago, Great Fosters was a Royal hunting lodge in the heart of Windsor Great Forest. A hotel since 1931, it is now a scheduled Grade I Historic Building retaining all the atmosphere and character of a past era. The house is set in 17 acres of formal gardens making it a particularly romantic venue for weddings. The menus offer a good standard of traditional fayre.

Tithe Barn Banquet: 200, Dinner Dance: 180, Reception: 200
The 15th century Tithe Barn just oozes character. Oak beams and posts support the high vaulted ceiling over a polished oak floor. There is a minstrel gallery, panelled walls hung with hunting trophies, a bar and a small stage. The room opens onto a large terrace which overlooks the magnificent grounds and water garden - perfect for summer receptions. Guests can be received in the adjoining Orangery or the Painted Hall.

Orangery Buffet: 80, Reception: 200
Added in 1989, the Orangery is linked to the Tithe Barn by the Painted Hall which features a hand painted ceiling and can itself accommodate 200 guests for a reception. The 18th century-style Orangery has arched windows opening onto a small terrace leading to the gardens. The suite has an entrance, foyer and facilities separate from the hotel.

**GREEN PARK HOTEL Half Moon Street, W1Y 8BP
Tel: 071-629 7522 Fax: 071-491 8971**

Literary Suite Banquet: 70, Dinner Dance: 60, Reception: 100
At lower ground floor level - there is a lift - the Literary Suite is a multi function L-shaped room that may be divided into three. The grey and pink colour scheme runs throughout and wooden lighting panels in the wall and ceiling give an illusion of daylight. The modern French cuisine contains interesting combinations of flavours and colours.

Claudes Banquet: 90, Dinner Dance: 80, Reception: 120
With its own entrance from Half Moon Street, Claudes is main hotel restaurant which can be hired for private and semi-private functions. The bar area is used for pre-dinner drinks and the conservatory, which has a tiled floor, makes a perfect dance area. The restaurant is made up of three houses so consists of connected areas all with a lovely homely feel.

**GROSVENOR HOUSE HOTEL Park Lane, W1A 3AA
Tel: 071-499 6363 Fax: 071-499 3901**

The Grosvenor House can offer a choice of banqueting rooms varying in size and style from the magnificent Great Room and Ballroom to the nine smaller banqueting suites of the newly

14

completed 86 Park Lane complex. A selection of the larger suites are described below. The highest standard of cuisine, presentation and service can be expected from the most experienced of banqueting staff. The service includes a complete party organising service so anything can be arranged by request. Guests can leave their cars either at the Grosvenor House Garage or the NCP car park on Park Lane.

Great Room Banquet: 1500, Dinner Dance: 1500, Reception: 2500
The largest hotel ballroom in the United Kingdom, the Great Room was once an ice rink and now caters for the most lavish of events. It is extremely flexible for almost any occasion. It has its own entrance from Park Lane which leads down the Great Room foyer. There is also an entrance for heavy goods from upper Grosvenor Street via a lift capable of taking up to four tons. The Great Room is surrounded by a balcony with a balcony foyer which is used for receptions. A pair of sweeping staircase make a dramatic entrance into the main room which is lit by fabulous chandeliers.

The Ballroom Banquet: 550, Dinner Dance: 500, Reception: 1000
Smaller than the Great Room but just as sumptuous, the Ballroom also has its own entrance from Park Lane and separate reception foyer. A pair of staircases at one end lead to a small, half-level balcony. Venetian chandeliers hang from the pale blue ceiling while the walls are hand-painted in delicate creamy yellow with ornate plasterwork. The room can be easily divided into two by means of a soundproof sliding partition.

90 Park Lane Banquet: 60
Exclusive hire of the Grosvenor House's restaurant is reserved for the hotel's valued clients and society occasions. There is a private area and a small alcove for more intimate celebrations. With plush, deep sofas and upholstered armchairs, the restaurant is decorated with fabulous paintings, some of which are from Lord Forte's private collection.

86 Park Lane has its own separate entrance from Park Lane, but can also be reached via the hotel reception. Of the eighteen suites, nine are considered suitable for banqueting, ranging in capacity for a cocktail party from 50 to 170 guests. Each of the suites has its own special character and is accessed via double doors of American Cherrywood.

Albermarle Suite Banquet: 120, Dinner Dance: 100, Reception: 170
The room is very bright and airy with windows on three sides and views over Hyde Park. Chandeliers provide the evening lighting. The decor is blue and gold with red upholstered furniture and two central mirrored pillars.

Brook and Burlington Suites Banquet: 20 (Brook), 90 (Burlington), Reception: 50 (Brook), 120 (Burlington). These rooms have been decorated to compliment each other and are ideally used together. Both rooms have plenty of natural daylight, the Burlington with windows on three sides. The Brook has pale grey watered silk wall covering, floral drapes, a white marble fireplace and crystal chandeliers. It is connected to the Burlington by double folding doors. The Burlington has a delicate patterned wall covering, pale grey drapes with red cords and tassels, and chandeliers.

HAMPSHIRE HOTEL Leicester Square, WC2H 7LH
Tel: 071-839 9399 Fax: 071-930 8122

Penthouse Suite Banquet: 80, Dinner Dance: 60, Reception: 100
Away from distractions, on the 8th floor, with views over London which include such sights as Big Ben and Nelson's Column, is the aptly named Penthouse Suite. The air-conditioned, square shaped suite is self-contained with its own cloakrooms and has a portable dance floor and stage. The walls are panelled in walnut and oak and the carpet and chairs are blue. The room is dominated by a huge, square crystal chandelier in the centre. The cuisine is French with a full and exciting menu and impressive wine list. There is no car park at the hotel but a car parking service is offered.

Hotels

HEATHROW PARK HOTEL Bath Road,
Longford,
West Drayton, Middx UB7 0EQ
Tel: 081-759 2400
Fax: 081-759 5278

Aviation Suite *(Right)*
Banquet: 450, Dinner Dance: 450,
Reception: 600
The six magnificent crystal chandeliers which
enhance the elegance of this room can be taken
down if necessary providing full flexibility.
The suite can be divided into three equal
sections - Wright, Scott and Mollison. There is
a floor to ceiling loading bay hidden by a huge
Austrian blind, making this an ideal venue for
a theme party where large props are required.
There is a central dance floor and the decor is
pale pink with panelled walls, mirrors and
blue upholstered chairs. In-house catering
provides good English fayre. Outside specialist caterers that have been recommended by the hotel
are permitted to use the facilities.

Longford Suite Banquet: 220, Dinner Dance: 220, Reception: 240
As in the Aviation Suite, an Austrian blind hides the access door to the car park. The Longford Suite
is decorated in pastel shades with limed oak half panelled walls, mirrors and chandeliers. The room
can be divided into two sections. It shares the foyer reception area with the Aviation Suite and can be
used in conjunction with it.
There are other suites available for smaller private parties.

HEATHROW PENTA HOTEL Bath Road, Hounslow, Middx TW6 2AQ
Tel: 081-897 6363 Fax: 081-897 1113

Wessex Ballroom Banquet: 500, Dinner Dance: 450, Reception: 500
The Wessex Ballroom has its own private entrance and reception area, the Wessex Lobby, which
can be used separately on occasions. It is decorated in deep pinks with chandeliers recessed into
panels in the ceiling. The room can be divided into two. The award-winning Master Chef has
produced some interesting and exciting menus.

Sir Francis Drake Room Banquet: 150, Dinner Dance: 150, Buffet: 220, Reception: 250
As it's name suggests, this room is a replica of a ship's wood-lined interior, with a large central
pillar adding to the atmosphere. It can be accessed by a private entrance if required making it ideal
for theme nights, discos or casino evenings. On the lower ground floor there are several smaller,
modern suites which can be used for entertaining. There is also a private section at the back of the
restaurant which can seat 200 or 150 for a disco.

HENRY VIII HOTEL 19 Leinster Gardens, W2 3AN
Tel: 071-262 0117 Fax: 071-706 0472

Anne Boleyn Suite Banquet: 65, Dinner Dance: 65, Reception: 120
This unusual room has a high ceiling, bare brick walls and clever use of mirrors between arches
creating the impression of space. Behind the curtain at one end of the room are glass doors which
can be opened for access to the indoor swimming pool making this an ideal venue for a Caribbean
party or similar. The in-house catering arrangements appear to be very flexible towards the
clients requirements.

HILTON NATIONAL WATFORD Elton Way, Watford, Herts WD2 8HA
Tel: 0923 35881 Fax: 0923 220836

Hertford Suite Banquet: 350, Dinner Dance: 300, Reception: 400
The bright and airy Hertford Suite has a pretty pink, blue and grey colour scheme. Windows on three sides ensure plenty of natural daylight, crystal chandeliers provide the evening lighting. For smaller numbers, the large bar and reception area would be separated from the main room by curtains. For larger functions, when the whole suite would be used, the reception would be in the Crystal Suite. There is a separate canopied banqueting entrance from the car park (300 spaces). The catering is of an exceptionally high standard with the added advantage of a separate kosher kitchen. For Sunday functions in particular, it is advisable to book well ahead.

Crystal Suite Banquet: 130, Dinner Dance: 100, Reception: 200
The mirrored Crystal Suite has a similar colour scheme to the Hertford Suite decorated with pretty silk flowers. It has its own bar and cloakrooms, and high windows on two sides supplying natural daylight.

HOLIDAY INN
SWISS COTTAGE
128 King Henry's Road,
Swiss Cottage, NW3 3ST
Tel: 071-722 7711
Fax: 071-586 5822

Adelaide Suite
Banquet: 300, Dinner Dance: 270,
Reception: 400

The suite has a private entrance leading to the reception foyer. Just off the foyer, there is a smaller room, the Park Suite, which is suitable for VIP receptions. The Adelaide Suite, is decorated in pastel shades of pink and blue, with variable down-lighting, crystal wall lights and a large dance floor. It can

be divided into three sound-proofed sections for smaller functions. The hotel specialises in Barmitzvah's and themed parties and also offers a complete wedding package. As well as providing a flexible selection of international cuisine, the hotel has a kosher kitchen for use by approved kosher caterers. There is a free car park under the hotel.

HOTEL CONRAD Chelsea Harbour, SW10 0XG
Tel: 071-823 3000 Fax: 071-351 6525

Henley Rooms Banquet: 200, Dinner Dance:170, Reception: 250
The Hotel Conrad was opened in 1990 in a unique setting overlooking the prestigious Chelsea Harbour marina. The Henley Rooms, on the lower ground floor, can be accessed either from the hotel foyer or from a separate entrance in the marina, particularly useful for guests arriving by river bus. Designed by David Hicks to a nautical theme, the rooms have a red, blue and cream colour scheme with light wood panelling, flush chandeliers and views over Chelsea Harbour. The rooms can be divided into two or three, with direct access to the reception area and cloakrooms. There is a wide selection of English and French menu suggestions and an extensive wine list. The hotel also has a superb in-house florist. There is a car park under the hotel.

Hotels

HOTEL RUSSELL Russell Square, WC1B 5BE
Tel: 071-837 6470 Fax: 071-837 2857

Wharncliffe & Woburn Suites Banquet: 380, Dinner Dance: 350, Reception: 650
The hotel is an impressive example of late Victorian architecture. The foyer reflects the grandeur of the early 1900s, retaining the original Italian marble features and huge sparkling crystal chandelier. The foyer leads directly to the Woburn Suite, once the original Wintergarden and now the reception room for the majestic Wharncliffe Suite. A stunning ballroom, the Wharncliffe Suite is bathed in natural light from windows running the length of the room. Stone maidens stand on high marble pillars to support the pale blue and cream decorative panelled ceiling. There is a large, central dance floor that can be carpeted when not required and a band stand set into an alcove. Dark blue velvet drapes match the upholstery on the chairs. In-house catering offers a good selection of traditional menus as well as complete wedding packages and theme parties. Outside caterers are allowed in on Sundays only.

HYATT CARLTON TOWER   On Cadogan Place, SW1X 9PY
Tel: 071-235 5411 Fax: 071-235 9129

The Ballroom Banquet: 300, Dinner Dance: 270, Reception: 500 plus
This chic, modern ballroom is decorated with peach moire wall covering in white painted panels and a pretty green and peach floral carpet. The huge, recessed crystal chandeliers and mirrors at each end make this room bright and comfortable. It can be divided into two or three smaller areas with a portable dance floor for complete flexibility. There is a separate ballroom entrance and reception foyer but for larger ballroom functions, the reception could be held in the Drawing Room overlooking Cadogan Gardens. A very high standard of catering is provided. There is a car park beneath the hotel.

_____ *Hotels*

HYDE PARK HOTEL 66 Knightsbridge, SW1Y 7LA
Tel: 071-235 2000 Fax: 071-235 4552

All the function rooms of this elegant Edwardian hotel are on the ground floor and all have the advantage of natural daylight. The hotel is renowned for the excellence of its international haute cuisine and fine wines and in addition offers a complete wedding package.

The Ballroom Banquet: 275, Dinner Dance: 230, Reception: 450
The Ballroom is decorated in the grand style, with sparkling chandeliers, gilded mirrors, and elegant drapes in blue and peach with delicate pastel walls. It has its own street entrance complete with red carpet, foyer and marble staircase. There is a small covered terrace commanding endless views over Hyde Park. The Ballroom can be used in conjunction with the adjacent Knightsbridge Suite.

Knightsbridge Suite Banquet: 160, Reception: 225
The Knightsbridge Suite compliments the Ballroom perfectly, matching the decor and style and used together, the two rooms can accommodate up to 700 standing guests. The room can be divided into two by means of heavy silk curtains and is ideal for weddings.

The Park Suite Banquet: 60, Dinner Dance: 40, Reception: 120
The room has a drawing room ambience, dominated by a large 18th Century painting. One wall is mirrored, reflecting the sparkle from the crystal chandeliers. The adjoining Loggia, overlooking Hyde Park can be used for the reception. This has its own entrance from the park (though special permission is needed to use it).

King Gustav Adolf Suite Banquet: 70, Dinner Dance: 70, Reception: 150
This suite consists of two rooms connected by sliding double doors, providing a distinguished yet flexible venue for smaller functions. Chandeliers, paintings, gilded mirrors and mahogany furniture are set off by the delicate pastel colour scheme and floral drapes and swags.

(FOUR SEASONS) INN ON THE PARK   Hamilton Place, Park Lane, W1A 1AZ
Tel: 071-499 0888 Fax: 071-499 5572

The Ballroom Banquet: 400, Dinner Dance: 325, Reception: 750
This gracious ballroom has hand-painted murals on the delicately carved wood panelling. The windows overlooking Hamilton Place provide good natural daylight with rectangular crystal chandeliers contributing towards the evening atmosphere. Situated on the first floor, it can be divided to form two separate rooms. A particular feature of the international range of banqueting menus, is Japanese cuisine offered by in-house chef Junji Aida.

Oak Room Banquet: 80, Dinner Dance: 60, Reception: 150
Formality combines with luxury in this comfortable oak-panelled room. It can be used as the reception room to the Ballroom or can combine with the smaller Pine Room.

Pine Room Banquet: 40, Reception: 60
The intricately carved pine panelling is original 18th century as is the marble fireplace. The Pine Room is separated from the Oak Room by a mirrored wall and doorway and can be used as the reception room for both the Oak Room and the Ballroom.

Park Room and Garden Room Banquet: 100, Dinner Dance: 80, Reception: 300
The Park Room is the galleried reception area for the Garden Room and leads directly into it. The elegant Garden Room, with its marbled walls and hand-painted mural, opens onto a picturesque garden which is illuminated at night. These rooms are usually hired together and are perfect for weddings.

19

Hotels

INTER-CONTINENTAL HOTEL 1 Hamilton Place, Hyde Park Corner, W1V 0QY
Tel: 071-409 3131 Fax: 071-493 3476

The Grand Ballroom Banquet: 800 (Westminster 360, Piccadilly 220),
Dinner Dance: 700 (Westminster 360, Piccadilly 150),
Reception: 1000 (Westminster 800, Piccadilly 400, Apsley 150)

The Apsley, Piccadilly and Westminster Suites combine to make up the Grand Ballroom - a modern, versatile suite with green and deep pink wall panels. The Ballroom entrance from Hamilton Place leads you up a sweeping staircase to the reception foyer and cloakrooms. The cuisine is superb, the banqueting selection is most impressive as is the wine list. There is a car park under the hotel.

KENILWORTH HOTEL Great Russell Street, WC1B 3LB
Tel: 071-637 3477 Fax: 071-631 3133

Kenilworth Suite Banquet: 110, Dinner Dance: 80, Reception: 150
Made up of the Edwardian and Victorian Rooms, The Kenilworth Suite, on the ground floor, is a self-contained banqueting area. The pale grey walls are hung with limited edition prints, with yew panelling, deep blue oriental carpets and floral chintz drapes at the windows. Chandeliers are set into a low, corniced ceiling. As with all the suites, there is controllable air-conditioning and lighting. Traditional English menus can be chosen from a selection ranging from cocktail snacks to elaborate dinner menus.

Bloomsbury Suite Banquet: 130, Dinner Dance: 100, Reception: 160
On the lower ground floor, the Bloomsbury Suite is very similar to the Kenilworth except that it has no natural light. It divides into the Russell and the Shaftesbury Rooms with its own bar and cloakroom. There are two other rooms on this level for smaller functions.

Louis XV Room Banquet: 40, Reception: 60
Directly opposite the bar on the ground floor is the Louis XV Room. It has original pine panelling and fireplace and a magnificent stained glass dome from which hangs a crystal chandelier. The antique furniture and paintings give this room a luxurious drawing room atmosphere.

KENSINGTON PALACE HOTEL De Vere Gardens, Kensington, W8 5AF
Tel: 071-937 8121 Fax: 071-937 8121

Duchess Suite Banquet: 160, Dinner Dance: 140, Reception: 250
A separate street entrance leads through to the elegant Duchess Suite, tastefully decorated in pale peach moire panelled walls, peach and blue carpet and drapes, and blue upholstered furniture. There is plenty of natural daylight and the suite can be easily divided into two. The foyer and facilities are shared with the adjacent Countess, Princess and Baroness Suites which can be used for pre-dinner drinks. All the banqueting suites at the Kensington Palace Hotel are fully air-conditioned. The head chef can cater for any type of function and offers a good selection of menus.

Marchioness Suite Banquet: 100, Dinner Dance: 100 (with lobby), Reception: 100
The lobby of the Marchioness Suite, situated on the lower ground floor, can be used for a drinks reception, buffet or dance area. The suite is decorated in pale blue and peach with limed oak woodwork. On the same level and of similar size is the Park Suite, a modern wood-panelled room which can be divided into two.

KENSINGTON PARK HOTEL De Vere Gardens, W8 5AG
Tel: 071-937 8080 Fax: 071-937 7616

Broadlands and Chartwell Suites Banquet: 120 (Broadlands 80, Chartwell 50),
Dinner Dance: 120 (Broadlands 80, Chartwell 50), Reception: 220 (Broadlands 150, Chartwell 70)
The Broadlands and Chartwell Suites can be hired together or individually. They share a private street entrance and grand staircase leading to the reception foyer, with its striking Italian marble

Kensington Park Hotel Continued....

floor and limed oak double doors to each suite. The decor in each room is similar with limed oak wall panels, mirrors, and floral carpets, though the Broadlands is predominantly pink and the Chartwell green. Both have natural light and air-conditioning. For smaller functions, the adjoining Harewood Suite can seat 30 for dinner and there are a number of smaller suites on the lower ground floor. A full range of menus for all types of meals is offered as well as a Complete inclusive wedding package.

LANGHAM HILTON
1 Portland Place, W1V 3AA
Tel: 071-636 1000
Fax: 071-323 2340

In 1865, when the Langham Hotel first opened, it was the largest building in London. It quickly established itself as one of London's most fashionable meeting places until in 1940 structural war damage forced its closure. After more than three years of painstaking reconstruction the hotel was opened in march.

The Ballroom Banquet: 300, Dinner Dance: 250, Reception: 500
The exquisite white and gold Ballroom retains many of its original Victorian features. The ornate panelled ceiling is decorated with Wedgwood rosettes and the pillars are topped with gold leaf. Huge frosted chandeliers light the Ballroom at night; daylight is supplied through windows that open onto a secluded garden terrace, which could be used for a summer reception or tented for a summer disco. Otherwise, the Ambassador's Room can be used for the reception. Several smaller suites are available for private dining. First class traditional cuisine is served - menus being individually discussed with the client. There is also a kosher kitchen for use by specified kosher caterers. An NCP car park with 1000 spaces is very near by.

LONDON EMBASSY HOTEL 150 Bayswater Road, W2 4RT
Tel: 071-229 1212 Fax: 071-229 2623

Mezzanine Suite Banquet: 120, Dinner Dance: 120, Reception: 200
This lovely, bright suite has windows running the whole length of one side which open onto a terrace overlooking Kensington Park. Situated on the first floor, it is entered via its own reception area. It is decorated in peach and grey with grey wood panelling and co-ordinating chairs and carpet. There are chandeliers as well as discreet flourescents making the lighting variable. The room can be divided into three sections. The hotel has a small private car park. Discos are not allowed here.

LONDON HILTON 22 Park Lane, W1A 2HH
Tel: 071-493 8000 Fax: 071-493 4957

Grand Ballroom Banquet: 1000, Dinner Dance: 850, Reception: 1000
Ten crystal chandeliers illuminate this impressive ballroom. The blue and coral decor is enhanced with rosewood panels. The room can be divided into two or three smaller areas each with access to the Foyer, which makes an ideal reception area combined with the adjoining Dome Room. The suite is situated on the first floor via an escalator and Grand Staircase from a seperate street entrance. There are several smaller suites available as well as an executive Business Centre and Meeting 2000.

Hotels

LONDON MARRIOTT HOTEL Grosvenor Square, W1A 4AW
Tel: 071-493 1232 Fax: 071-491 3201

Westminster Suite Banquet: 500, Dinner Dance: 500, Reception: 900
Comprising the Eaton, Chester and Belgrave Rooms, the Westminster Suite is a versatile modern function room. The large, concealed loading bay, high ceiling and pillar free space make this an ideal venue for a theme party where large props are required. Located on the ground floor, this air-conditioned suite has a permanent dance floor, a striking pink panelled ceiling and full height sunburst design doors. The international cuisine has a strong New World influence. There is an NCP car park under the hotel. Other suites are available for smaller functions.

LONDON REGENTS PARK HILTON 18 Lodge Road, St John's Wood, NW8 7JT
Tel: 071-722 7722 Fax: 071-483 2408

Dennis Compton Suite Banquet: 150, Dinner Dance: 120, Reception: 175
This suite is attractively decorated in pinks, greys and blues with an elegant pink ceiling. There is natural daylight and a permanent marble dance floor in the centre which can be covered when not in use. For large dinners and dances, the adjoining Tom Graveney Suite is used for the reception. The two suites share their own foyer and street entrance from St John's Wood Road. Catering is in-house.

Wellington Suite Banquet: 120, Reception: 175
The Wellington Suite is on the first floor and can be divided into three rooms of equal size. Decorated in blues, greens and greys, there is natural daylight and a low ceiling.

MANSION HOUSE AT GRIM'S DYKE Old Redding, Harrow Weald, Middx HA3 6SH
Tel: 081-954 4227 Fax: 081-954 4560

Music Room Banquet: 95, Dinner Dance: 90, Reception: 150
The Mansion House, built in 1878, was the former home of W.S.Gilbert. Set among 110 acres of woodland, it is approached via a long wooded drive. Among the Music Room's impressive features are a listed barrel ceiling in stencilled plaster, a Cornish alabaster fireplace standing 15 feet high and a minstrels gallery. Not surprisingly, Gilbert and Sullivan soirées are a speciality. The gardens or the Library Bar can be used for the pre-dinner reception. The imaginative English cuisine is renowned and beautifully presented. There is parking for 100 cars.

Azalea Suite Banquet: 70, Dinner Dance: 65, Reception: 90
The Azalea Suite has direct access from the car park and has its own private cloakroom and bar area. The windows overlook the extensive grounds and the inglenook fireplace gives this room immense character. There are other rooms available for smaller parties.

Rose Garden Marquee Banquet: 300, Dinner Dance: 160, Reception: 240
Every year, Between May and October, the marquee is set up in the magnificent grounds at Grim's Dyke. The rouched cream silk linings, arched windows, chandeliers and wall sconces make this an imposing and elegant venue for a summer function. Outside caterers may use the marquee by arrangement.

MAY FAIR INTER-CONTINENTAL HOTEL Stratton Street, W1A 2AN
Tel: 071-629 7777 Fax: 071-629 1459

Crystal Room Banquet: 320, Dinner Dance: 220, Reception: 500
The Crystal Room has its own entrance from Berkeley Street and an adjoining reception area on the lower ground floor. The sumptuous pink ballroom has cream silk moire wall panels and velvet drapes dressing tinted mirrored arches. Three glittering rectangular chandeliers are set into mirrored recesses and cover most of the ceiling. This is a wonderful room for a very special occasion such as a wedding. The French style cuisine is of an exceptionally high standard, with a particularly good vegetarian selection. Outside caterers may be used only on Sundays. There are

May Fair Intercontinental Hotel Continued....

several smaller suites available, in particular the Lansdowne and Devon Suites which can accommodate 60 for dinner, 120 for a reception. In addition, there is a private theatre which seats 310 and a health club with pool, sauna and gym.

LE MERIDIEN LONDON 21 Piccadilly, W1V 0BH
Tel: 071-734 8000 Fax: 071-437 3574

Georgian Suite   Banquet: 250, Dinner Dance:210, Reception: 400
All the banqueting suites at Le Meridien are on the first floor. The Georgian Suite is a gorgeous Adam-style ballroom decorated in pale blue and white with elaborate plasterwork on the walls and ceiling. The room has windows at one end providing natural daylight, though some of the windows are false, while brass chandeliers provide the evening lighting. The smaller adjacent Adam Room is similarly decorated and can be used for the reception. There is a huge selection of set menus to choose from, including menus for theme parties.

Edwardian Suite Banquet: 350, Reception: 300
The Edwardian Suite is modern and versatile and can be divided into two self-contained suites. Simply decorated in pastel shades with light wood detail, the suite has French windows overlooking Piccadilly. Another smaller suite, the Regency, is also available.

MOSTYN HOTEL
Bryanston Street,
W1H 0DE
Tel: 071-935 2361
Fax: 071-487 2759
John Adam Room
(Right) Banquet: 120, Dinner Dance: 80, Reception: 150
The John Adam Room is located on the ground floor of the Georgian building which dates back to the mid-18th century and still retains many of the original features. The room has natural daylight and an ornate decor picked out in pastel shades of pink and blue. A crystal chandelier is suspended from the magnificent ceiling. It has its own private street entrance and reception room with a bar. In-house catering offers

innovative menus and outside caterers are permitted by negotiation. There is NCP parking for 200 cars. The restaurant is also available for private use and can seat up to 80 people.

Bryanston Room Banquet: 60, Dinner Dance: 50, Reception: 100
The Bryanston Room is situated on the first floor and, though smaller than the John Adam Room, is just as grand. The original Georgian features include the ornate ceiling, fire surround and doorway. The decor is a delicate combination of pale green, lilac and peach. There is natural

daylight and air-conditioning. It can be used in conjunction with the smaller Portman Room via an inter-connecting door.

Portman Room Banquet: 30, Reception: 40

Adjacent to the Bryanston Room is a smaller version of it, the Portman Room. It has pale green watered silk wall panels that are edged with lilac and peach and the heavy drapes are deep green. The ceiling and the fireplace are reminders that this was once a grand Georgian house.

ONSLOW HOTEL 109/113, Queen's Gate, SW7 5LR
Tel: 071-589 6300 Fax: 071-581 1492

Kensington Suite Banquet: 60, Reception: 90

The Kensington Suite, on the lower ground floor, is simply but tastefully decorated in muted shades with a low ceiling and natural daylight. It can be divided into two separate suites, Manson and Brompton. Pre-dinner receptions may be held in the cocktail bar on the ground floor. There is a good selection of set banqueting menus.

The Brasserie on Queen's Gate Banquet: 120, Dinner Dance: 80

Abundant natural daylight, marble effect wall covering and a colour scheme of cream, pink and turquoise make this a popular venue for weddings. A private section of the Brasserie may be separated and hired for smaller parties. The head chef has some innovative and creative menu suggestions on offer.

The Bank Discotheque Banquet: 200, Dinner Dance: 200, Reception: 250

As complete contrast to the tranquil ambience of the Onslow Hotel, The Bank is a maize of red and black, onyx effect pillars and low ceilings. It has its own street entrance from Old Brompton Road and is available for private hire on Sunday and Monday evenings and every day until 7pm.

PARK LANE HOTEL Piccadilly, W1Y 8BX
Tel: 071-499 6321 Fax: 071-499 1965

Ballroom Suite Banquet: 600, Dinner Dance: 550, Reception: 1000

The private entrance from Piccadilly leads through the spectacular Art Deco Silver Gallery down to the foyer of The Ballroom. A masterpiece of Art Deco design, The Ballroom incorporates a separate reception area with bar and a large balcony area. The resplendent decoration includes metal murals, tinted mirrors, green and silver balcony railings and frosted glass chandeliers. The suite has a built in stage and dance floor and is fully air-conditioned, as are all the banqueting suites at the Park Lane Hotel. The Ballroom and Silver Foyer have recently been attentively refurbished. The standard of cuisine is exceptionally high with a good choice of menus and an extensive wine list. In addition, the Park Lane Hotel has a separate kosher kitchen which can serve any one of the banqueting suites under strict supervision. Special bedroom rates are offered for guests attending a dinner dance. There is private covered parking for 180 cars opposite the main entrance to the hotel.

Tudor Rose Room Banquet: 200, Dinner Dance: 150, Reception: 250

Access to the Tudor Room is from the hotel's Palm Court Lounge on the ground floor. The suite is elegantly decorated with pale blue moire wall fabric and blue and gold furnishings. There is a large, central dance floor and a pretty mirrored 'window box' back-drop for a top table. It can be used in conjunction with the adjoining Oak Room.

Oak Room Banquet: 80, Dinner Dance: 50, Reception: 140

Adjoining the Tudor Rose Room, the Oak Room was originally the gentlemen's smoking room. The rich oak panelling and elaborate ceiling decoration provide a traditional ambience. The room is lit by silvered chandeliers and wall lights.

PORTMAN INTER-CONTINENTAL 22 Portman Square, W1H 9FL
Tel: 071-486 5844 Fax: 071-935 0537

Ballroom Banquet: 400, Dinner Dance: 380, Reception: 700
The pink panelled Ballroom divides into three self-contained, sound-proof rooms that may be used individually or combined. Windows overlooking the terrace provide natural daylight and huge rectangular chandeliers and wall-lights illuminate the room for evening functions. The adjoining Montague Suite can be used for receptions. The Ballroom has its own separate entrance from the hotel forecourt and shares a foyer with several smaller suites, all on the first floor. An interesting and varied range of International meat, fish and vegetarian menus is offered. There is NCP parking at the hotel with 300 spaces.

RAMADA HOTEL 10 Berners Street, W1A 3BE
Tel: 071-636 1629 Fax: 071-580 3972

The Edwardian splendour of the hotel features magnificent marble decor, glittering chandeliers and ornate plasterwork particularly evident in the grand entrance hall and the restaurant where there is a private area - the Fabergé Suite - which seats up to 35. The hotel has excellent facilities for the disabled including specialised bedrooms and a lift to all floors. Set menus suggestions are supplied by the in-house caterers offering mainly traditional cuisine.

Berners Suite Banquet: 160, Dinner Dance: 120, Reception: 200
The self-contained, lower ground floor suite is made up of the York Room (often used for dancing or a small reception), Berners East and Berners West. Each room has its own entrance from the private foyer and can be used individually or combined. The decor is continued through the whole suite - beige suedette walls, blue carpet - and all rooms have natural light and air-conditioning.

Empire Room Banquet: 80, Reception: 100
On the first floor, the Empire room has a delicate beige and pale pink colour scheme, moulded cornice and brass chandeliers. It connects with one of the bedrooms which can be used as a cloakroom. Pre-dinner drinks can be served on the balcony area overlooking the foyer. The Empire Room is the perfect setting for wedding receptions.

RAMADA INN WEST LONDON 47 Lillie Road, SW6 1UQ
Tel: 071-385 1255 Fax: 071-381 4450

Thames Suite Banquet: 1450, Dinner Dance: 1200, Reception: 1750
The Thames Suite is one of the largest venues of its kind in London with no obstructions and a huge loading bay providing access for even the largest props for a theme party. If it is too large for your needs, the suite can be divided into three sections, named Twickenham, Wimbledon and Richmond. Each can accommodate 350 for a banquet, 300 for a dinner dance and 500 for a reception. The suite, located on the ground floor, has its own entrance, foyer, bar, cloakroom, toilets and kitchen and a built in dance floor. It is fully air-conditioned and decorated with beige walls, red carpet and crystal chandeliers. There is NCP parking for 130 cars under the hotel. The selected banqueting menus offer English cuisine or you can bring in outside caterers if preferred.

REMBRANDT HOTEL Thurloe Place, SW7 2RS   Tel: 071-589 8100 Fax: 071-225 3363

King Suite and Queen Suite Banquet: 160 (King), 60 (Queen)
Dinner Dance: 150 (King),40 (Queen) Reception: 250 (King), 100 (Queen)
Known collectively as the State Rooms, the King Suite and the adjacent Queen Suite are situated on the ground floor with their own reception area. Both enjoy natural daylight and are fully air-conditioned. The King Suite can be divided into four sound-proofed areas for complete flexibility. The similarly decorated Queen Suite divides into two and is often used as the reception room for functions in the King Suite. Both rooms are purpose built and ideal for private functions. The in-house catering can produce a varied international cuisine, though outside catering is permitted for more specialist fayre.

Hotels

RITZ HOTEL
Piccadilly, W1V 9DG Tel: 071-493 8181 Fax: 071-493 2687

Cesar Ritz created The Ritz Hotel in 1906 and the standards he set then are still meticulously preserved today. Head Chef Keith Stanley offers a combination of excellent English and French cuisine. Live music is allowed but definitely no discos. Apart from the rooms described here, The Ritz Hotel can also offer a number of smaller rooms for private dining.

Marie Antoinette Suite *(Above)* Banquet: 50, Reception: 80
Opposite the Palm Court is the exquisite Marie Antoinette Suite, a replica of a room at the palace of Versailles. There are ornate gold leaf mouldings on the walls, mirrors at either end, and one hanging over a grand marble and gold fireplace. The room is lit by wall sconces and a central chandelier.

Palm Court Banquet: 50, Dinner Dance: 100, Reception: 150
Facing the Piccadilly entrance is the Palm Court, a wonderful extravagance of gold leaf, marble, chandeliers and mirrors in the style of Louis XVI. Every Friday and Saturday, the Palm Court revives the Big Band era of the 20s, 30s and mid 40s. Alternatively, it may be hired for a private function.

The Ritz Restaurant Banquet: 130
A more elegant and opulent restaurant in London would be hard to find. The frescoed ceiling is hand painted, as is the mural behind the statue of Neptune, while garlands of gold leaf hang between chandeliers. Private use of the restaurant is reserved for very special occasions and can be used in conjunction with the Marie Antoinette Suite and Italian Garden.

**ROYAL GARDEN HOTEL 2-24 Kensington High Street, W8 4PT
Tel: 071-937 8000 Fax: 071-938 4532**

Palace Suite Banquet: 600 (Buckingham 300, St. James 250)
Dinner Dance: 500 (Buckingham 200, St. James 160)
Reception: 800 (Buckingham 550, St. James 350)

As well as its own street entrance, The Palace suite has its own concourse, reception area, two bars and cloakrooms. It is lined in dark wood with blue upholstery and modern chandeliers. The suite lends itself particularly well to themed evenings as there are very wide direct-access doors making it easy to transport props and the floor can support heavy items such as cars. The hotel can arrange a variety of themes as well as provide three-dimensional sets of many London scenes. The room is air-conditioned, as are all the banqueting rooms at the hotel, and can be split into two, The Buckingham Suite and The St. James Suite. The French haute cuisine is supervised by executive chef David Nicholls.

Kensington Suite Banquet: 90, Dinner Dance: 60, Reception: 120
The Kensington Suite, on the lower ground floor, has direct access from Kensington High Street or the hotel lobby by lift. The Victoriana style decor in neutral shades includes gold beaded wall panelling and crystal chandeliers. The low ceiling gives this room an exclusive feel. There is a dance floor under a section of carpet. The room can be split into two separate parts (Victoria and Albert) suitable for a reception in one followed by dinner in the other.

Balmoral Suite Banquet: 120, Dinner Dance: 90, Reception: 150
On the mezzanine floor, the Balmoral Suite overlooks Kensington High Street and can be used in conjunction with the smaller Sandringham and Osbourne Suite which shares the same concourse. Both suites are simply decorated in soft tones with an attractive pattered carpet.

**ROYAL LANCASTER HOTEL Lancaster Terrace, W2 2TY
Tel: 071-262 6737 Fax: 071-724 3191**

Nine Kings Suite Banquet: 1500, Dinner Dance: 1300, Reception: 1800
This is probably the most versatile suite to be found in London. It can be divided into numerous soundproofed areas using advanced electronics. A team of technicians are on hand at all times. Even the magnificent crystal chandeliers are retractable allowing use of high-tech lighting as an alternative. The lavish use of wood, marble and mirrors in the interior design are set off by the striking royal blue paisley carpet. The foyer reception area is similarly decorated but with the addition of back-lit stained glass. There is a private street entrance for the Nine Kings Suite and the Westbourne Suite which can be used together. Executive Chef, Remy Fougere, a member of the Academie Culinaire Française, takes care of the banqueting requirements and offers a full range of menus. There is parking for 120 cars.

Westbourne Suite Banquet: 900, Dinner Dance: 550, Reception: 1000
The warm, opulent Westbourne suite is decorated with classically redesigned tapestries in muted shades, complete with blue Italian marble pillars and a domed ceiling. It can be divided into four separate rooms, each individually accessed or can be combined with the Nine Kings Suite with which it shares a street entrance.

Gloucester Suite Banquet: 80, Dinner Dance: 70, Reception: 200
This elegant Rococo style suite is decorated in delicate green and peach and has a private foyer. It can be divided into two sound-proofed rooms, one slightly larger than the other. Smaller suites are also available.

27

THE SAVOY Strand, WC2R 0EU
Tel: 071-836 4343 Fax: 071-240 6040

Since its creation in 1889 by Richard D'Oyly Carte, The Savoy has remained one of the world's most glamorous hotels. The hotel offers a flexible range of banqueting suites, each with its own individual character and appeal. In addition to the rooms listed here, there are eight smaller private rooms, seven of which are named after Gilbert and Sullivan operas. The banqueting rooms can be approached from the Strand or River Entrances. Parking can be arranged in the Savoy's Adelphi Garage. The Savoy's reputation for high standards of cuisine, wine and service is well deserved.

Lancaster Room Banquet: 500, Dinner Dance: 400, Reception: 800
The French chateau-style ballroom is a glittering combination of crystal chandeliers, mirrored panelling, ornate plasterwork and a hand-painted cloud-effect ceiling. The walls are Wedgwood blue and ivory and heavy blue drapes dress the stage. The ballroom can be used in combination with the adjoining Parlour Room or nearby River and Abraham Lincoln Rooms.

Abraham Lincoln and Manhattan Rooms Banquet: 240, Dinner Dance: 180, Reception: 400
This suite of rooms is completely self contained, with its own cloakrooms and easy access from the River Entrance. It is decorated in Art Deco style and has a sprung dance floor and purpose built wall divide.

River Room Banquet: 120, Dinner Dance: 120, Reception: 350
Redecorated by David Hicks, the River Room has a strong theatrical feel and dramatic views over the Thames. White marble walls are broken with red panels, grey and red carpet and marble pillars.

SELFRIDGE HOTEL Orchard Street, W1H OJS
Tel: 071-408 2080 Fax: 071-409 2295

Selfridge Suite Banquet: 290, Dinner Dance: 228, Reception: 450
The Selfridge Suite can be divided into the Cotswold, Cheviot, Cleveland and Chiltern Rooms by means of sliding, soundproofed panels. These panels are concealed behind colour co-ordinated curtains when not required. The suite is fully air-conditioned. Located off the cedar panelled lounge on the first floor, the suite is decorated in golden yellow tones with a soft coloured red and yellow carpet around a central dance floor lit by crystal chandeliers. The wide selection of interesting menus is very flexible and can cater for all dietary requirements. Through their own wine company, they can offer a full choice of fine wines, ports and brandies. There is an NCP car park under the hotel.

SELSDON PARK HOTEL Sanderstead, South Croydon, Surrey CR2 8YA
Tel: 081-657 8811 Fax: 081-651 6171
Selsdon Park Hotel is an impressive ivy-clad country house set in 200 acres of rolling parkland. The excellent leisure facilities include an 18 hole championship golf course, tennis courts, croquet lawn, open-air swimming pool and an indoor tropical leisure centre. Apart from the rooms described below, there are several other rooms, varying in size and style, available for private dinners or receptions. The traditional English and Continental style cuisine is of a high standard with the emphasis on fresh produce and good service. There is a 250 space car park at the hotel.

Tudor Room Banquet: 180, Dinner Dance: 155, Buffet: 200, Reception: 250
The largest function room at Selsdon Park, the Tudor Room opens directly onto the terrace overlooking the golf course - ideal for a summer reception. Alternatively, guests can be received in either the Essex Room or the smaller Kent Room. The decor is traditional with a distinctive Tudor style ceiling and wood panelled walls.

Essex Room Banquet: 140, Buffet: 120, Reception: 200
With direct access to the car park, the Essex Room has leaded light windows overlooking the grounds at the side of the hotel. The room is simply decorated in beige and green with a large tapestry on the wall.

Selsdon Park Hotel Continued....

Tropical Leisure Complex Buffet: 100
A modern addition to the hotel, this is strictly for lovers of the heat, wonderful for winter parties. Guests can have drinks around the poolside bar or cross the little wooden bridge to the pool island, then go upstairs to the Tropical Lounge where the buffet is served. The complex is decorated with tropical plants, flamingoes and pink striped loungers and umbrellas. Beach wear is recommended!

SHERATON PARK TOWER 101 Knightsbridge, SW1X 7RN
Tel: 071-235 8050 Fax: 071-235 8231

The Trianon Banquet: 160, Dinner Dance: 150, Reception: 250
The Trianon is a graceful crescent-shaped room with full height picture windows leading out to a private garden terrace overlooking Lowndes Square. The terrace, with its pretty shrubbery and ornamental fountain, is a delightful setting for pre-dinner drinks and, as it is very popular for weddings, makes an ideal backdrop for photographs. The Trianon room itself has a delicate peach colour scheme, brass chandeliers and mirrored pillars. The creative team at the Sheraton Park Tower are experienced party planners who specialise in weddings and themed events. The cuisine is of a very high standard and the menus are exciting and flexible. There is NCP parking under the hotel.

SHERATON SKYLINE HOTEL Bath Road, Hayes, Middx UB3 5BP
Tel: 081-759 2535 Fax: 081-750 9150

International Ballroom Banquet: 450, Dinner Dance: 400, Reception: 600
The modern ballroom has beige panelled walls with a red border, a red and brown carpet and mirrored rectangular chandeliers. It can be divided into two or three sections and has direct loading access from outside. Either the adjacent Canadian Room, which can seat 100 for dinner, or part of the Patio Caribe could be used for pre-dinner receptions. A good selection of French and traditional cuisine is offered as well as an impressive range of speciality themed evenings. There is free parking space for 425 cars.

Patio Caribe Banquet: 300
The focal point of the hotel, the famous Patio Caribe is an extensive indoor tropical garden, complete with palms, surrounding a swimming pool and circular bar under a glass roof. This exotic setting is lit by gas lanterns at night and is perfect for a whole range of themed events. A resident steel band is available for Caribbean parties.

Diamond Lil's Banquet: 160, Dinner Dance: 120
Diamond Lil's Saloon is an authentic reconstruction of a Montana barn dating back to the Klondyke days. The Wild West theme is carried through with red and white check tablecloths and saloon doors. The resident cabaret could be included and charcoal grills and draught beer are a speciality.

SHERLOCK HOLMES HOTEL Baker Street, W1M ILB
Tel: 071-486 6161 Fax: 071-486 0884

Baker Street Banquet: 50, Dinner Dance: 40, Reception: 80
On the lower ground floor, the Baker Street suite is a fully air-conditioned long and narrow room, skilfully decorated with soft pink suede-effect and pine-finished walls. The room inter-connects through double doors with the Devonshire suite which can be used for dancing or on its own for smaller functions (35 dinner, 50 reception). The cloakroom and toilet facilities are on the same level as well as some smaller suites. There is NCP parking behind the hotel.

Hotels

SOPWELL HOUSE HOTEL AND COUNTRY CLUB Cottonmill Lane, Sopwell,
St Albans, Herts AL1 2HQ Tel: 0727 864477 Fax: 0727 44741

Sopwell House is an attractive venue with much to offer, so is included even though St Albans lies just outside the area covered in this book. The elegantly refurbished 18th century manor house is set amidst 11 acres of grounds and includes a new country club/health centre and a purpose built conference and banqueting wing in keeping with the character of the hotel. The contemporary English and French cuisine is of a high standard, with an exciting selection of menu suggestions. A complete party planning service is offered.

St Albans Suite *(Above)* Banquet: 320, Dinner Dance: 220, Reception: 500
The St Albans Suite, in the new wing, is totally self-contained with its own entrance, marble foyer, panelled lounge and bar. The ballroom has full ash panelling, rectangular crystal chandeliers and a built in dance floor. It can be divided into two or three smaller areas by means of ash partitions. Large French windows open onto the terrace leading to a Japanese Bridge over a miniature pond and landscaped gardens. A marquee can be set up here for 600 or more guests - ideal for summer balls or barbecues. Conveniently situated on the ground floor, the suite has full facilities for the disabled. Smaller suites are available.

Magnolia Conservatory Banquet: 100
The split level conservatory restaurant is only available for weddings and private lunches on Saturdays until 5.30pm. Mature magnolia trees grow in the conservatory which has fine views over the terrace and courtyard - perfect for 'al fresco' drinks and dining.

STAFFORD HOTEL St James's Place, SW1A 1NJ
Tel: 071-493 0111 Fax: 071-493 7121

Wine Cellars *(Right)*
Banquet: 40
Reception: 60
Wine Tasting: 60
The 300 year-old working wine cellars are situated under the quiet mews behind the hotel. Guests are led through the hotel kitchens and dimly lit cellar passages to a white walled, stone floored chamber. 350,000 bottles are stored in the cellars, so it is hardly surprising that this is a very popular venue for wine tastings. The cellars are candle lit and have a faint musty smell creating an authentic ambience. At the far end of the room, there is a smaller area for pre-dinner drinks,

separated by a wrought iron gate. No dancing is allowed in the wine cellars, background music only, and no stag nights. The cuisine is of an exceptionally high standard, offering a choice of traditional English and gourmet French menus and a selection of over 200 fine wines.

Sutherland Room Banquet: 40, Reception: 75
In total contrast, this elegant, green drawing room has a traditional homely atmosphere, complete with Victorian marble fireplace and pictures on the walls. There is no natural light but an artificial window is cleverly lit from the outside. There is a small adjoining room, the Stage Room, which connects the Sutherland Room to the Restaurant and can provide space for one extra table, if required. Pre-dinner drinks can be served in the adjoining Panel Room, a comfortable mahogany panelled reception room with a pink marble fireplace and brass light fittings.

Restaurant Banquet: 50
The gracious pink and white Restaurant can be hired for exclusive use, seating up to fifty guests on tables of various sizes. Windows at the rear of the room overlook a small ornamental courtyard featuring a statue of Aphrodite. A large crystal chandelier hangs from the hand-painted ceiling and the marble fireplace enhances the warm, relaxing ambience.

STAKIS ST. ERMIN'S HOTEL Caxton Street, SW1H 0QW
Tel: 071-222 7888 Fax: 071-222 6914

Ballroom & Balcony Room Banquet: 240 (280 with balcony), Dinner Dance: 140, Reception: 350
The grand, elegant Ballroom retains many of its original late 19th century features. A glittering chandelier hangs over a large central dance floor and handsome marble pillars support the ornate ceiling. The Balcony Room is the reception area, reached via the scalloped gallery over-hanging the Ballroom. In-house catering is excellent and well presented. Menus can be chosen from an imaginative selector or tailor-made. Kosher caterers can be brought in on Sundays only.

Hotels

ST. JAMES COURT Buckingham Gate, SW1E 6AF
Tel: 071-834 6655 Fax: 071-630 7587

The elaborate Edwardian architecture of St James Court has been restored to its original elegance and is located very close to Buckingham Palace. Adjoining the hotel is the Conference & Banqueting Centre with access either from the hotel or from an independent entrance from Buckingham Gate. This entrance leads into a smart lobby with an oriental staircase to the reception area on the first floor. The Centre's own kitchen offers a complete range of reception and banqueting menus in addition to gourmet French and Chinese cuisine from the hotel's restaurants.

Edwardian I *(Right)*
Banquet: 150, Reception: 250

Without being overwhelming, the rich mahogany panelled walls and sparkling chandeliers hung from a barrelled ceiling make this a perfect setting for an elegant and dignified function. It has direct connection to Edwardian Room II via two sets of double doors.

Edwardian Room II
Banquet: 50, Reception: 60

Decorated in similar style to the adjoining Edwardian Room I, this room can be used as the reception area to functions in the larger suite. The walls are panelled in mahogany and deep, rich red to match the carpet.

Taj Room Banquet: 40, Reception: 60
The exotic interior of the Taj Room features intricate, lemon stained woodwork, Eastern design fabric wall covering and blinds, and three amber glass chandeliers. The large windows, overlooking Buckingham Gate, provide plenty of natural light.

Elizabethan Room Banquet: 20, Reception: 60
A small, sophisticated suite consisting of two conventional size adjoining rooms, both decorated in blue and cream with heavy deep blue drapes, swags and tails.

Courtyard *(Right)*
Banquet: 150, Reception: 400

At the centre of St James Court is a half acre courtyard, planted with trees, evergreens and flowering shrubs in green and blue tiled gardens, paved in white York stone. The central fountain is said to have been donated by Queen Victoria. The magnificent terracotta frieze which surrounds the Courtyard is reputedly the longest in the world and depicts scenes from several of Shakespeare's plays. A unique setting for al fresco functions in London, the Courtyard can be covered with a marquee for those who have no faith in the British summer.

STRAND PALACE HOTEL Strand, WC2R OJJ
Tel: 071-836 8080 Fax: 071-836 2077

Burleigh Suite Banquet: 230, Dinner Dance: 200, Reception: 300
Established since 1909, the Strand Palace retains many of the original Art Deco features, such as the splendid marble and steel staircase which leads down to the suite foyer from the separate street entrance. The foyer serves the Burleigh Suite as well as the two smaller suites, the Drake and the Essex. The Art Deco Burleigh Suite has its own reception area which opens to the L-shaped main room by means of folding doors. There is a large central dance floor and a piano is available. A full range of banqueting menus, mostly English , is offered, as well as complete wedding packages.

TOWER THISTLE HOTEL St Katharine's Way, E1 9LD
Tel: 071-481 2575 Fax: 071-488 4106

The Tower Suite Banquet: 230, Dinner Dance: 175, Reception: 350
Access to the Tower Suite can be either from the hotel foyer or from a separate entrance facing Tower Bridge. The foyer and cloakrooms are on the ground floor leading to the reception area on the first floor, with a magnificent view over the river. The modern ballroom has a small dance floor and can be divided easily into two. The highly professional banqueting team provide a wide range of mainly traditional menus which are very flexible. The hotel has its own car park with 110 spaces.

VANDERBILT HOTEL 68-86 Cromwell Road, SW7 5BT
Tel: 071-589 2424 Fax: 071-225 2293

Victoria & Albert Suites Banquet: 100, Dinner Dance: 100, Reception: 125
The Victoria and Albert Suite is situated on the lower ground floor and can be divided into two. The modern red decor is enhanced by light oak woodwork. Two small skylights allow some daylight in and chandeliers provide the evening lighting. The adjoining foyer is shared by some smaller suites, including the Milton and Cromwell, which is decorated in the same way and is often used for the drinks reception. As well as offering a choice of international menu selections, the head chef is able to create dishes of any nationality to match a theme such as Japanese and Caribbean.

WESTBURY HOTEL Bond Street at Conduit Street, W1A 4UH
Tel: 071-629 7755 Fax: 071-495 1163

Mount Vernon Room Banquet: 100, Dinner Dance: 80, Reception: 130
The Mount Vernon Room is attractively decorated with hand-painted panelling, a pale green moulded cornice and deep pink carpet. A crystal chandelier hangs over the central dance floor, the specialist lighting is particularly soft. The room can be partitioned into two, offering separate reception and dining areas. The hotel offers excellent standards of French cuisine and service and will provide interesting set menus.

Pine Room Banquet: 80, Dinner Dance: 60, Reception: 110
This elegant, pine panelled room has a gilded stucco ceiling, gleaming chandelier and a stately ambience. The Westbury Hotel also has two smaller suites available for private dining - the Regency Room, serviced by the restaurant, and the gorgeous Brighton Room, modelled on the Brighton Pavilion.

WESTMINSTER HOTEL 16 Leinster Square, W2 4PR
Tel: 071-221 9131 Fax: 071-229 3917

Boulevard Brasserie Banquet: 120, Dinner Dance: 100, Reception: 120
Although the Boulevard Brasserie is actually below ground level, it is extremely light, bright and airy, possibly due to the clever use of mirrors and colour - pale grey and peach. There is a huge matching marble buffet counter and separate bar area. A marble dance floor is available if required. The cuisine is French and English specialising in buffet events to cover a variety of dietary needs and fashions. Outside caterers may hire the venue.

Hotels

WALDORF HOTEL The Aldwych, WC2B 4DD
Tel: 071-836 2400 Fax: 071-836 7244

Palm Court *(Above)* Reception: 500
Well known for it's tea dances, the Palm Court may be used alone for a private cocktail party or as the reception room and dance area for larger functions in the adjoining Adelphi Suite. This impressive Edwardian lounge is on two levels, the upper is a balcony on three sides and the lower is where the dancing takes place. The floor is marble and the ceiling is of frosted glass allowing some natural daylight through. The decor is green and cream and, as its name suggests, potted palms are all around.

Adelphi Suite Banquet: 420, Dinner Dance: 420, Reception: 800
The Waldorf Hotel, opened in 1908, retains much of its authentic Edwardian splendour and this is reflected in the Adelphi Suite, located directly off the famous Palm Court. Its original features include tall pillars along each side, a high ceiling, glass chandeliers and a built-in dance floor. The decor is cream and pale green and the full length windows are dressed with pink and green drapes. The suite can be divided into three areas, each with separate access to the Palm Court. The selection of banqueting menus caters for almost every occasion though they are always eager to try new ideas and will tailor a menu to your specific requirements.

Charter Suites Banquet: 280, Dinner Dance: 230, Reception: 400 (both suites)
Divided into Suites One and Two, the Charter Suites have their own private entrance and cloakroom facilities. Situated on the lower ground floor, Charter Suite One is used for the reception for larger parties. With fewer guests, the reception can be held on the balcony of the larger suite. The suites are both air-conditioned and decorated in pale blue and white with mirrors, crystal chandeliers and ormolu wall lights. Charter Suite Two has pillars on either side, a built-in dance floor and an alcove with a portable stage. The balcony - only four steps up - has an unusual feature of decorative shop windows. Being totally self-contained, these suites are very popular for weddings.

WHITES HOTEL Lancaster Gate, W2 3NR
Tel: 071-262 2711 Fax: 071-262 2147

The Grill Room Banquet: 70, Dinner Dance: 70, Reception: 100
The restaurant of this luxury Victorian hotel facing Kensington Gardens is available for exclusive hire. The two areas of the L-shaped restaurant are connected by an archway. The larger,

Whites Hotel Continued....

front area has an elegant glass domed ceiling and intricate moulding, the other has an attractive tented ceiling and a mirrored arch. Antique crystal chandeliers illuminate the peach and terracotta furnishings and the pale ragged walls hung with paintings and mirrors. Pre-dinner drinks are served in the pale yellow panelled bar.The restaurant has a separate entrance via a glass canopy as well as access from the hotel foyer. A very high standard of traditional English cuisine is beautifully served - menus are tailor-made to suit individual clients. There is parking for 25 cars in the cobbled forecourt.

WOODLANDS PARK HOTEL Woodlands Lane, Stoke D'Abernon, Cobham, Surrey KT11 3QB Tel: 037284 3933 Fax: 037284 2704

Prince of Wales Suite (Lancaster and Cornwall Suites)
Banquet: 300 (Lancaster - 180, Cornwell - 90)
Dinner Dance: 250 (Lancaster - 150, Cornwell - 80)
Reception: 400 (Lancaster - 250, Cornwell - 150)

Woodlands Park is a carefully restored Victorian mansion set in 10 acres of grounds just 45 minutes from central London, between junctions 9 and 10 of the M25. The Prince of Wales Suite, which divides into the Lancaster and Cornwell Suites, has a separate entrance, private bars and cloakrooms. The suite is half-panelled in mahogany with cream moire walls and deep blue carpet matching the gold-fringed drapes. French windows open onto the terrace for summer receptions. A wide variety of high quality traditional cuisine and wines may be chosen from the menu selector.

Banqueting Suites

Often tied to catering firms, banqueting suites are designed specifically to provide efficiently run functions. At multi-suite venues, there are likely to be several events taking place simultaneously, but meticulous planning by experienced staff will ensure that each is kept entirely separate and will not affect your function in any way.

THE BREWERY Chiswell Street, EC1Y 4SD
Tel: 071-606 4455 Fax: 071-638 5713

The original Whitbread Brewery was the creation of Samuel Whitbread, built over a period of 30 years in the 18th century. The building was converted into suites in 1976 retaining many of the original Georgian architectural features. The in-house caterers have prepared an impressive a la carte menu and selected buffet and canapé menus. The cuisine is predominantly French though they are able to prepare special menus for themed parties or specific dietary requirements. The cellar at The Brewery stocks an extensive selection of fine wines, ports and draught beers. A complete party planning service is offered. The Brewery is closed every August for redecoration.

The Porter Tun Banquet: 700, Dinner Dance: 550, Reception: 1200
Originally used for the brewing of porter, this magnificent room has the largest King-Post timber roof in Europe with a clear span of 20 metres over an unobstructed solid oak floor. The Hind's Head Bar is set on a raised balcony which is used for receptions for smaller functions. For larger parties, the George III Room is used for the reception. The Porter Tun is the perfect setting for medieval banquets.

King George III Banquet: 420, Dinner Dance: 330, Reception: 700
Also known as the Overlord Room, the King George III has an unusual barrel-vaulted ceiling, exposed brickwork, mahogany woodwork and is lit by 18th century-style brass lanterns. It has direct access to the adjoining Queen Charlotte room where guests can be received.

Queen Charlotte Banquet: 180, Dinner Dance: 120, Reception: 250
Decorated in a similar way to the King George III, this room also has a barrel-vault ceiling, softened by Georgian crystal chandeliers.

Sugar Rooms Banquet: 100, Dinner Dance: 100, Reception: 150
The Sugar Rooms are always sold as a pair and are very popular for weddings. The upper Sugar Room, overlooking the cobbled courtyard, has an original Queen-Post roof and is nicknamed "The Chapel". This is where all the sugar used for fermentation was once kept. The best crystal, china and silverware are used in this room which is decorated with Whitbread family portraits. The Lower Sugar Room is where the reception and dancing take place. It is decorated in the same Georgian style as the upper room - primrose walls, turquoise and yellow drapes - with original lights from the brewery cellars.

Smeaton's Vaults Banquet: 130, Dinner Dance: 130, Reception: 250
The inter-connecting King and Queen Vaults feature the original copper pipes that used to carry beer from the Porter Tun. The King Vault has a barrel-vaulted ceiling and a gallery on three sides. The Queen Vault contains part of the original gallery walkway and has a fixed bar. Either room can be used for dancing.

James Watt Banquet: 80, Reception: 120
This is where the beer used to be kept, hence the sloping floors for rolling barrels. A collection of menus from the 1920's and 30's decorate the walls which are half panelled in limed oak.

City Cellars Banquet: 50, Dinner Dance: 40, Reception: 80
Comprising two adjoining rooms, the City Cellars were formerly the Directors' Dining Rooms. The reception room has a fixed bar, barrel ceiling, and exposed London brick. The dining room has panelled walls and six pillars in a circle around a small dance floor.

CAFÉ ROYAL 68 Regent Street, W1R 6EL Tel: 071-437 9090 Fax: 071-439 7672

The Café Royal has been a famous venue for social occasions since it first opened in 1865. It is now one of Europe's largest and most versatile banqueting venues, containing 21 suites, varying in size and style. The suites are available for any occasion from a quiet dinner party to a lavish ball for up to 1500 (by combining several floors). A selection of the larger suites are described below. The catering is of a high standard offering a varied selection of traditional and international menus and an excellent wine list. The Café Royal has an experienced team of banqueting managers available to discuss your requirements.

Empire Napoleon Suite *(Right)*
Banquet: 650, Dinner Dance: 550,
Reception: 1000
Occupying the whole of the fourth floor, this grand ballroom sparkles with mirrors and crystal chandeliers. it has an impressive pan-elled ceiling, large central dance floor (carpeted when not required) and a balcony at one end. A separate reception area could be curtained off.

Dubarry and Dauphin Suites
Banquet: 360, Dinner Dance: 300,
Reception: 600
The larger of the two, the Dubarry Suite has an elegant lofted ceiling, crystal chandeliers, mirrored arches and red furnishings. It is perfectly complimented by the adjoining Dauphin Suite, used for pre-dinner receptions.

Elysee Suite Banquet: 220, Dinner Dance: 180, Reception: 300
The main attraction of this suite is the central dance floor, surrounded by a low wall supporting marble pillars - perfect for a dinner dance or disco party.

Pompadour Suite Banquet: 120, Dinner Dance: 90, Reception: 200
The sumptuous Pompadour suite was originally a restaurant in the late 1800s. Decorated in Louis XV style, the room features an exquisite hand-painted and gilt panelled ceiling and mirrored wall panels. Floor to ceiling windows overlook Regent Street.

**THE ELIZABETH SUITE Barrington House, 59/67 Gresham Street, EC2V 7EY
Tel: 071-606 7344 Fax: 071-606 2881**

The banqueting rooms at the Elizabeth Suite are all situated on the lower ground floor and vary in size and style. Dishes from all over the world can be provided by the in-house caterer. Outside caterers may use the facilities by arrangement. Street parking is unrestricted after 6.30pm.

The Spanish Room Banquet: 350-400, Dinner Dance: 375, Reception: 700
Entrance to the room is via a balcony with a staircase to either side. There is a large central dance floor, a bar at the far end and a stage to one side. The Spanish look comes from the deep red and gold furnishings and the ornate wood effect plaster work on the walls and ceiling. Decorative mirrors enhance the pillars in the room which is lit by Spanish chandeliers.

Golden Hind (Incorporating Drake, Raleigh and Grenville) Banquet: 80, Reception: 150
Sometimes used for receptions for functions in the Spanish Room, the Golden Hind can be divided into four separate areas, each with its own entrance from the corridor. The walls are half panelled in dark oak with white brick effect above. In addition the oak panelled, split level Library can accommodate 40 seated or 50 for a reception.

Banqueting Suites

GROSVENOR ROOMS   92 Walm Lane, Willesden, NW2 4YQ
Tel: 081-451 0066/7/8 Fax: 081-459 7676

The three banqueting suites that make up the Grosvenor Rooms are each self-contained with their own bars and cloakrooms. There is a private car park on site. The suites are available for hire to outside caterers or you may choose the in-house banqueting service which has over 50 years catering experience of Continental, Asian and kosher cuisine as well as offering an outside catering service.

Grosvenor Suite *(Right)*
Banquet: 500
Dinner Dance: 350
Reception: 700

The central staircase off the main foyer leads to the Grosvenor Suite with its deep pink furnishings, a mirrored arch and pillars. The room divides into two separate areas, one for reception and dancing and the other for dining.

Executive Suite
Banquet: 180
Dinner Dance: 180
Reception: 240

The   royal blue reception room, which is also used for dancing, leads through to the deep pink dining room with its floor to ceiling carpeting and gleaming chandeliers.

Pearl Suite
Banquet: 140
Dinner Dance: 140
Reception: 220

Appointed directly off the main foyer on the ground floor, the mirrored Pearl Suite has two central pillars, a small dance floor and two bars.

KING DAVID SUITE   32 Great Cumberland Place, W1H 7DJ
Tel: 071-723 7933 Fax: 071-402 0399

Banquet: 450, Dinner Dance: 400, Reception: 1000
Located close to Marble Arch, the King David Suite contains all the necessary up-to-date facilities. Situated on the lower ground floor, reached via a marble staircase or lift, the suite has a reception room that can be used alone for smaller functions (dinner dance: 90, reception: 150). Both rooms have a neutral decor of beige and brown with marble effect wall covering, lit by crystal chandeliers and wall lights. The mirrored arches along the side walls are decorated with ornate mouldings. The catering is provided solely by V. Schaverien Caterers Ltd (see Caterers) who own the suite and offer an extensive variety of excellent kosher cuisine as well as a complete party planning service. There is NCP parking opposite the suite in Great Cumberland Place.

NEW CONNAUGHT ROOMS Great Queen Street, WC2B 5DA
Tel: 071-405 7811 Fax: 071-831 1851

The New Connaught Rooms have been a popular venue for meetings and banquets for more than 200 years. Now restored to its original splendour, the venue offers a choice of 27 rooms - some self-contained, others inter-connecting - varying in size, style and grandeur. The in-house caterers are highly experienced and provide a full range of international menu suggestions, or will tailor a menu to suit any theme or requirement. Outside caterers are allowed in on Sundays only. The following are a selection of the larger suites.

Grand Hall Banquet: 600,   Dinner Dance: 500, Reception: 600
At the top of the sweeping staircase, is the Grand Hall and the adjoining Balmoral Suite. Interconnected by four doors, the two rooms used together can seat up to 1000 for a banquet. Otherwise, the Balmoral may be used for a reception, though for larger functions, the Edinburgh Suite is used. The impressive Grand Hall has an elaborate ceiling that soars to a height of 40 feet, with four huge crystal chandeliers.

Banqueting Suites

New Connaught Rooms Continued....

Edinburgh Suite Banquet: 330, Dinner Dance: 180, Reception: 350
The striking blue decor of the Edinburgh Suite is continued through to the adjoining Drawing Room where guests can be received. Both rooms, on the first floor, benefit from plenty of natural daylight.

Cornwall Suite Reception: 330, Dinner Dance: 200, Reception: 350
Often sold with the adjacent Crown Room, the Cornwall is the least ornate of the two, with pink and grey colour scheme, panelled ceiling, chandeliers and windows on three sides. Used for the reception, the Crown Room features a superb domed ceiling with a glass skylight and ornate criss-cross plasterwork. The decor here is pale blue and white with chandeliers and natural light. A dinner dance for 80 could be held in the Crown Room which has its own dance floor. Both rooms are on the second floor.

Connaughts Brasserie Banquet: 200, Dinner Dance: 150, Reception: 300
The ground floor restaurant is open to the public during the day so is only available for exclusive hire in the evening or at weekends. With its own street entrance, the Brasserie has a 1920's style with a gorgeous hand-painted ceiling, polished wood floor and wooden bar.

ROYAL MAJESTIC SUITE 196 Willesden Lane, NW6 7PR
Tel: 081-459 3276/0567 Fax: 081-451 0920

Banquet: 240 Dinner Dance: 220 Reception: 350
This purpose built banqueting suite is smartly decorated in grey and peach with two huge crystal chandeliers hanging from the barrel ceiling. The walls are half panelled in light oak with high windows on two sides providing natural daylight. There is a large dance floor and a stage. Upstairs, the reception room is similarly decorated and may be used separately for smaller functions - 72 for dinner or dinner-dance, 150 for a cocktail party. It has a fixed bar and dance floor, barrel ceiling and natural light. In-house caterers Helen and Richard Goide, have a long standing reputation for excellent kosher cuisine and attentive service. They are experienced party planners and offer a complete package. There is limited parking in the forecourt but unrestricted parking in the street.

ROYAL OVER-SEAS LEAGUE
Park Place, St James's Street,
SW1A 1LR
Tel: 071-408 0214
Fax: 071-499 6738

Over-Seas House is situated in the heart of St James's at the end of a quiet street. It is an elegant building which comprises two period houses and a 1930's extension, so offering a variety of rooms of different size, shape and atmosphere. The catering is traditionally English.

The Rutland Room, *(pictured above right)* overlooks the League's private garden and Green Park, and is decorated in the Georgian style of the building. This is just one of the four rooms available for parties of up to 50 guestsand provides enviable surroundings for a special evening in London.

In the more modern part of the building, there are two halls which can accommodate much larger groups. The larger of the two, the **Hall of India** caters for up to 250 people for a cocktail party or buffet, or 200 for a dinner.

Royal Overseas League Continued....

St. Andrew's Hall   *(Right)*

Banquet: 80
Dinner dance: 60
Reception: 150
One of the larger venues at Overseas House, St.Andrews Hall has an optional dance floor, and a stage area which can be set up for a cabaret or disco for a really good party. The large windows down one side of the room provide plenty of natural light for daytime functions. St Andrew's Hall and the Hall of India may be booked jointly for a dinner dance for 200 guests.

SYON PARK CONFERENCE AND BANQUETING CENTRE
Syon Park, Brentford, Middx TW8 8JF
Tel: 081-568 0778 Fax: 081-568 4308

The Conference and Banqueting Centre comprises five inter-connecting rooms, varying in size, all overlooking the gardens at Syon Park and each with their own terrace area. The rooms can be used individually or combined to accommodate a maximum of 500 for a banquet or dinner dance and up to 1000 for a reception. Town & County provide a high standard of traditional English catering. The three larger rooms are described.

Garden Room Banquet: 146, Dinner Dance: 146, Reception: 300
Used mainly for weddings, the pretty green and white Garden Room has a built-in dance floor and patio doors to the terrace. The Conservatory Lounge could be used for a pre-dinner reception.

Camellia Room Banquet: 110, Dinner Dance: 100, Reception: 200
This bright and airy conservatory-style room is decorated in green with trellis work and an attractive, shaped wooden ceiling. The adjoining Camellia Lounge and bar could be used for the reception. The Camellia Room is available all day on Saturday and any evening.

Lakeside Room Banquet: 130,Dinner Dance: 130, Reception: 280
Fortunate guests might see peacocks around the lakeside terrace. The room has blue furnishings, brass chandeliers and a wooden beamed ceiling. It shares an entrance with the Terrace Room.

WALBROOK CONFERENCE & BANQUETING CENTRE
Buckersbury House, Walbrook, EC4N 8EL
Tel: 071-621 0315

Banquet: 220 Dinner Dance: 200, Reception: 500 (with Cotillion Restaurant)
On the lower ground floor of Bucklesbury House, the Walbrook uses modern equipment to create a party atmosphere, including sophisticated lighting effects, dance floor, bar and stage. The suite can be used in conjunction with either the smart, Regency style Cotillion Restaurant or the more modern BBs Brasserie which has its own disco and can accommodate 150 people for a buffet. Catering is by Graisons who also offer a complete party planning service, or you can choose outside caterers if preferred.

Restaurants

If food is the highest priority at your party, a restaurant might be your best choice of venue. You will be able to try out the menu beforehand and be confident that the quality of the meal will be consistent.

APOLLONIA RESTAURANT
25 Church Road, Stanmore, Middx HA7 4AR Tel: 081-954 5060   Fax: 081-954 0934

Banquet: 200, Dinner Dance: 175

Apollonia is a well established venue for parties and functions with over fifteen years excellent reptutation. It specialises in French and Continental cuisine. Menus are tailor-made when you take over the whole venue for a party and guests are offered desserts from an impressive selection on the trolley. Decorated in smart fresh pink and grey, with some unusual personalised features, this is an excellent 'local' venue for a party. The management has vast experience in party planning and will enthusiastically arrange the whole party package, down to the finest detail. They also have other venues which are suitable for smaller parties.

LA BASTIDE 50 Greek Street, W1V 5LQ
Tel: 071-734 3300

La Bastide Salon Banquet: 50, Reception: 100
On the first floor of this gracious Georgian town house, above the restaurant, is the original drawing room, now the salon. The decor is in keeping with the period - pale grey walls and dusty pink drapes - creating a refined yet informal ambience. The room is lit by brass chandeliers, with natural lighting from both sides of the room. The walls are hung with prints and a large oil painting of the restaurant. The salon can be divided into two and is available seven days a week. Live music and dancing are not allowed. Modern and classical French cuisine is served from the same kitchen as the renowned restaurant.

BEEFEATER BY THE TOWER OF LONDON Ivory House, St Katharine's Dock,
East Smithfield, E1
Tel: 071-408 1001 Fax: 071-629 4623

Banquet: 500, Dinner Dance: 500
Situated in the historic vaults of Ivory House, the Beefeater provides a perfect setting for a medieval banquet. Guests are welcomed by King Henry VIII and his court, served by wenches and entertained by minstrels, the court jester, jousting knights and other royal entertainers. A five course banquet is served accompanied by jugs of wine and ale. Alternatively, you can choose to have a buffet and arrange your own entertainment. The vaults have eight bays which each hold fifty people, so it is ideal for both private and semi-private parties.

THE BELVEDERE Holland House, Holland Park, W8
Tel: 071-602 1238

Banquet: 132, Dinner Dance: 132, Reception: 180
Situated in the heart of Holland Park, The Belvedere is the Old Summer Ballroom of Holland House which dates back to around 1850. The building has an elegant country house feel. There are plenty of bright windows showing off views over the park. The restaurant is on two levels, the main eating area below and the reception area upstairs. The dance floor can be situated upstairs for larger functions or downstairs for dinner dances for up to 80. Menus can be chosen from an à la carte banqueting selector and extensive wine list. The cuisine is renowned for its excellence.

COATES KARAOKE BAR & RESTAURANT 45 London Wall, EC2M 5TE
Tel: 071-256 5148 Fax: 071-382 9373

Karaoke: 200, Pizza Reception: 200
The City of London's only full time karaoke bar has an ultra-modern high-tech design. The bar area features a long, curved, marble and neon bar with video screens and a specialised speaker system. A thriving pizza business (mainly at lunchtimes) allows popular, inexpensive food to be supplied at all private parties. Coates is available for exclusive hire every night of the week.

CORNEY & BARROW 19 Broadgate Circle, Broadgate, EC2M 2QS
Tel: 071-628 1251 Fax: 071-382 9373

Reception: 300
A unique modern curved terrace bar in a stunning location overlooking England's only open-air ice rink in winter and a concert area in summer. The light grey and pink decor is enlivened with excellent lighting and many 'City' touches (televisions, world time clocks, STX phones). On either side of the bar there are open balconies, overhung with greenery, where you can hire Jumbrellas (giant white umbrellas) which look extremely elegant. The bar can be hired exclusively at weekends and semi-private areas at other times.

Restaurants

CORNEY & BARROW   118 Moorgate, EC2M 6UR
Tel: 071-628 2898 Fax: 071-382 9371

Banquet: 100, Dinner Dance: 70, Reception: 250
Downstairs, beneath the Champagne Bar, the restaurant features a spectacular sunken, oval bar of polished American walnut. Designed by Julyan Wickam, it has a low red ceiling, blue carpet, comfortable black chairs and an in-built dance floor. The imaginative international menu and extensive wine list will not disappoint. The restaurant is available for parties at weekends and evenings.

CORNEY & BARROW
44 Cannon Street,
EC4N 6JJ
Tel: 071-248 1700
Fax: 071-382 9373

Banquet: 100-150
Dinner Dance: 100-200
Reception: 200

This pretty, split level restaurant is located below the wine bar via an impressive angled steel and black slate staircase. The soft, rose-coloured walls and alcoves give this room a warm, almost romantic atmosphere. The slate floor of the upstairs wine bar is perfect for discos. The cuisine is basically English with some interesting touches added. As with all the Corney & Barrow restaurants, the wine list is exceptional. The restaurant is available for parties from Monday to Saturday though only semi-private during the week when the wine bar is open to the public.

DICKENS INN BY THE TOWER   St Katharine's Way, E1 9LB
Tel: 071-481 1786

For 130 years the building was a spice warehouse, then in 1969 it was moved, brick by brick, to its present site and opened as an inn the following year. The original facade, with its wooden balconies and geranium-filled window boxes, now faces St Katharine's Docks and Tower Bridge. The cuisine is traditional English offering a choice of eight set menus which are very flexible.

Nickleby Suite Banquet: 110, Dinner Dance: 110, Reception/Buffet: 110
On the first floor, the Nickleby Suite includes a large reception bar and views over both sides of the dock. It is a traditional room with exposed brick walls, a wooden floor and a vaulted, beamed roof decorated with a maritime theme - fishing nets, lobster pots, anchors, even a small rowing boat. It has its own kitchen, cloakroom and lift.

Great Expectations Banquet: 100, Dinner Dance: 100
An open-air balcony runs along the whole length of this room, used for receptions or extra tables in summer. Being on the second floor, there are magnificent views of the docks from three sides of the room. Like the Nickleby Suite, it has a vaulted, beamed roof, wooden floor, exposed brick walls and maritime decorations with the addition of a 'shop window' recess. There is a bar, a piano and an open plan kitchen.

44

L'ESCARGOT 48 Greek Street, W1V 5LQ
Tel: 071-437 2679 Fax: 071-437 0790

Barrel Vaulted Room Banquet: 46, Buffet: 80, Reception: 80
On the second floor, the bright and airy Barrel Vaulted Room has a splendid glass roof. The walls are pale green contrasting with the deep blue carpet. The ground-floor Brasserie can also be hired on occasions and can seat up to 90 but works better using the front section for a reception and seating 70 in the back. The cuisine has an excellent, well deserved reputation. Guests can select from a menu with three or four choices. The exceptional wine list includes a selection of New World wines.

Banqueting Room *(Above)* Banquet: 30, Buffet: 50, Reception: 50
Accessed from the reception, so by-passing the Restaurant and Brasserie, the private Banqueting Room, on the first floor, is beautifully decorated in 18th century style with pale green panelled walls, deep blue carpet, peach drapes and matching upholstered chairs. There is a large fireplace and a crystal chandelier hanging from the listed moulded ceiling.

FREDERICK'S RESTAURANT   Camden Passage, Islington, N1 8EG
Tel: 071-359 3902 Fax: 071-359 5173   Party Organiser - Sue Evans

Whole Restaurant Banquet: 135, Dinner Dance: 125, Reception: 175
For a Sunday party, Frederick's is an ideal venue when the entire restaurant is available for private functions. The delightful Garden Room, with it's high domed ceiling, and the conservatory give direct access to a picturesque patio and garden: a country idyll in the heart of town. From Monday through to Friday, the Garden Room is available for parties for up to 85 (65 minimum). The smaller private dining room, The Clarence Room, on the first floor can seat up to 26 or 45 for a cocktail party every day except Sunday. Frederick's is well known for the originality of the menu and high quality of the French cuisine as well as its comprehensive wine list.

THE GREENERY 28 The Minories, EC3N 1DD
Tel: 071-621 0315

Banquet: 240, Dinner Dance: 170, Reception: 300
A few steps lead down to the bar area decorated with hanging greenery and trellis work. This can be separated from the restaurant by a curtain until dinner is announced. The garden-room theme is continued through the restaurant with green grass-paper walls, green trellis ceiling and mirrored pillars. The large dance floor is carpeted over when not in use and has some sophisticated lighting equipment above it to create a variety of moods and effects. Two private areas can be curtained off for smaller functions, one in the bar area and one in the restaurant, each able to seat up to 70 people. The cuisine is international with a strong English influence.

MONKEY BUSINESS 35 The Piazza, Covent Garden, WC2
Tel: 071-379 5803

Banquet: 200, Dinner Dance: 200, Reception: 300
Past the safari jeep at the entrance and down the stairs, you will find yourself face to face with a life-size African elephant in the heart of the jungle. The safari hut in the centre of the restaurant houses the raised bar. Beside it, there is a jungle train where you can eat while watching videos through the windows. Elsewhere, there are hanging baskets of greenery, murals depicting jungle

46

Monkey Business Continued....

scenes and even the occasional monkey just hanging around. A large screen projects pop videos, unless you would prefer something else. There is a small dance floor at the back of the restaurant which is licensed for dancing until 2am. The food is American/Mexican specialising in Cajun Creole from the five Gulf states of Mexico.

NEW SERPENTINE RESTAURANT Hyde Park, W2
Tel: 071-402 1142

Banquet: 140, Dinner Dance: 140, Reception: 250
The restaurant consists of two interlinking hexagonal buildings, set on the edge of the Serpentine with stunning views over Hyde Park. The terrace area may be used for receptions or extra seating in summer. The two rooms, which can be used individually or together, have white "tented" roofs and glass walls. The venue is not available at weekends during the summer and all events must finish by midnight. There is ample parking in the Serpentine car park. The restaurant is run by Leith's Good Food (see Caterers) who present an exceptionally high standard of modern and inventive cuisine.

ORMONDS'S 91 Jermyn Street, SW1Y 6JT
Tel: 071-930 2842

Banquet: 250, Dinner Dance: 200, Reception: 300
Ormond's consists of two separate inter-connecting venues - the restaurant and the club (the entrance for which is at 6 Ormond Yard, off Duke of York Street). Each is self-contained and sound-proofed and can be hired individually or combined. The Jermyn Street entrance is guarded by a uniformed doorman. Stairs lead down to the restaurant which has a bar, bare brick walls, wooden floors and subdued lighting. Wooden screens can divide the room into separate areas. Dancing can take place at the back of the restaurant, or (for larger numbers) downstairs at the club. The dark green discotheque can seat 80 for dinner. It has a bar, dance floor, air-conditioning, the latest disco equipment and a wind machine. The cuisine is French, there are set party menus though they can provide anything the customer wants. Both venues are available for hire any day of the week up until 3am.

QUAYSIDE RESTAURANT World Trade Centre, International House,
1 St Katherine's Way, E1 9UN Tel: 071-481 0972 Fax: 071-488 3482

Banquet: 150, Dinner Dance: 130, Reception: 200
This stylish restaurant has a wonderful view over St Katharine's Dock and a terrace for alfresco events. Bare brick walls work well with the attractive maroon and grey colour scheme and there is a comfortable bar lounge with a piano. Adjoining the restaurant is Drew's Private Room which could accommodate 60 for a lunch or dinner and 80 for a buffet reception. The exclusive modern French cuisine is first class and well presented.

SCHOOL DINNERS RESTAURANT 1 Robert Adam Street, W1M 5AG
Tel: 071-486 2724 Fax: 071-935 8262

Banquet: 100, Dinner Dance: 100, Reception: 100
This legendary restaurant is great fun and makes a unique party venue. The walls are lined with memorabilia to transport you back to your school days. Guests are served by stocking-clad sixth formers, though more sedate uniforms can be worn if the occasion needs to be toned down. A disco is provided and extroverts can really show off using the latest Karaoke equipment. The food is a great deal better than anything you would have had at school, but don't worry, Spotted Dick and custard is still on the menu.

Restaurants

SPICE MERCHANT
Coburg Hotel,
129 Bayswater Road,
W2 4RJ
Tel: 071-221 2442
Fax: 071-229 0557

Banquet: 120
Dinner Dance: 80
Reception: 120
The Spice Merchant is the exciting new restaurant at the recently refurbished Coburg Hotel. It is situated on the lower ground floor and has its own street entrance. The split-level modern interior has pale walls with a warm brown tiled frieze, attractive Indian prints and a large, central dance floor which is carpeted when not in use. The finest Indian cuisine is served with an emphasis on quality. The service and presentation are also excellent. Set party menus are available, though these are very flexible. There is an NCP car park next door.

THE VEERASWAMY 99-101 Regent Street, W1 8RS
Tel: 071-734 1401 Fax: 071-439 8434

Banquet: 120, Dinner Dance: 80, Reception: 40-60 Buffet 150
London's oldest Indian restaurant, the Veeraswamy is an L- shaped first floor room, beautifully decorated in pastel shades and Indian artwork. There is a bar and small reception area for pre-dinner drinks. The cuisine is classical Indian of the highest standard. The private Bengal Room on the second floor, can accommodate 40 seated or 60 buffet.

Many of the halls are extremely old and richly decorated, often with traditional panelling and ornate mouldings, but there are also some modern halls which are equally as suitable for even the most prestigious of occasions.

APOTHECARIES' HALL Blackfriars Lane, EC4V 6EJ
Tel: 071-236 1180 Fax: 071-329 3177

Great Hall Banquet: 146, Reception: 250
The building has altered little since it was rebuilt following the Fire of London in 1666. The whole building may be hired, comprising the courtyard, entrance hall, Great Hall and two anterooms - the Court Room and the Parlour. The Great Hall and anterooms are all on the first floor, reached via a stately oak staircase. The Hall is panelled in dark oak and hung with large portraits of distinguished members of the Society. Stained glass windows provide some natural light, huge brass chandeliers hang from the high Adam-style ceiling. At one end, there is a small minstrel gallery - at the other, an ornately carved screen. Either of the adjacent anterooms can be used for the reception. Both are hung with portraits and furnished with antiques. The Court Room is fully oak panelled, the Parlour is half panelled in pine and houses a collection of antique drug jars and pill tiles. Party Ingredients (see Caterers) handle all the catering arrangements. No dancing is allowed in the building which is available from Monday to Friday until 11pm and on Saturday for weddings until 5pm. There are three NCP sites within three minutes walk.

BUTCHERS' HALL   87 Bartholomew Close, Smithfield, EC1A 7EB
Tel: 071-600 5777 Fax: 071-600 2777

Reception Hall Reception: 150,
This beautiful room was designed by Algernon Asprey and contains the striking glass screen depicting the Four Seasons designed and engraved by John Hutton. It serves as the reception area for functions in the Great Hall and the Court Suite. No smoking is allowed in the Reception Hall. Chester Boyd Ltd (see Caterers) take care of all the arrangements.

Great Hall *(Right)*
Banquet: 160,
Dinner Dance: 120,
Reception: 250
The Great Hall is a majestic room with an Adam style ceiling, beech panelling and crystal chandeliers. The South wall is dominated by the colourful Aubusson tapestry, presented by the Vestey family. A recent portrait of the guild's Patron, The Queen Mother, was commissioned and donated by a liveryman and now hangs in the Hall. There is abundant natural light from windows on two sides. Music and dancing is allowed until 11pm but no discos.

Court Suite Banquet: 80, Reception: 100
By sliding open the dividing doors, the Small and Large Court Rooms become the Court Suite. This L-shaped room on the first floor is half-panelled in Australian Black Bean and receives natural light from windows on two sides.

The Taurus Suite Banquet: 80, Reception: 100
On the lower ground floor, this suite has its own Sheraton furnished reception area. The walls are decorated in pale green rag work with a blue carpet.

FARMERS' & FLETCHERS' LIVERY HALL   3 Cloth Street, EC1A 7LD
Tel: 071-606 2204/5 Fax: 071-600 1059

Livery Hall Banquet: 120, Dinner Dance: 250, Reception: 250
The first purpose built livery hall to be built in the last 200 years, Farmers' & Fletchers' is tastefully decorated throughout in pale cream with crests from both companies displayed on the panelled walls. The hall is beautifully lit by chandeliers and is fully air conditioned. Removable screens separate the Hall from two adjoining rooms which can be easily adapted to suit any occasion. Food and drink is supplied by the in-house caterers.

FOUNDERS' HALL
1 Cloth Fair, EC1
Tel: 071-600 5777
Fax: 071-600 2777

Banquet: 75, Reception: 100
Completed in 1987, the Hall was specifically designed with modern functions in mind. Overlooking the ancient Priory Church of St Bartholomew-the-Great, the room is light, beautifully decorated and well appointed. There are five circular windows, each displaying a sculpture, and shields of past masters are hung on a wall of gold.
Earlier shields are displayed in a glass case. The red walls, carpet and upholstery contrast dramatically with the striking black bog ash dining furniture. Lighting is concealed in the unusual chrome ceiling. The Parlour is used as the reception room for the main hall or for small dinners parties for up to 25 guests. Catering is by Chester Boyd Ltd (see Caterers) who can provide a wide range of menu suggestions or produce one to the clients requirements. Music and dancing are allowed by arrangement but no discos. There is metered parking outside or an NCP a minute's walk away.

GLAZIERS HALL 9 Montaque Close, London Bridge, SE1 9DD
Tel: 071-403 3300 Fax: 071-407 6036

Banqueting Hall Banquet: 270, Dinner Dance: 200, Reception: 500, Balls: 400
Dating from about 1808, the listed building was reopened after restoration in 1978. The Banqueting Hall is half panelled in oak with a polished wooden floor and is lighted by three large crystal chandeliers. It is overlooked by the River Room on the first floor which can be used for the reception. A list of recommended caterers is supplied but Glaziers Hall reserve the right to supply all the bar and wine requirements.

The River Room Banquet: 120, Dinner Dance: 50, Reception: 250
Wonderful views across the Thames are provided through five massive floor to ceiling arched windows. The room forms an enclosed balcony overlooking the Banqueting Hall. The River Room is carpeted in the same red carpet that is used throughout the building. Two further rooms can be combined with the River Room for extra capacity - The Library and the Court Room.

MERCHANT TAYLORS' HALL Threadneedle Street, EC3
Tel: 071-588 7606 Fax: 071-528 8332

Great Hall Banquet: 280, Dinner Dance: 160, Reception: 600
The first Merchant Taylors' Hall was built on the present site in the 14th century. The Hall has twice been destroyed by fire but the original walls survived and have been incorporated in the restoration. The Hall features rich mahogany panelled walls, ash and lime panelled ceiling,

stained glass windows, and brass chandeliers. A Renatus Harris organ is in place on the gallery that runs right around the hall. No discos are allowed in the Hall which is available on weekdays, though Saturdays are sometimes possible by special arrangement. Merchant Taylors' Catering provide a high standard of traditional cuisine and are happy to cater to the customers special requirements.

Parlour Banquet: 80, Reception: 170
The reconstructed 17th century Parlour is panelled in oak and contains some wonderful Regency furniture and paintings of past masters. The elaborate ceiling is decorated with coat of arms. The Parlour is carpeted over a polished floor. Windows look out onto the cloistered courtyard where it is possible to have a summer reception for up to 200.

**STATIONERS' HALL Ave Maria Lane, Ludgate Hill, EC4M 7DD
Tel: 071-248 2934**

Livery Hall Banquet: 200, Dinner Dance: 172, Reception: 400
The Hall was completed in 1673 on the site of the previous hall destroyed in the Great Fire. It is oak-panelled and has a splendid oak carved screen at one end. The stained glass windows represent various important figures and events and are flood-lit from the outside at night. Brightly coloured flags and armorial shields decorate the room. There is a minstrels gallery from which there are excellent acoustics. A piano is available. Caterers must be chosen from the approved list. The Hall and other rooms are not available for six weeks during August and September and Christmas week.

The Stock Room Banquet: 45, Reception: 70
The oak-panelling and carving date back to the 17th century. Armorial shields, mainly of past masters, stretch right around the room above the frieze. There are stained glass windows and portraits on the walls. This room is often used for wine tastings for which it is ideal. Dancing is possible in this room but a maintenance fee of £200 will be charged. The small anteroom is available for private luncheons or dinners for up to 20. The wonderfully ornate Court Room, with its fine plaster work and gilding, and original carved pine mantlepiece looks out onto the garden. It may be used for a pre-dinner reception but no eating or smoking is allowed in this room.

**WATERMENS HALL 18 St Mary-at-Hill, EC3R 8EE
Tel: 071-283 2373 Fax: 071-283 0477**

The Court Room Banquet: 35, Reception: 60
Built in 1780 in the classical style, the building is the only genuine Georgian Hall in the City. The perfectly preserved Court Room, on the first floor, has original features which include a delicately ornate ceiling, stained glass window, marble fireplace and pine half-panelling. The magnificent crystal chandelier. This room can be used for small dinners or cocktail parties or as the reception room to the Freemen's Room.

The Freemen's Room Banquet: 72, Reception: 110
In 1983, the Freemen's Room was constructed from rooms of the house next door together with a new kitchen. The walls are pale green, the ceiling is blue, the mouldings are picked out in white and the curtains are of navy blue velvet. The red carpet is decorated with gold dolphins, the motif of the Watermen. On the far wall, a cabinet houses a colour display of Watermen's uniforms. Only background music is allowed, no dancing. The catering is by Payne & Gunter (see Caterers). The building is closed during August each year.

Grand Halls

Banquet: 400, Reception: 600

The Palladian architecture of Banqueting House was designed by Inigo Jones as part of the old Palace of Whitehall. Today, it still has the status of a Royal Palace and as such, does not allow private functions but is limited to hire by charities, cabinet members and reputable companies, subject to the discretion of the Historic Royal Palaces Agency. The hall is dominated by the magnificent painted ceiling by Rubens. At the far end of the room is the Victorian throne from the royal collection. A gallery surrounds the room and it is lit by natural daylight and brass chandeliers. There is no smoking or dancing allowed in the main hall. Any outside caterers may be used (a recommended list is available) but meals may not be cooked on the premises, although there are facilities for re-heating. Downstairs, the Crypt is available for hire for a reception of up to 300 guests.

DUKE OF YORK'S HEADQUARTERS
Kings Road, Chelsea, SW3 4RY Tel: 071-730 5513 Fax: 071-730 0033

Cadogan Hall *(Above)* Banquet: 300, Dinner Dance: 250 (500 with marquee), Reception: 350
The hall provides an extremely flexible space which can easily be decorated to spectacular effect
with just a little imagination. The facilities make transformation from hall to ballroom easy. The
beamed, vaulted ceiling can support hanging adornments or even interior tenting. The hall has
a gallery at one end, reached via a spiral staircase, a polished wooden floor, natural light through
high windows and a separate reception area. The capacity of the hall can be increased by simply
adding a marquee alongside. For even larger functions, a marquee can be erected on the lawn
(Pictured Below). The choice of caterers is left up to you, most of the top caterers and party planners
have worked at the venue. Parking space within the grounds is limited but car passes can be ob-
tained for bridal parties, principal guests and VIPs.

DULWICH COLLEGE   Dulwich Common, SE21 7LD Tel: 081-693 3433 Fax: 081-693 6319

Dulwich College was founded in 1619 though the present buildings, set in extensive grounds, dates from 1866. With the variety of rooms available for hire ranging in style from classical to contemporary and the added option of a marquee for 250 in the grounds, the college is an extremely versatile venue for any type of event. The availability of the 250 seat theatre and of the Pavilion and sports facilities, both indoor and out, make this a popular venue for club and corporate hospitality events. Dulwich College is available during holiday periods and offers a full catering service. Alternatively, outside caterers could be used. There is ample parking space in the grounds.

The Great Hall Banquet: 250, Dinner Dance: 200, Reception: 500-600
The medieval style hall was modelled on Westminster Hall with a spectacular painted hammer-beam roof and dark red and gold decor. Natural light is provided by traceried windows at both ends. Two side rooms, one on either side of the hall, are available for VIP receptions or small cocktail parties. Two imposing stone staircases lead down to the Lower Hall on the ground floor which is used for receptions. Leather Chesterfield sofas give this classical hall a feeling of intimacy. The main double doors face the front drive of the College, approached through wrought iron gates from the road. Smoking is not allowed in the Great Hall.

KING'S COLLEGE LONDON
Strand, WC2
Tel: 071-351 6011
Fax: 071-352 7376

Great Hall
Banquet: 220, Dinner Dance: 200,
Reception: 500
Three pairs of double doors lead from the elegant, stone flagged entrance foyer to the recently refurbished Great Hall, a classical style room with tall pillars, brass chandeliers and a polished Irish oak floor. Powder blue full length drapes dress the windows on three sides of

the hall. There is a moveable stage and two grand pianos. Receptions could be held in the smart Council Room on the first floor. Weddings can be performed in special circumstances in the gorgeous 140-year-old chapel, complete with organ, ornate panelling, oak pews and domed alter. You could either choose the in-house catering or make your own arrangements. The Great Hall may be hired every day between July and the end of September and at weekends between October and April. All functions must end by 1am.

PORCHESTER CENTRE Queensway, W2 5HS
Tel: 071-792 2823

Banqueting Hall Banquet: 450, Dinner Dance: 450, Reception: 630
From the exterior of this Grade II listed building, you would not imagine that it houses one of the grandest and best preserved Art Deco ballrooms to be found. Built in 1929, it has mahogany panelled walls, dark blue velvet drapes fringed with gold and an ornate ceiling with crystal chandeliers. The oak parquet dance floor is surrounded by discreet arched recesses with a nine metre stage at one end. It has its own street entrance and is approached by a grand marble staircase with ornamental bronze and wrought iron ballustrading. The Small Hall downstairs can serve as the reception area. Caterers may be chosen from a list approved by the centre.

Turkish/Russian Baths Banquet: 100, Reception: 250
Marble tiled floor, freized walls and a gold mettalic hanging ceiling which overlooks a plunge pool - an ideal venue for an unusual party reception.

ROYAL AERONAUTICAL SOCIETY 4 Hamilton Place, W1V 0BQ
Tel: 071-499 3515 Fax: 071-499 6230

Argyll Room Banquet: 120, Dinner Dance: 60-120, Reception: 150
This beautifully preserved Georgian house is located just off Park Lane and has been home to the Earl of Lucan, the Duke of Wellington and Lord Granville. The grand marble staircase leads to the Argyll Room on the first floor. It is a long, elegant room decorated in pale cream with a gilt ormolu cornice and huge gilded mirrors over two white marble fireplaces. At either end are large bow windows, one opening onto an outside terrace overlooking Hyde Park. A small adjoining anteroom can be used for serving drinks or a buffet. The in-house catering is by a well established reputable firm. Occasionally, outside caterers may be used for special dietary needs such as kosher.

STANLEY HOUSE King's College London, 552 King's Road, Chelsea, SW10 0UA
Tel: 071-351 6011 Fax: 071-352 7376

Hamilton Suite Banquet: 100, Dinner Dance: 75, Reception: 200
The suite consists of three inter-connecting rooms which overlook the garden where a marquee could be erected for larger summer functions. Sir William Hamilton, who owned the house, was secretary to Lord Elgin, hence the frieze of plaster casts of the Elgin Marbles in the main room. The room is decorated in Wedgewood blue and white with a wood strip floor for dancing. The adjoining rooms may be used for pre-dinner drinks and receiving. The suite is available for hire all year round except between 23rd December and 2nd January. Functions must end by 1am. You may either make your own catering arrangements or use the services of the in-house caterers.

ST. BARTHOLOMEW'S
HOSPITAL
West Smithfield, EC1A 7BE
Tel: 071-601 8019
Fax: 071-601 7899

The Great Hall
Banquet: 190, Reception: 250
Designed in the 1730's by James Gibbs, the Great Hall at St Bartholomew's remains virtually unaltered and is one of the most imposing venues of its kind. The hall has an ornate gilded ceiling with concealed lighting, stained glass windows and plenty of natural daylight. There are three marble fireplaces in the hall, one of which may be used for an open fire in winter. The walls are decorated with portraits and name plaques. At the far end of the hall is the Guild Room, a cedar-panelled anteroom which may be hired separately for smaller dinner parties. The Treasurer's Room, at the opposite end, can be used either as a cloakroom or small reception area. The approach to the Great Hall is via the famous Grand Staircase, decorated with murals by William Hogarth. The in-house catering department at St Bartholomew's can offer a selection of menus at competitive prices or, alternatively, you may choose from a list of approved caterers. As the hall is within the hospital precinct, there is no loud music or dancing allowed and parties must finish by 11.45pm. There is an NCP car park adjoining the hospital entrance.

Houses and Stately Homes ─────────────────

The atmosphere of a party at these venues is that of being welcomed into a private home. Some are very grand, while others are more homely. If the whole house has been hired, guests are free to wander around from room to room.

APSLEY HOUSE Piccadilly, W1
Tel: 071-938 8366   Fax: 071-938 8341

Waterloo Gallery, Portico and Piccadilly Rooms Banquet: 110, Reception: 200
Number One London, as it is known, was the residence of the first Duke of Wellington and is now run by the Victoria and Albert Museum. Remarkably, the house has survived along with its original furnishings and the Iron Duke's outstanding collection of paintings. The banqueting rooms are on the first floor via the Grand Staircase. The Waterloo Gallery is the setting for the annual Waterloo banquet. Being 90 feet long, it can seat up to 80 on a long oval table or 110 on round tables. The Portico and Piccadilly Rooms are available with the Waterloo Gallery for receptions for 200. The rooms are all elaborately decorated with silk damask wall coverings, gilded ceilings and glittering chandeliers. The remaining rooms are open for guests to view, a guided tour can be arranged. Smoking and the use of candles are not permitted and no dancing is allowed - background music only. There is no parking at Apsley House though there are two NCP's nearby. The house is available only ten times a year so bookings are sometimes taken three or four years in advance. Black tie functions are preferred. Caterers must be selected from an approved list.

BROCKET HALL Welwyn, Herts AL8 7XG
Tel: 0707 335241 Fax: 0707 375166

Banquet: 150 (60 on Prime Minister's State Dining Table), Dinner Dance:150,Reception: 400
Although Welwyn is a little further to ask your guests to travel, be assured that they will not be disappointed. Brocket Hall is one of the most magnificent venues within easy reach of London. The house, built in 1760, is the home of the present Lord and Lady Brocket, having been bought by the first Lord Brocket in 1921. Previously, Brocket Hall has been the home of two Prime Ministers - Lord Melbourne and Lord Palmerston. Brocket Hall is let out with the exclusive use of the house and grounds. During certain months of the year, all bookings have to be of a residential nature. Pre-dinner drinks are usually served in the Morning Room and the Drawing Room. Dinner is served in the spectacular Ballroom with its hand painted barrel ceiling, gilded mouldings, sparkling chandelier, and huge fireplace. The gold fabric walls are hung with mirrors on one side and a collection of paintings which includes the famous portrait of George IV by Reynolds. By using the Dining Room and the Family Dining Room, numbers for banqueting can be increased by up to 70. After dinner, guests have the use of the Library, with its rare Chippendale bookcases, and the Billiard Room, hung with a fine collection of hunting trophies. Downstairs, the Boardroom can be used for dancing and is where breakfast is often served. Each of the rooms is lavishly furnished with antiques and works of art. There are 46 bedrooms, each with its own individual style, on three floors of the house and in the Stable Annex. The Prince of Wales Hall is a 9,000 square metre struc-ture that can be erected in the grounds to accommodate up to 600 guests. The grounds offer a host of sporting and leisure activities, such as ballooning, boating and fishing, Landaus are available for rides around the estate. Brocket Hall has its own team of chefs who will suggest menus individually with the client. The cuisine is superb and the service impeccable.

BURGH HOUSE   New End Square, Hampstead, NW3 ILT
Tel: 071-431 0144

Music Room Banquet: 40, Buffet: 90, Reception: 90
This handsome Queen Anne house, built in 1703, is home to the local museum and library. Though added to the house much later, the pine panelled Music Room contains many of the original early 18th century features including the marble fireplace. The room is entered through double doors from the hall, which is used for pre-dinner drinks. Windows on two sides overlook the pretty, terraced garden which is used with the Music Room in summer. Sedate background music is allowed but nothing loud and no dancing or smoking. The Music Room is available for hire every day except Wednesday and Sunday afternoons, though the house and gardens are open to the public

Burgh House Continued....

during the day. Catering is handled exclusively by the Burgh House Buttery who specialise in home-style cooking. The Buttery can cater for parties of 40 seated or 90 for a finger buffet and the Library is available for parties of up to 25 guests.

30 PAVILION ROAD Knightsbridge, SW1X 0HJ
Tel: 071-823 9212 Fax: 071-823 8694

Banquet: 120, Dinner Dance: 120, Reception: 250, Wedding: 200, Fork Buffet: 160
30 Pavilion Road is a private 18th Century mews house which was created specifically for parties by the catering company, Searcy's (see Caterers), a name by which the house is also known. Guests enter the elegant stone-flagged hall from where the Georgian serpentine staircase leads to three rooms on the first floor. The Library is a handsome pine-panelled room, ancestral portraits hang from the walls, leather-bound books and ledgers line the shelves, a fire glows in the open fireplace. This leads to the anteroom, decorated in subtle florals, with a chandelier and parquet flooring which continues through a large archway to the magnificent Ballroom. This room is decorated in a delicate yellow with glittering gilded mirrors, curlicue wall sconces, oil paintings and an 18th century chandelier. The house is brightened by natural daylight in all the main rooms. The whole house may be hired or, for smaller functions, just a part of it. Overnight accommodation for hirers may be provided at the Roof Garden Rooms above.

QUEEN'S HOUSE   National Maritime Museum, Romney Road, SE10 9NF
Tel: 081-312 6714 Fax: 081-312 6632

The five-year, £5 million restoration of the Queen's House, also known as the 'House of Delights', was completed in 1990. The house was built by Inigo Jones in the 17th century and became the home of Queen Henrietta Maria, the wife of Charles I. As well as the suites listed below, other areas available for receptions include the barrel-vaulted basement Treasury and, in summer, the open-air Loggia. Marquees could be erected in the grounds for larger functions. Viewing of the exquisite Royal Apartments may be arranged for your guests. In summer, the house may only be hired in the evening, but certain areas are available during the daytime in winter. Smoking, candles and loud music are not permitted in the building, though dancing is sometimes possible. Caterers must be selected from an approved list. There is parking space for 100 cars.

Henrietta Maria Suite Banquet: 120, Dinner Dance: 100, Reception: 300
The suite consists of the Great Hall, a perfect forty foot cube with a stunning painted ceiling, and two adjacent anterooms each hung with Van de Veldes. The first floor gallery surrounding the Great Hall leads to the Royal Apartments. Access is either from the horseshoe staircase and terrace facing the Thames at the front of the house or from the cobbled courtyard between the two parts of the house.

Van de Velde Suite Banquet: 50 + 50, Reception: 150
At the back of the house, with views across the Royal Park to the Old Royal Observatory, is the Van de Velde Suite consisting of the Orangery and two flanking anterooms. These contain an unrivalled collection of 17th century Dutch marine paintings from which the suite takes its name.

SPENCER HOUSE 27 St James's Place, SW1A 1NR
Tel: 071-409 0526

Banquet: 120, Reception: 600 (whole house), 250 (ground floor only)
The London home of the Spencer family was re-opened in November 1990 following an extensive restoration programme. The house was built in 1756 for the first Earl Spencer and was often the setting for lavish entertainments. Now returned to its former glory, this outstanding venue

Houses and Stately Homes

Spencer House Continued....

may be hired as a whole or in part for the purpose for which it was originally intended. The Great Room on the first floor is decorated with bronzed medallions representing music, wine, love and female beauty under a green and white gilded barrel ceiling and lit by glittering chandeliers. The room overlooks Green Park and is a perfect setting for a dinner for up to 120 guests. The whole of the ground floor, which includes the exquisite Palm Room, the library, the dining room and the terrace, could be used for a cocktail party for 200, or the dining room could be hired on its own for a dinner party for up to 24 guests. Smoking is restricted and only background music, such as a string quartet or harp, would be permitted. The catering is extremely grand and menus are individually tailored to the clients requirements. Arrangements for kosher catering can be made only by the management.

THE WILDERNESS 19 Inner Park Road, Wimbledon Common, SW19 6ED
Tel: 081-788 3146

Banquet: 55, Reception: 120
This elegant house, built in 1840, has the peaceful atmosphere of a luxury family home, which, in fact, it is. Downstairs, the hall leads through a small anteroom - ideal for receiving guests - to the beautiful yellow Drawing Room. This opens onto a lovely secluded garden with a terrace, lawns and a formal fish pool. A marquee in the garden could seat an extra 130 guests. Also on the ground floor, there is a small dining room which may be used for buffets or small dinner parties for up to 14. The upstairs drawing room can be used for pre-dinner drinks. The reception rooms have log fires burning in winter and are tastefully furnished with antiques and paintings. If an overnight stay is required, there are three double bedrooms available, one with a four poster bed. The house is a perfect setting for weddings and garden parties. Only background music is permitted out of respect for the neighbours. You can choose from a list of recommended caterers or make your own arrangements.

High insurance costs make museums and art galleries expensive to hire but the dramatic effect of a priceless back-drop will leave a lasting impression on your guests. Catering facilities are often limited so you will need to use caterers who know what they are doing. Most of the museums and art galleries do not allow smoking or even candles on the tables, and in some, music is restricted to suitable background music.

BRITISH MUSEUM Great Russell Street, WC1B 3DG
Tel: 071-636 1555 Fax: 071-323 8480

Of the many rooms of the British Museum, the ones listed here are the most suitable for private parties. Some of the other rooms may be used for pre-dinner drinks or after dinner coffee. Museum experts may be hired to provide private viewings and arrangements can be made for the museum shop to be open. Smoking, dancing and recorded music are not allowed in the museum, though appropriate live background music is acceptable. Choose either the in-house catering company or from a list of approved outside caterers. Parking is available for VIPs only.

The Nereid Room *(Right)*
Banquet: 250
Reception: 350
The reconstructed 4th century Ionic facade which dominates the room is known as the Nereid Monument. It takes the form of a small Greek temple showing female sculptured figures in wind-blown draperies between the columns. A collection of sculptures and friezes are displayed around the gallery. The adjacent Duveen Gallery, where the Elgin Marbles are displayed, is sometimes used for serving after-dinner coffee and can be used

together with the Nereid Room to accommodate 800 standing guests. The Roman Room is often used for pre-dinner drinks.

Egyptian Sculpture Gallery Reception: Up to 700
This large gallery houses some of the museums most massive treasures including the gigantic granite head of Ramesses II. Guests can mingle among the impressive display of sculptures that range from life-size to colossal.

Japanese Galleries Reception: 250
Situated on Level 5 from the North Entrance, the modern, air-conditioned galleries displays Japanese treasures. Exhibitions are changed regularly. At the entrance to the galleries there is a replica of an authentic Japanese tea room. The light wood and off-white decor reflects the characteristics of Japanese culture and creates a peaceful atmosphere.

DICKENS' HOUSE 48 Doughty Street, WC1N 2LF
Tel: 071-405 2127

Library Reception: 50
Now a museum, this was Charles Dickens' home at the turning point of his career. The basement library, lined with cases containing editions of Dickens, is just large enough for an early evening drinks party for up to 50 standing guests. The rest of the museum is open for visiting. No smoking is allowed except in the garden and food and drink can only be consumed in the basement. You can choose your own caterers though kitchen facilities are limited. The library is available for hire in the evenings from Monday to Friday. All bookings are taken at the discretion of the curator.

Museums and Art Galleries

DULWICH PICTURE GALLERY   College Road, SE21 9AD
Tel: 081-693 5254 Fax: 081-693 2456

Banquet: 200, Reception: 300/400
First opened in 1814, the Dulwich Picture Gallery is the oldest in the country and displays a magnificent collection of Old Masters including works by Canaletto, Poussin, Rembrandt and Rubens. It consists of five main galleries, interlinked by wide arches, and various side galleries. Natural light is supplied through skylights. Surrounded by five acres of grounds, the Gallery offers the opportunity to hold larger functions in a marquee. Smoking and dancing are not allowed in the Gallery. There is a small list of approved caterers to select from, though any outside caterer may be used for marquee functions. There is unlimited parking space on both sides of the Gallery.

FREUD MUSEUM 20 Maresfield Gardens, Hampstead, NW3 5SX
Tel: 071-435 2002 Fax: 071-431 5452

Dining Room & Conservatory Banquet: 15, Reception: 75
The home of Sigmund Freud, from his exile from Vienna in 1938 until his death a year later, was maintained by his daughter, Anna who bequeathed the house as a museum when she died in 1982. The study and library contain Freud's belongings from Austria exactly as he left them. Both floors of the house may be used but food and drink may only be consumed in the dining room, conservatory and garden, and smoking is only allowed in the garden. Tours of the house can be arranged by the museum staff. You must organise your own caterers. Cutlery, crockery and glassware must all be brought in.

IMPERIAL WAR MUSEUM   Lambeth Road, SE1 6HZ
Tel: 071-416 5000 Fax: 071-416 5374

Atrium Banquet: 350, Dinner Dance: 350, Reception: 700
The elegant award winning new museum houses a unique collection of historical war exhibits. Artillery, tanks and naval exhibits are displayed on the ground floor of the glass-domed atrium, while aircraft from both world wars are suspended overhead. For smaller functions, the Boardroom on the first floor can accommodate 50 for a dinner or 70 for a reception. Smoking is not allowed in the main exhibit hall. A list of recommended caterers is supplied by the museum.

INSTITUTE OF CONTEMPORARY ARTS The Mall, SW1Y 5AH
Tel: 071-930 0493 Fax: 071-873 0051

The Nash and Seminar Rooms Banquet: 120, Reception: 300
Recently refurbished, the elegant Nash Room has full height windows leading onto balconies overlooking The Mall with views over St James's Park and Whitehall. It is decorated in pale grey with white pilasters and cornices and a wooden floor. Double doors lead to a small anteroom with a richly decorated domed ceiling and plaster mouldings. This room connects the Nash Room to the plainer Seminar Room and serves as a reception area for both. There is a private entrance in Carlton House Terrace which leads directly up to the reception rooms on the first floor. Guests attending a function here are welcome to view exhibitions in the ICA galleries. The two large galleries are occasionally available for private events. Discos and loud music are not allowed. In-house catering offers a full service ranging from finger buffets to champagne banquets - vegetarian food is a speciality.

KEW BRIDGE STEAM MUSEUM Green Dragon Lane, Brentford, Middx TW8 0EN Tel: 081-568 4757

Steam Hall Banquet: 100, Dinner Dance: 100, Reception: 150
Built in 1838, this Grade I listed museum contains the original waterworks' steam engines in working order. A balcony runs along one side of the hall, overlooking the dance area and the engines which can be working during the party, or part of it. The specialist lighting adds a dramatic touch,

Kew Bridge Steam Museum Continued....

ideal for a Victorian themed evening. There is an adjoining area, the Water Hall, which is basically a large, empty hall which can be dressed up if a larger dining area is required. The museum is available in the evenings only from Wednesdays to Saturdays, though some Sundays are negotiable. There is a noise limiter in operation so no loud rock bands are allowed. Caterers can be selected from a recommended list or you can choose your own. There is parking for 40 cars.

LEIGHTON HOUSE MUSEUM 12 Holland Park Road, W14 8LZ
Tel: 071-602 3316

Banquet: 86, Reception: 150
Built around 1865, Leighton House was the home of the great classical painter, Frederic Lord Leighton. He later added the Arab Hall to show off his collection of blue and gold Islamic tiles and mosaics. The dining room on the ground floor has access to the garden which can be used for summer receptions. Upstairs, the main studio can be used for cocktails and dinner parties with the addition of the Silk Room if extra space is needed. Guests have access to all the public rooms but smoking is restricted to the Arab Hall and the dining room. No dancing is allowed, no amplified music and no 18th or 21st birthday parties. The house is available from 6.30 to 11 on any evening except Sunday. Leith's Good Food (see Caterers) take care of all the catering needs.

LONDON TOY & MODEL MUSEUM 21/23 Craven Hill, W2 3EW
Tel: 071-262 7905 Fax: 071-262 9450

Clockwork Cafe Banquet: 50, Reception: 200-300
The multi-galleried museum features a collection of mainly Victorian and Edwardian teddy bears, dolls, toys and models, some of them working, extending over the ground and lower ground floors of two Victorian houses and out to the partly covered garden. The cafe and main entrance area are best for finger buffets and the large garden could be used for summer barbecues. There is also a small room downstairs suitable for a disco. Smoking is only allowed in the garden. The museum is available for hire any evening from 6.30 to midnight. In - house catering is available.

LONDON TRANSPORT MUSEUM Covent Garden, WC2E 7BB
Tel: 071-379 6344 Fax: 071-836 4118

Museum Banquet: 70, Reception: 400
The unique collection of historic vehicles makes the museum a fascinating and highly original setting for a party. Guests can put themselves in the driving seat of a London bus or a Circle Line tube train, or step back in time to admire a Victorian steam train or horse bus. The museum's recently refurbished lecture theatre is available for daytime hire seating up to 70. Smoking is allowed in the lecture theatre and reception area only. The three recommended catering companies for the museum are London Transport Catering, Moving Venue and Squires (see Caterers).

MALL GALLERIES 17 Carlton House Terrace, SW1Y 5BO
Tel: 071-930 6844 Fax: 071-831 7830

Main Gallery, East Gallery and North Gallery Banquet: 30-250, Reception: 50-500
Run by The Federation of British Artists, the galleries offer several options for private functions. Located near Admiralty Arch, they are entered from The Mall. The galleries house several exhibitions during the year and these provide a lovely backdrop for social events. They are available for hire only after 5pm, either separately or in any combination. The Main Gallery is an extensive modern area for larger functions. The East Gallery, to the other side of the foyer, is smaller room but just as simple. Leading off from the Main Gallery is the North Gallery which is smaller still and is divided by two central arches. Any outside caterers may be used and the galleries will supply a list of recommended companies on request. Background music only is acceptable - dancing is not allowed. There is parking for 200 cars within 50 metres.

Museums and Art Galleries ────────────────

Mall Galleries Continued......

Bradshaw Room Banquet: 70, Reception: 120
The Bradshaw Room is entered through an imposing portico at 17, Carlton House Terrace. The staircase leads from the reception area to the lovely Nash Regency room on the first floor. It is simply decorated in beige and white with a brown carpet, ornate mouldings on the walls and ceilings and a pine and marble fireplace. The small adjacent boardroom may be used in conjunction with the Bradshaw Room bumping the maximum numbers up to 150 for a reception. As with the galleries, no dancing is allowed - background music only - and you can choose your own caterers.

MUSEUM OF LONDON London Wall, EC2
Tel: 071-600 3699 Fax: 071-600 1058

Reception/Buffet: Lord Mayor's Coach Gallery: 300, Medieval Gallery: 150,
                     18th Century Gallery: 80, Imperial Capital Gallery: 250
Over 2000 years of London's history is represented in this museum which is a fascinating venue for a party. A party using the whole museum can be arranged for your guests but are better concentrated in specific. The Medieval Gallery has show cases displaying hundreds of objects that once belonged to Londoners between the 5th and 15th centuries. The 18th century Lord Mayor's Coach is displayed in the largest gallery. A smaller area which includes the coach can be screened off for smaller parties of 50 or 60 guests. In summer, the tiered Garden Court can be used with the Coach Gallery or Imperial capital Gallery for a garden party for up to 100. The 18th Century Gallery contains period costumes and doors from Newgate Prison amongst its displays. All the displays are well lit at night and provide a variety of atmospheres and moods. There is also a lecture room available for hire for up to 270 people. There are some restrictions on the type of music allowed and smoking is restricted in the museum. Milburns are the in-house caterers but you may organise your own.

MUSEUM OF THE MOVING IMAGE   South Bank, SE1 8XT Tel: 071-928 3535

TV Studio Banquet: 50, Dinner Dance: 50, Reception: 180
 Since its opening in 1988, the Museum has become a popular and unique venue for parties. The TV

Museum of the Moving Image Continued....

Studio is available any evening from 6pm. Guests can arrive from 6.00 for pre-dinner drinks in the Colonnade or tour the Museum ending up in the TV Studio when the party begins. Here guests can fly over London, read the news from an autocue or be interviewed by Barry Norman. Then they could visit Hollywood and take part in their own screen test. The MOMI actors could be hired to mingle and entertain. A full party planning service can be provided. The in-house caterers offer a full service and are happy to cater to themes. Smoking is restricted to certain areas. Ample parking is available in the South Bank complex.

NATIONAL ARMY MUSEUM Royal Hospital Road, SW3
Tel: 071-730 0717

Art Gallery Banquet: 120, Reception: 500,
Various galleries of the museum recalling the history of the British army can be hired for cocktail parties but the Art Gallery is ideal for a dinner or larger reception. The room is long and narrow, hung with a priceless collection of military paintings. Tours of the museum can be arranged and security can be provided for VIP guests. The museum is available every evening from 6pm though caterers can have access earlier. Smoking and dancing are not allowed but background music is permitted. A list of recommended caterers is supplied or you can choose your own.

NATIONAL PORTRAIT GALLERY 2 St Martin's Place, WC2H 0HE
Tel: 071-306 0055 Fax: 071-306 0056

The Stuart Room *(Right)*
Banquet: 70, Reception: 300,
The Stuart Room is part of the impressive suite which houses the magnificent Tudor and Stuart Collection, and provides a unique and historic venue for evening receptions and small dinner parties. The Tudor Room can seat 30 to 40 for dinner around an oval table or may be used for drinks before dinner in the Stuart Room. The spectacular red-damask 18th Century Gallery is similarly available for dinner parties of up to 70 guests. As with all the galleries available for hire here, there is no smoking or dancing allowed. Caterers must be chosen from an approved list. The galleries are only available for evening hire, including week-ends. A private viewing of a special exhibition can often be included, by request.

Museums and Art Galleries

Edwardian & Victorian Galleries Reception: 250, Buffet: 220
This superb suite of rooms has period decor, hung with pictures of 19th Century sitters forming part of a national collection. The Long Gallery will seat 100 guests or 200 if using the adjoining inter-linking rooms. Used alone, the Edwardian gallery will accommodate 60 for dinner or 100 for a reception.

NATURAL HISTORY MUSEUM Cromwell Road, SW7 5BD
Tel: 071-938 8934 Fax: 071-938 8934

Central Hall Banquet: 450, Dinner Dance: 400, Reception: 1000
The Victorian cathedral-like architecture of the unique "Waterhouse Building" with the added attraction of the huge model dinosaur skeleton dominating the hall make this a dramatic and unique venue. Floodlighting, outside and in, and clever decoration (no balloons allowed though) transform this major attraction into a stunning party setting at night. The huge stone staircase can act as a stage for a band, or an entry point for a marching band or cabaret. It is probably the only museum party venue where smoking is allowed. An adjoining Gallery, is available for the reception, though the Mammal Gallery can also cater for receptions for up to 150 guests. The museum is available for private hire on any evening from 6pm except for Christmas day. You can choose to use caterers from an approved list.

Earth Galleries Banquet: 130, Dinner Dance: 130, Reception: 400
Previously known as the Geological Museum, the Earth Galleries are entered from Exhibition Road. The main gallery houses the museum's collection of minerals, gems and decorative stones with a huge stone wall at the far end. Light pours in from the very high glass roof but clever lighting can be used to create the right atmosphere. The New Exhibition Area, known as The Link as it joins the Earth Galleries to the Natural History, is a dramatic white gallery displaying fossils and minerals. No red wine is allowed in here to protect the white terrazzo floor. Several other galleries are also available for receptions. In addition, there is a lecture theatre which can seat up to 200, suitable for a presentation to be followed by a reception or dinner in the galleries. This has a separate street entrance.

ROYAL ACADEMY OF ARTS Piccadilly, W1V 0DS
Tel: 071-494 3976 Fax: 071-434 0837

Private Rooms   Banquet: 100 (Corporate Members only)
                      Reception: 350 -1000 (depending on exhibition)
Receptions at the Royal Academy are only available as part of a private view of an exhibition and dinners are only permissable for Corporate Members of the Royal Academy. The Reynolds Room is the largest of the 18th century private rooms on the first floor of Burlington House. This elaborately gilded room is hung with Academy works, as are the two other inter-connecting rooms in this suite - the ornate Saloon and the Council Room with is richly painted ceiling. Adjoining these rooms is the less elaborate Architectural room which has a vaulted ceiling. Other galleries might be available depending on the exhibitions showing at the time. Milburns, who operate the Royal Academy restaurant, can handle the catering or you might prefer to choose from the recommended list of outside caterers. No smoking is allowed anywhere in the building.

ROYAL AIR FORCE MUSEUM
Grahame Park Way, Hendon, NW9 5LL
Tel: 081-205 2266

Britain's national museum of aviation provides a unique party venue. There are a number of areas in the museum that may be used, varying in capacity and several areas may be used together for more flexibility. Guests can have a private viewing of the exhibition. There is no smoking in the museum. Clients have their choice of caterers.

Royal Air Force Museum Continued....

The Dermot Boyle Wing Banquet: 150 - Low Gallery, 300 - High Gallery ,
Dinner Dance: 100 - Low Gallery, 150 - High Gallery, Reception : 200- Low Gallery
The Dermot Boyle Wing is divided into the Low Gallery and the High Gallery with a reception area
in between. Each may be used separately or could be combined to accommodate up to 400 guests.
The Low Gallery is an L-shaped room , decorated with war artists' paintings. It could be used as
a reception room for the High Gallery which is literally a 'black box' with a high ceiling and huge
loading door, making it an excellent venue to decorate for a theme party.

Battle of Britain Hall *(Right)*
Banquet: 270
Reception: 400
Here you can dine under the
wings of the huge, white Sunder-
land sea-plane surrounded by many
other exhibits in the hall. There is
full disabled access and toilets. Other
areas that are suitable for parties
include the E-Pen where the old
British and enemy war planes are
housed, the Mezzanine overlooking the E-Pen, and Wings Restaurant.

SCIENCE MUSEUM Exhibition Road, South Kensington, SW7 2DD
Tel: 071-938 8184 Fax: 071-938 8112

Banquet: 300, Dinner Dance: 300, Reception: 2000
With 200,000 different objects spread over five floors, the museum offers the opportunity to
choose a relevant backdrop for any corporate function. The East Hall on the ground floor is suitable
for dinner dances. Company logos could be projected onto screens suspended above a working
steam-driven Lancaster Mill Engine. The blue carpeted area at the back of the East Hall, Gallery
5, can seat 300 when it is not being used for temporary exhibitions. The first floor Space Gallery
would suit a reception or buffet for 250 around the Apollo 10 space capsule. On the third floor,
the Aeronautics Gallery features an impressive collection of aircraft and engines, some suspended
overhead, and can accommodate 250 for dinner and 400 for a reception. Several other galleries
could be used as well as the more formal Fellows Room and anteroom (130 dinner, 200 reception)
and a well equipped Lecture Theatre, both of which are available for daytime or evening functions.
The galleries, however, are for evening functions only. Smoking is not allowed in any of the
galleries. Daytime catering is by the in-house caterers. For evening functions, choose from a list
of recommended caterers. The museum is not available for hire by private individuals.

THEATRE MUSEUM   1E Tavistock Street, Covent Garden, WC2E 7PA
Tel: 071-938 8366 (Special Events Office, V & A)

Paintings Gallery Banquet: 70, Dinner Dance: 70, Reception: 150 - 300
The Theatre Museum, housed in part of the Old Flower Market of Covent Garden, now displays the
national collection of theatrical material. The Paintings Gallery, on the lower ground floor, is a
mirrored re-creation of an Edwardian theatre foyer where the Museum's collection of paintings is
displayed. The ground floor area is a fantasy stage setting by Anthony Holland. It is suitable for
a cocktail reception for up to 150 or a dinner for 60 in the Bandstand or for a reception for 300 with
the Paintings Gallery. There is also a fully equipped Studio Theatre available for hire. Small tours
of the Museum can be arranged during a reception or before dinner. Smoking is restricted in some
areas of the Museum. Caterers may be chosen only from the approved list. The Museum is available
for private hire on Mondays at lunchtime and from 6.30 to 11pm, and on other evenings from 10pm
to midnight. There is no parking at the Museum.

Museums and Art Galleries

VICTORIA & ALBERT MUSEUM Cromwell Road, South Kensington, SW7 2RL
Tel: 071-938 8366 Fax: 071-938 8341

With twelve acres of galleries contained in this fine Victorian building, there are many possibilities for entertaining surrounded by the wonderful works of art on display. As well as the galleries mentioned, it may be possible for other rooms to be hired for receptions. Entrance can be either from Cromwell Road or Exhibition Road. Small tours of the museum can be arranged and it is possible for the shop to remain open. Smoking is not permitted anywhere in the museum except in the New Restaurant. Milburns are the in-house caterers but outside caterers may be chosen from the approved list only and all equipment must be hired through the caterer.

The Gamble Room *(Right)*
Banquet: 150, Reception: 350
Dating back to the mid 19th century, the Gamble Room is completely tiled with ornamental ceramics by Minton and an enamelled ceiling. The stained glass windows incorporate the Royal arms, quotations from the Bible and the Ingoldsby legends. Decorated pillars support high arches in the centre of the room. Statues of Diana and Venus flank a magnificent fireplace. Music, preferably of the period, is allowed in this room, but no dancing. The adjoining Morris Room may be used for the reception.

The Morris Room Banquet: 40, Reception: 80
This deep green and gilt room contains panel paintings (representing signs of the zodiac) and stained glass windows by Sir Edwin Burne Jones. The Morris Room and the Gamble Room are available everyday lunchtimes and evenings.

The Raphael Cartoon Court Reception: 600
The famous cartoons by Raphael depicting the Acts of the Apostles are housed here, on loan from the Queen. There is a Renaissance fountain in the centre, also statues and well heads all under a huge barrel vault ceiling. No dancing, but some music may be considered. Prospective clients must make a written proposal to the director for approval.

The Dome Area *(Right)* Banquet 250 - 300,
Reception: 100-700
Used as the main entrance foyer during the day, but ideal for an evening reception when guests may also view the Medieval Treasury. Music is allowed here, but again, no dancing.

Pirelli Garden Reception: 700
This Italianate garden, opened in 1987 is a spectacular venue for a summer party. The trees are floodlit at night as is the fountain. There are two slightly raised lawn areas. Music is allowed here.

New Restaurant and Painted Room Banquet: 150,
Dinner Dance: 150, Reception: 300
The modern, white paint and bare brick restaurant is a stark contrast to the opulence of some of the other areas of the museum but provides a versatile venue for an evening party. The adjoining Painted room seats 40 and is deco-
rated with five modern trompe l'oeils depicting the great ages of interior design. The room is lit by a massive chandelier.

HMS BELFAST   Morgans Lane, Tooley Street, SE1 2JH
Tel: 071-403 6246 Fax: 071-407 0708

Launched in 1938, the last survivor of the Royal Navy's big gun ships is now permanently moored on the Thames as a floating museum, run by the Imperial War Museum. Various areas of the ship are available individually or you can hire the whole ship (up to 450 people for a cocktail reception). The Quarter Deck is only protected from the elements by an awning, so is only available between May and September for receptions for up to 350. A launch is available to collect up to a hundred guests at a time from anywhere on the river. The catering is by Ring and Brymer. A complete party package is offered for a minimum of 40 guests.

Ships Company Dining Hall Banquet: 144, Dinner Dance: 96, Reception: 240
Apart from the pipes, posts and portholes, there is a large dance floor here so it is ideal for a dinner dance or disco. The Ward Room may be used for pre-dinner drinks in winter, or the Quarter Deck in summer.

The Gun Room Banquet: 60, Reception: 120
The Gun Room is the latest addition, with luxurious fittings decorated with dark oak and relaxing shades of blue.

Ward Room and Ante Room Banquet: 50 (Horseshoe style), Reception: 80
The Ante Room was originally the officers mess and has a bar and fixed seating. It serves as the reception room for dinners in the Ward Room which is decorated in a similar style - beige walls and traditional dark red carpet. Smaller parties can be held in the Admiral's Quarters.

CABINET WAR ROOMS
Clive Steps, King Charles Street,
SW1A 2AQ
Tel: 071-930 6961
Fax: 071-582 5374

Banquet: 50 (Conference Room)
Reception: 200 (Whole venue)
The underground emergency accommodation used by Winston Churchill and the British Government during the Second World War makes a very unusual and atmospheric venue for a party. Guests can wander through the narrow corridors and view the

various rooms and offices still displaying their original maps and charts on the walls, old-fashioned typewriters and telephones on the desks, with sound effects piped through if you want. Alternatively, you could choose to have popular 40s music played. The whole venue can be hired any evening after 6, but the Conference Room, which was once the Cabinet War Rooms main underground telephone exchange, can be used for both daytime and evening functions. Outside caterers may be brought in for evening functions but for daytime functions in the Conference Room, choice is limited to one of a small number of approved caterers. Parking is the only problem here, so public or organised transport is recommended.

CHESSINGTON WORLD OF ADVENTURE
Leatherhead Road, Chessington, Surrey KT9 2NE
Tel: 0372 724720 Fax: 0372 725050

Chessington Manor Banquet: 150, Dinner Dance: 150, Reception: 200 plus
Chessington Manor, formerly known as The Burnt Stub Mansion House is situated in the heart of Surrey's finest countryside and lends itself to a variety of day and evening activities. With a choice

Tourist Attractions

of four rooms, functions of all sizes can easily be accommodated. The largest of these is the Great Hall which is very popular for Jacobean Banquets, with leaded light windows overlooking garden and an adjoining bar, it is an excellent choice for larger functions. The Buckingham Room is a bright delicate room and can seat 70 for an evening function. The inter-connecting Nell Gwynne Bar can serve as a reception area and the front hall could be used for dancing. Finally the King Charles Room, oak-panelled in Jacobean style, can seat upto 60 people for a variety of functions. All your requirements can be provided in-house. Outside caterers may be used for Marquee events in the grounds.

Black Forest Château *(Right)*
Banquet: 300
Dinner Dance: 250
Reception: 400
Set in Transylvania, one of the many themed areas of the park, hire of the Black Forest Château can be combined with a ride on the Vampire, the UKs first hanging roller-coaster. Guests could be greeted by Count Dracula as they enter the Château's raised walkway. The Château is decorated with Bavarian village scenes but could easily be themed for a horror party. Summer 'al fresco' events can take place in the village square.

Chessington World of Adventures consists of various themed areas which can be used for parties and which could accomodate the use of the rides. Various other venues throughout the park are available, from themed evenings in Chessington Manor to a taste of the Orient in the Mystic East. We can tailor each event to your own special requirements.

CUTTY SARK
King William Walk,
Greenwich, SE10 9HT
Tel: 081-858 3445

The Tween Deck
Banquet: 80, Reception: 170
The world's only surviving tea clipper was built in Dumbarton in 1869 and has been in dry dock at Greenwich as a museum since 1957. The complete ship is hired out for functions and guests can wander around the three decks. The Lower Hold contains a unique collection of merchant ship figure heads. In summer, drinks can be served in the

Photograph by kind prmission of Moving Venue

open air on the Weather Deck. Parties take place on the 'Tween Deck where tables can be arranged around the exhibits. This deck has direct access from the dockside. Caterers may be chosen from a recommended list or you may choose your own subject to discussions with the functions manager as catering facilities are limited. Smoking, discos and dancing are not allowed on board the ship which is available for evening hire only. There is parking space alongside.

LONDON DUNGEON   28-34 Tooley Street, SE1 2SZ
Tel: 071-403 7221 Fax: 071-378 1529

Banquet: 100 (silver served), Seated Buffet: 300, Finger Buffet: 400, Disco: 100-400
This outrageous horror themed venue is definitely not for the squeamish. The realistic tableaux depicting the darker side of medieval London provide a blood-curdling backdrop to themed events. Actors are on hand to fit in with the theme and 'entertain' your guests. The caterers, The Moving Venue (see Caterers) can provide theme food starting with 'eyeball cocktails' (lychees in cassis and sparkling wine) in the smoke filled reception area. Guests can then continue through the dark, musty museum to the buffet and dancing areas. The venue is available any evening from 7.30 in summer and 6.30 in winter.

LONDON ZOO Outer Circle, Regent's Park, NW1 4RY
Tel: 071-586 3339 Fax: 071-722 3333

Regency Suite Banquet: 250, Dinner Dance: 250, Reception: 320
On the first floor, overlooking the illuminated fountains with the Zoological Gardens beyond, is the Regency Suite, the zoo's traditional banqueting venue. The suite is light and bright and stylishly decorated in pink and blue with floral panels matching the upholstery on the chairs. The room can be divided into three sections by curtains, with a fixed bar in one section suitable for a drinks reception. Alternatively, the adjoining cherry tree courtyard may be used for an evening reception or barbecue. It is also possible to erect a marquee on the lawns for up to 600 people. Parking is convenient, unlimited after 11am, and there is a private guest entrance. Guests can even arrive by barge from Little Venice to the zoo's private jetty. The zoo's hospitality caterers offer a complete choice of menus and bar options, with full silver service available.

The Aquarium, Reptile House, Insect House & Butterfly Forest
Dinner: Aquarium - 150, Reptile House - 80
Buffet: Aquarium - 200, Reptile House - 100, Insect House & Butterfly Forest - 60
Reception: Aquarium - 250, Reptile House -180, Insect House & Butterfly Forest - 100
 These three unique and exciting venues are available any evening, after 6.30. Discos are allowed in the Aquarium only as volume is not a problem here but as constant subdued lighting has to be maintained, no flashing or strobe lights are allowed. The Aquarium is made up of three linked halls containing illuminated tanks and is close to the main zoo entrance. The Reptile House is a large open square with central exhibits, opposite the main gate adjacent to the Aquarium. The Insect House, on the north side of the zoo via the east tunnel, is an attractive T-shaped hall with interesting exhibits on both sides, leading to the Butterfly Forest which recreates the butterflies' natural habitat where they can fly freely. Background music or suitable 'jungle' sounds are available on request.

MADAME TUSSAUD'S Marylebone Road, NW1 5LR
Tel: 071-935 6861 Fax: 071-935 8906

Banquet: 300, Dinner Dance: 250, Reception: 450
Madame Tussaud's world famous exhibition of wax portraits provides a unique and exciting venue for private functions. Various areas and combinations can be used. For example, cocktails could be served in 200 Years of Madame Tussaud's and/or in The Garden Party among such personalities as Joan Collins, Michael Caine and Dame Edna Everidge, followed by dinner in the Grand Hall in the more prestigious company of world leaders and heads of state, past and present. After dinner, dancing could take place in the Grand Hall or a disco could be set up in the chilling Chamber of Horrors. By Word of Mouth (see Caterers) organise the catering, though kosher catering can also be arranged. Madame Tussaud's is available any evening after 7pm, by which time parking in Marylebone Road is no problem. Smoking is restricted.

Tourist Attractions

ROCK CIRCUS London Pavilion, Piccadilly Circus, W1
Tel: 071-734 7203 Fax: 071-734 8023

Banquet: 150, Dinner Dance: 150, Buffet Disco 250, Reception: 350
Opened in 1989, Rock Circus is the world's only permanent tribute to the great stars of rock and pop. Around fifty rock stars are portrayed in the exhibition, as wax or bionic figures, or in photographic or video form. Guests are issued with headsets which pick up the music system that brings the exhibits alive. The main party area is around the central display on the third floor where guests can join company with the likes of Elvis Presley, Little Richard, Stevie Wonder and Elton John. On the fourth floor, is the Revolving Theatre, where the auditorium revolves between 'acts' to face three different stages. This is normally used for the audio anamatronic show but could be used for presentations. By Word of Mouth (see Caterers) provide the catering or you can make your own arrangements. No smoking is allowed in the exhibition.

TOWER BRIDGE Tower Road, SE1 2UP
Tel: 071-403 3761

Daytime Reception: 200, Evening Reception: 300 each walkway
Tower Bridge offers a truly unique setting for corporate receptions with unbeatable views of the Thames and the London skyline from 140 feet up. The two high level walkways that link the tops of the main towers of the bridge are fully enclosed and glazed but despite heaters being installed, they can still be cold and draughty during the winter months, so are recommended for summer events only. Both walkways may be hired for evening receptions to finish by 9pm (9.30pm if less than 200 attending), though the East Walkway may also be hired for daytime functions. The walkways are not available at weekends and between December and April. Only background music is allowed and smoking is not permitted anywhere on the bridge. As facilities are limited, it is recommended that caterers are selected from a list that have successfully catered for events in the past. Only corporate bookings will be accepted.

WINDSOR SAFARI PARK Winkfield Road, Windsor, Berks SL4 4AY
Tel: 0753 830886 Fax: 0753 861045

St. Leonard's Mansion Banquet: 120, Dinner Dance: 100, Reception: 150
Dating back to 1760, St Leonard's Mansion is set on a hill overlooking the Park and the surrounding Windsor countryside. Once owned by the Duke of Gloucester, the Mansion still retains its original elegant style and authentic decor. A patio runs the width of the back of the Mansion and can be used during the summer for receptions and barbecues. Of the three rooms available for hire, the John Kennedy is the largest. It has windows on three sides with access to the terrace, and a small dance floor. The elaborate off-white and gold decor is repeated in each of the rooms with ornate panelled walls and hand carved finishes. A stags head trophy hangs over the open fireplace. The room is carpeted in red, unlike the Gloucester Room which has a polished parquet floor. The Gloucester can accommodate 50 for a banquet and 120 for a reception. The third room, the Waldegrave, is used mainly for conferences. There is a separate wood panelled bar area. A marquee could be erected in the grounds for larger parties - up to 1000 people. There is a variety of traditional menus ranging from informal buffets to more formal banquets.

The Africa Lodge Banquet: 150, Dinner Dance: 150, Reception: 200
Available mainly at Christmas time, the restaurant is an unusual African-style Safari Lodge on three levels with a patio overlooking the park. The interior is all wood with exposed timbered ceilings, a large dance floor and a bar. It is decorated with African artifacts and makes an authentic setting for African themed parties.

Make use of all the available facilities, such as lighting and sound, to create the right atmosphere for your function.

THE HIPPODROME
Hippodrome Corner,
Leicester Square, WC2 7SH
Tel: 071-437 4837
Fax: 071-434 4225

Auditorium
Banquet: 375, Dinner Dance: 375, Reception: 1650
This bright and exciting famous high-tech nightclub can be hired in part or whole, day or night. Decorated in black, chrome, leather and mirrors, the Hippodrome is a mass of the most up-to-date technology available. The auditorium has a central, mechanically raised dance floor and stage with stage lift, lasers, videos, a back projection screen and advanced sound and lighting systems. A balcony runs around three sides of the auditorium where there is a restaurant that can cater for 140 for a banquet or dinner dance and 450 for a reception. The Stage Bar, in the centre of the club, can cater for a reception for up to 300. The Star Bar, a private room with antique furniture and a 'distressed' decor, offers a more relaxed atmosphere and can hold 100 guests for a reception. There is a choice of 4 set banqueting menus and 14 example buffet menus though they often cater to the clients specific requirements. Occasionally, they will allow outside caterers the use of their two fully equipped kitchens.

JONGLEURS AT THE CORNET
49 Lavender Gardens,
Battersea, SW11 1DJ
Tel: 071-924 3080
Fax: 071-924 5175

Banquet: 300
Dinner Dance: 225
Reception: 350
Jongleurs is a hugely popular cabaret venue primarily for fringe comedy. The wonderfully 'seedy' decor - black panelled walls, wooden floor and vaulted ceiling - can be transformed into just about anything by the expert Jongleurs set designers. They can arrange for a cabaret to be specially scripted for the event or just organise a disco, if you prefer. There is a separate bar area for a pre-dinner drinks. The venue is not available for private hire on Friday or Saturday nights when it is used for the comedy club. International cuisine is prepared in-house or you may choose outside caterers from an approved list.

LE PALAIS 242 Shepherd's Bush Road, Hammersmith, W6 7NL
Tel: 081-748 2812 Fax: 081-741 4994

Banquet: 500, Dinner Dance: 500, Buffet:1200, Reception: 2300
The 'Hammersmith Palais' is a spacious and versatile venue that is truly multi-function. Based around a huge split level auditorium, a balcony runs around three sides with a private box for a group of twenty VIPs. Other areas may be sectioned off for different size parties - the Balcony

Nightclubs

Le Palais Continued....

Bar takes 450, the Cocktail Bar 200 and the Stage Bar 300. There is a giant thirty foot screen video wall for simultaneous filming and projection of events. It houses the very latest in sound and lighting systems and is decorated in bright, clashing pinks, greys and silver with chrome and velvet furniture. It is available for private hire on Sunday, Monday and Tuesday nights and up to 9pm on other evenings and every day during the day. Private parties can also take place on public nights in certain areas of the venue.

LIMELIGHT
136 Shaftesbury Avenue, W1V 7DN
Tel: 071-434 0572 Fax: 071-434 3780

Dome Bar Banquet: 110 (150 with gallery), Reception: 300 (350 with gallery)

Formerly a Presbyterian church, built for John Wesley in 1754, Limelight re-opened in September 1990 after extensive refurbishment. The Dome Bar features a 150 feet high gold domed ceiling from which hangs a massive chandelier. Surrounding the dining area, at mezzanine level, is the Gallery Bar which could be used for a pre-dinner reception. There is direct access to The Club on the lower ground floor where up to 200 guests could be invited to a buffet and disco. The Private Dining Room and Study are suitable for smaller parties. A brasserie menu is offered six days a week. It is possible to hire the whole building or just a part of it for up to 650 guests.

TALK OF LONDON Drury Lane, Parker Street, WC2
Tel: 071-568 1616 Fax: 071-568 6845

Banquet: 350, Dinner Dance: 350

At the New London Theatre, on the first floor, is a luxurious cabaret theatre. Carefully arranged in a circular layout on split levels, each guest has an uninterrupted view of the entertainment. There is a dance floor, hydraulic stage and a bar area which can be separated by curtains. A complete evening's entertainment can be provided which includes a floorshow, cabaret and dancing to a top show band. Alternatively, you can provide your own entertainment. A four course dinner is usually served, chosen from a selection of traditional style menus. There is an NCP car park next door.

XENON 196 Piccadilly, W1V 9LG
Tel: 071-734 9344/5 Fax: 071-734 3416

Banquet: 600, Dinner Dance: 220, Reception: 800

Xenon is a lavishly equipped discotheque with a sophisticated sound and lighting system including simultaneous projection and lasers. Features include a hydraulic stage, waterfalls and fountains alongside the dance floor and three bars, one of which is in the private area on the first floor which can accommodate 150 guests. A complete range of banqueting and buffet menus is offered, or you could choose an outside caterer.

See also:
Onslow Hotel
Ormonds

THE BAFTA CENTRE 195 Piccadilly, W1V 9LG
Tel: 071-465 0277 Fax: 071-734 1009

Banqueting Suite Banquet: 200, Reception: 200
The headquarters of the The British Academy of Film and Television Arts comprises varied and elegant hospitality areas and state-of-the-art theatres. The first floor reception foyer, overlooking Piccadilly, leads into the main suite which has full height windows with views onto St James's Church and Jermyn Street. Modern, deep blue "flying saucer" ceiling lights contrast dramatically with the pale walls and ornate moulded frieze. By clever use of screens, which are mirrored on one side, the room can be adapted to comfortably seat 50 guests. Background music only, either piped or live, is allowed in the banqueting suite with dancing in the club area on the second floor. There are two theatres available for hire - The Princess Anne Theatre (200 seats each endowed by famous personalities), and The Run Run Shaw Theatre (30 seats). The highest culinary standards are achieved by Roux Restaurants Ltd, sole caterers at the BAFTA Centre.

ROYAL ALBERT HALL Kensington Gore, SW7 2AP
Tel: 071-589 3203 Fax: 071-823 7725

This grand Victorian architectural masterpiece is a dramatic and historic venue for a prestigious function. Apart from the Hall, there are a number of private rooms available which vary tremendously in style and capacity. All the catering at the Hall is by Brookes, a subsidiary of THF, with a full range of traditional English menus. The following is a selection of the larger rooms.

Hall Banquet: 2200, Dinner Dance: 2200
Probably one of the largest and most impressive venues in London, the famous hall can be laid out in tiers of long tables with round tables in the arena. The boxes and balcony can also be utilised. The arena, or part of it, can be used for dancing, and the stage for cabaret. No smoking is allowed in the auditorium. Bookings for the Hall are taken up to five years ahead. The Gallery, which runs around the auditorium with full view of the stage and arena, can hold 450 people for a cocktail party before or after a concert or event.

Elgar Room Banquet: 150, Reception: 225
The Victorian style, split level room is located on Balcony level. There are windows on three sides with views over Hyde Park. The room is richly decorated with marbled stairs and columns, pastel velour walls and dramatic fringed drapes and swags. An ornate frieze runs around the upper level incorporating the "A" for Albert.

Victoria Room Banquet: 90, Reception: 130
Also at Balcony level, the Victoria room has its own reception room and bar. Full height windows overlook the Victoria Memorial. It is decorated with paintings and red velvet drapes in the original style of the period.

Prince Consort Room Banquet: 90, Reception: 150
As this room is used as a restaurant during concert times, such as the Proms, it is only available for private hire at other times. At Grand Tier level, it is an unusual curved shaped room with windows overlooking the Royal College of Music and original mosaic flooring.

ROYAL OPERA HOUSE Bow Street, Covent Garden, WC2E 9DD
Tel: 071-240 1200 Fax: 071-836 1762

Crush Room Banquet: 100, Fork Buffet: 300, Reception: 350
The present theatre, which was opened in 1858, is the third to be built on this site, the previous buildings having been completely destroyed by fire. It became the Royal Opera House in 1892 and is today one of the finest and best-loved opera houses in the world. The grand staircase leads to the elegant Victorian Crush Room with its high, panelled ceilings, glittering chandelier and deepest pink furnishings. It is decorated with huge paintings, mirrors and statues, a twin staircase leads to the balcony. The mirrored bar area can be separated by curtains. The Crush Room is available for

Theatre Banqueting Rooms ———————————

Royal Opera House Continued....

daytime hire or after evening performances. In-house catering offers an extensive range of food and wines.

THEATRE ROYAL, DRURY LANE   Catherine Street, WC2B 5JF
Tel: 071-836 3687 Fax: 071-836 6465

Grand Salon Banquet: 120, Reception: 250
The oldest theatre in the world, the Theatre Royal, Drury Lane is the fourth to be built on the same site over a period of three and a quarter centuries. The present building was built in 1812 a retains a wealth of original features including the magnificent Rotunda and an impressive pair of double staircases which lead to the Grand Salon on the first floor. The salon is decorated with deep pink moire wall covering and velvet drapes at the tall windows. Marble columns are topped with gilded mouldings and glittering crystal chandeliers hang from the high ceiling. There is a long wooden bar, portable stage and baby grand piano. Catering is by Crown who also run the theatre restaurant.

Country Clubs ———————————————

HAMILTONS MIDDLESEX & HERTS COUNTRY CLUB
Country Club, Old Redding, Harrow Weald, Middx HA3 6SD
Tel: 081-954 7577 Fax: 081-954 3466

Fountain Suite Banquet: 180, Dinner Dance: 140-150, Reception: 250
This self-contained suite is set in seven acres of landscaped grounds, overlooking its private garden with a fountain centrepiece. It is approached from the car park via a canopied path past the swimming pool (use of which is reserved for club members). There is a separate reception room with a bar and this room can be used alone for smaller functions. The adjoining main room has a bar, dance floor and built in disco equipment. Larger informal parties, for around 500 to 600 people, can be catered for using the club area on specified days. A marquee can also be set up in the grounds. The resident head chef, Jacques Degageaux, can cater for all styles of function. Kosher or other specialist outside caterers are permitted to use the facilities by agreement.

HURLINGHAM CLUB Ranelagh Gardens, SW6 3PR
Tel: 071-736 8411 Fax: 071-731 1289

All Banqueting Rooms Banquet: 700 Dinner Dance: 450 (600 with marquee) Reception: 1000
Set amidst 42 acres of grounds along the banks of the Thames, this beautiful Georgian mansion is very much in demand for grand summer balls but all events must be sponsored by a member of the Club. All the banqueting rooms, with the exception of the Drawing Room, can be interconnected and may be used individually or in any combination, so are adaptable for almost any size of function up to the maximum numbers above. Some of the rooms though, are not suitable for dancing. The in-house caterers will tailor a menu to suit individual clients and are able to adapt to any style or theme. The Club is not available for hire on Sundays. There is ample parking space in the grounds.

See also:
Sopwell House Hotel & Country Club
Selsdon Park Hotel

You should make sure that your guests understand the need for punctuality as moving venues usually depart and return at pre-determined times. Guests who arrive late or need to leave early could have problems!

CONCORDE c/o British Airways, Caledonian House, Gatwick Airport, West Sussex RH6 0LF
Tel: 0293 668213 Fax: 0293 668331

Banquet: 100
You and your lucky guests could enjoy a 100 minute round flight, which includes 20 minutes at supersonic speed, from Heathrow, Gatwick or in fact any international airport. The price, of course, is astronomical but includes the food, champagne, supersonic flight certificates and Concorde souvenirs. Any other aircraft from the British Airways fleet could also be chartered for private events.

THE ELIZABETHAN c/o Monrow House, 40-42 King Street, WC2E 8JS
Tel: 071-379 5042 Fax: 071-379 1225

Banquet: 148, Dinner Dance: 148, Buffet: 230, Reception: 260
The Elizabethan is a luxurious replica of a 1890's twin-decked Mississippi paddle steamer. The wood-panelled upper deck - the reception and entertainment area - has a sliding roof over the large dance floor and a unique upper-deck promenade. The lower deck, level with the pier, is a traditional dining saloon elegantly decorated in blue and peach. The seating is not fixed so the saloon can be arranged to suit both formal and informal events. All the food is prepared on board by the Elizabethan's own chefs who can cater for any event from canapes to gala dinners. A wide range of menu ideas is available. The Elizabethan can pick up from most central London piers from Putney to the Thames Barrier.

NATICIA Charing Cross Pier, WC2
Tel: 071-839 3572 Fax: 071-987 0291

Banquet: 276, Dinner Dance: 276, Reception: 300
The largest catamaran on the Thames, Naticia is designed for entertainment with the galleried upper deck overlooking the spacious dance floor below. There is a sliding sunshine roof and a bar on each level. Naticia is the flagship of the Catamaran Cruisers fleet which includes several smaller vessels for private hire. Catamaran Cruisers will organise the entire party, supplying all the food, drinks and entertainment to suit the event.

REGALIA Swan Lane EC4
Tel: 071-623 1805 Fax: 071-839 1034

Banquet: 150 Dinner Dance: 150 Reception: 250
This oak lined floating restaurant is a reconstruction of an 18th century livery barge. Regalia has three decks. The lower Orlop deck is the dining area which has a dance floor and a small stage, ideal for cabaret. The galleried mezzanine deck, which overlooks the Orlop deck, has the main bar. The open - air Masters Walk on the top deck is open to the public. In summer, the roof can be opened. Entertainment, food and drink can all be provided by Catamaran Cruisers.

THAMES LAUNCHES Lambeth Pier, Albert Embankment, SE1 7SG
Tel: 071-261 0291 Fax: 071-261 0291

Thames Launches are a private charter agency who will help you choose the most appropriate boat for your function from over 30 vessels operating on the Thames. They will arrange for you to view the boats which vary in style and size, and organise the catering through the Fitzrovia Catering Company.

Moving Venues

WOODS RIVER SERVICES PO Box 177, Blackheath, SE3 9JA
Tel : 071-481 2711 Fax: 071-480 6932

Silver Barracuda Banquet: 168, Dinner Dance: 168, Buffet: 200, Reception: 280
The flag ship of the Silver fleet, the Silver Barracuda is a luxurious two-decked vessel, with a 1920's Art Deco style interior. The top deck has comfortable cane furniture, a bar, an oval teak dance floor and a sliding roof for when the weather is fine. The lower deck can be adapted to suit different occasions. The central seating is removable to make way for buffet modules if preferred. The boat is refurbished annually so always looks fresh. The five star French cuisine is all prepared in the company's own kitchens with an emphasis on quality and versatility. Set menu suggestions are provided as well as self selection menus and a comprehensive wine list. Woods River Services can also provide an in-house disco and fun gaming tables. The embarkation point can be chosen from five piers along the Thames. There is a smaller boat in the Silver fleet - the Silver Dolphin which can accommodate 70 seated or 100 for a reception.

BALTIC EXCHANGE St Mary Axe, EC3
Tel: 071-623 5501 Fax: 071-623 6644

Trading Floor Banquet: 600, Dinner Dance: 600, Reception: 1000
Built in 1903, the Baltic Exchange is now the world's leading international shipping market. The spectacular panelled hall boasts marble pillars, polished floors, back-lit stained glass and exquisite domed ceilings. The hall is available for hire from Monday to Friday after 4.30pm when all trace of the day's trading is removed from sight. Some Saturday functions are allowed but no Sundays. Receptions can be catered for in-house. For more lavish events, there is a list of recommended caterers. The Queen's Room could be used for pre-dinner receptions.

Queen's Room Banquet: 200, Lunch: 120, Reception: 300
The Queen's Room was built for the directors of the exchange in 1956 and retains the style of that decade. It is located on the lower ground floor with a separate entrance at 14/20 St Mary Axe. An unusual feature of the wood panelled room is the hydraulically operated dividing wall which can disappear into the floor to dramatic effect. There is direct access to the Trading Floor above.

COTTONS ATRIUM Tooley Street, SE1
Tel: 071-626 3411 Fax: 071-623 9459

Banquet: 100, Reception: 200
The 100 feet high atrium is a very unusual riverside venue with spectacular views over the Thames and the City through a glass wall. It is filled with exotic greenery, a flowing water feature and the award winning sculpture "Dancers" by Allen Jones. As there is no in-house caterer, you can choose your own. There is parking for 100 cars but guests can also arrive by riverboat at the private pier. The atrium is available seven days a week, evenings only.

HAY'S GALLERIA Tooley Street, SE1
Tel: 071-626 3411 Fax: 071-623 9459

Banquet: 1000, Dinner Dance: 800, Reception: 1500
Formerly a Victorian wharf, the Galleria has been splendidly converted into a shopping mall with interesting arcades and a marvellous riverside view. It has a high glass barrel-vaulted roof which is open at one end onto the river so is only suitable as a summer venue. There is a large, water spouting sculpture of a ship in the centre which is dramatically spot lit at night. There is a private pier so that guests can arrive by river. Alternatively, there is parking for 100 cars. The Galleria is available on Friday and Saturday nights only. Choose your own caterers.

HOP CELLARS 24 Southwark Street, SE1 1TY
Tel: 071-403 6851

Banquet: 150, Dinner Dance: 120, Reception: 250
These unique function rooms have recently been created from the original Victorian cellars underneath the Hop Exchange building, dating back to 1868. The white brick cellars are fully carpeted and air-conditioned. In-house catering is provided with party menus offering banquets, informal dinner parties, buffets and canapés and an extensive wine list which includes draught beer.

HOP EXCHANGE 24 Southwark Street, SE1 1TY
Tel: 071-403 2573 Fax: 071-403 6848

Exchange Hall Banquet: 230, Dinner Dance: 200, Reception: 400
Recently restored to its original splendour, this 19th century building is full of decorative motives and real character. The hall has a striking terracotta and black stone floor under a glass vaulted roof. Around the perimeter there are three tiers of green wrought iron balconies decorated with details of hops in relief and red and white Kent horse shields. The hall is available for corporate functions only on any day except Sundays. There is no in-house catering so you can organise your own.

Somewhere Different

IMAGINATION GALLERY South Crescent, 25 Store Street, WC1E 7BL
Tel: 071-323 3300 Fax: 071-323 5810

Banquet: 100 plus, Reception: 250
Far from being a typical party space, the roof top gallery is designed for flexibility. It is on the 5th floor of the award winning Imagination building, with superb views over Bedford Square. Guests will take the lift to the 4th floor, walk up one flight then cross the steel bridge to reach the light, airy atrium. The decor is white and grey with chrome and black leather furniture and is lit by spotlights and plenty of natural light. The gallery encourages young artists, photographers and designers to display their work and can be used in conjunction with a viewing of a current exhibition. The in-house caterers provide set canapé menus or will tailor the menu to suit your requirements. The venue is available for hire any day or evening until midnight, but Sundays are discouraged.

LLOYD'S OF LONDON 1 Lime Street, EC3M 7HA
Tel: 071-623 7100 Fax: 071-626 2389

The Captain's Room Banquet: 350, Dinner Dance: 250, Reception: 800
This fascinating building has several options available for parties but the most flexible of these is the Captain's Room. The open plan restaurant is decorated in red with a white fabric sail effect perimeter and moveable colour co-ordinated screens. The unusual ceiling has large inset lights that look rather like speakers set into panels. The whole effect is very dramatic and becoming. The set menus veer towards the French style though they are very flexible and able to cater for any theme. The Captain's Room is available for private evening functions from Monday to Friday (set-up from 3pm). A private viewing of the underwriting room, not generally available to the public, is offered to guests. Liveried staff are available to act as guides.

Old Library Reception: 150
This really is an old library with the original oak panelling taken from a stately home. This room can act as the reception room for functions in the Captain's Room and can be used in conjunction with the Nelson Collection.

Nelson Collection Reception:150
The reception area of Lloyd's of London houses this priceless collection which includes part of Nelson's silver Nile dinner service. This area is suitable for cocktail parties or a reception for functions in the Captain's Room. Cocktails for up to 80 guests can also be served in the viewing gallery, on the 5th floor, which is connected to the Lloyd's exhibition.

MACHIN CONSERVATORY Ransome's Dock, 35-37 Parkgate, SW11 4NP
Tel: 081-874 8505 Fax: 071-928 9734

Banquet: 30, Buffet: 60, Reception: 100
This remarkable roof-top venue is a Victorian-style conservatory decorated with sculptures, two small internal fountains and exotic foliage. It leads out to a delightful roof terrace which is illuminated at night. The conservatory is available for hire by the hour seven days a week until midnight. No dancing or loud music are allowed - background music only. A recommended list of caterers is supplied or you can choose your own.

OBSERVER
Chelsea Bridge House,
Queenstown Road,
Battersea, SW8 4NN
Tel: 071-627 0700
Fax: 071-627 8154

Boardrooms
Banquet: 80
Reception: 130
The impressive Chelsea Bridge House has been home to the Observer newspaper since 1988. The three second floor boardrooms open up completely to form one large reception room suitable for corporate or private dinners, product launches, wine tastings and cocktail parties. The ultra modern grey and white rooms have large windows with views across Battersea Park. Parking is available either in Battersea Park or at The Observer. The Observer can organise everything from catering to background music. Alternatively, outside caterers could be used. The boardrooms may be hired at weekends, most evenings and sometimes during the day.

THE ORANGERY Holland Park, W8
Tel: 071-602 7344

Banquet: 70, Reception: 150
This Grade 1 listed building was added on to Holland House in the mid-1800s. The Orangery is a rectangular, white-painted conservatory with a flagstone floor and large arched windows which look out over the surrounding park. The adjacent lawn may also be hired and a marquee could be put up for larger parties. Amplified music is not permitted. All catering requirements are provided for by Leith's Good Food (see Caterers). There is parking for 65 cars situated in the park.

THE ROOF GARDENS 99 Kensington High Street, W8 5ED
Tel: 071-937 7994 Fax: 071-938 2774

Banquet: 240, Dinner Dance: 200, Buffet: 350, Reception: 420
Situated 100 feet above street level, on the sixth floor of what used to be Derry and Toms, there is one and a half acres of themed gardens complete with stream, palm trees and flamingoes! The options for private entertaining at the Roof Gardens are endless. The Spanish Garden, bordered by fountains could be used for summer receptions and barbecues. A buffet could be served in the adjoining Tudor Walkway. The alcoves of the Tudor Garden are perfect for small dinners or drinks receptions. A marquee could be erected over the square courtyard for safer summer functions. Inside, floor to ceiling windows opening out onto the gardens provide illuminated views of the English Woodland Garden by night. The room is arranged around a large sunken dance floor under an unusual mirrored mosaic ceiling. This unique venue is available for exclusive or selective hire anytime from Monday to Saturday except for Thursday and Saturday evenings. Their own brigade of chefs will provide anything from light buffets and barbecues to formal French cuisine. A complete party planning service is available, including valet parking if required.

Somewhere Different

THE SANCTUARY
12 Floral Street, WC2
Tel: 071-240 9635

Banquet: 150
Buffet: 350
Reception: 350
The only time that a man could accompany his lady to this famous health spa is if he is lucky enough to be invited to a function here. Various segments of the Sanctuary can be hired for private parties: the upstairs conference facilities and restaurant could be used for a breakfast buffet while the tropical swimming pool and relaxation area would suit an evening event, possibly themed to include a synchronised swimming display or a steel band for example. The in-house caterers will organise the party and provide excellent food and wine, though no spirits can be consumed on the premises. Outside caterers can be used in specific circumstances. Smoking is restricted to the gallery area only.

TOBACCO DOCK Pennington Street, E1
Tel: 071-702 6981 Fax: 071-481 1102

Banquet: 600, Dinner Dance: 600, Reception: 1000
Adjoining the new Tobacco Dock Shopping Centre, created from the original tobacco warehouses that have stood on this site since 1805, this unique venue is extraordinarily flexible for any type of function. The high vaulted glass roof gives the venue airy ambience, perfect for summer parties, but is difficult to heat sufficiently in winter. The atmospheric vaulted arches and plazas are particularly well suited to themed events. Each of the two plazas has a central pink water fountain and is surrounded by areas of various shapes and sizes, any number of which may be used at one time. In summer, pre-dinner drinks can be served on the outdoor piazza, where there are two pirate galleons on view. Access to the venue can be from any of three main entrances. AM & PM Catering and Moving Venue (see Caterers) have both successfully operated there on several occasions. There is a large car park on site.

WESTMINSTER
BOATING BASE
136 Grosvenor Road,
SW1V 3JY
Tel: 081-459 2461 (Victualling)

Edgson Room, Buttery and Pier
Banquet: 100
Dinner Dance: 100
Reception: 250 (400 with Marquee)
Buffet: 250
The base is set in a small park overlooking the Thames close to Victoria. On the first floor, the light and airy Edgson Room has a canopied balcony and is linked to the Buttery by a wide gantrywhich spans the atrium, the main entrance to the base. The most popular set-up in winter, when weather precludes the use of the Pier, is to have a buffet and bar in the Buttery, leaving the Edgson room free for dancing. The Pier is tented over during June, September and December and can combine with the Edgson Room and Buttery for maximum capacity. There are in-house catering facilities, but outside catering companies are welcome.

MARQUEE AND CATERING
EQUIPMENT HIRE

Marquees

Create or expand your own venue by hiring a marquee. It can be attached to your house or chosen venue in such a way that it would be difficult for your guests to tell where the building stops and the marquee begins. Alternatively, it could be erected free-standing on any suitable site. The most common and cost effective type of tentage is the traditional marquee which is supported by internal poles and external ropes, and is quick to erect and dismantle. A clear-span or frame tent has no internal supports and is usually either aluminium or steel framed. It will allow you to add windows and doors or even remove the walls if it's hot. A good marquee company will advise you as to which design is best suited to your project.

Bill Woodward of Neptunus Tent Rental highlights some helpful guidelines to follow when choosing a marquee hire company:

"Ask a hotel or organisation which regularly hires tents to recommend a suitable company. You can then approach that company mentioning how you came to hear of them. This will ensure that your enquiry will be serviced correctly. Before placing an order, try to view one of the company's projects. Photographs and brochures can be very misleading as to the current quality of the equipment.

When budgeting for your event, allow an extra 15% to cover the small details not at first envisaged. Where budgets are very restricted, try to hire from a company in your area to minimise transport and labour charges. National companies can be expensive by comparison due to their higher fixed overhead costs. If possible, try to get a comparative quote for like equipment to ensure peace of mind. It is advisable, when discussing payment schedules, to keep a percentage of the contract value for payment on completion of dismantling. This should ensure good service and minimise damage to the site for fear of compensation being deducted from the final payment.

With regard to the times of erecting the equipment, try to allow one extra day to cover any unforseen problems such as bad weather or delivery break-downs, which can happen to even the most efficient companies."

ALFRED BULL Woodbridge Meadows, By-Pass Road, Guildford, Surrey GU1 1BB
Tel: 0483 575492   Fax: 0483 573448

Alfred Bull have been covering events throughout the south of London for over 100 years. It remains a privately run business offering the very best of personal service supplying traditional marquees and clear-span frame tents in widths up to 40 feet and any length. Also lean-to extensions, covered walkways, flooring, beautiful coloured internal linings, dance floors, lighting, heating and a vast range of furniture to suit all needs.

ASHLEY MARQUEES 42 Mount View Road, North Chingford, E4 7EF
Tel: 081-529 3267

This company provides marquees of all sizes and equipment for various types of events throughout the country. Their luxury linings enhance the overall effect and create a warm and cosy atmosphere. Also awnings, walkways, dance floors, full flooring, lighting, carpets, tables and chairs.

C.F. BARKER & SONS 47 Osbourne Road, Thornton Heath, Croydon, Surrey CR7 8PD
Tel: 081-653 1988   Fax: 081-653 2932

Still very much a family firm, C. F. Barker & Sons have been operating in the South East for well over 50 years, They hire out marquees, frame tents and ancillary equipment for parties, weddings, barmitzvahs, corporate hospitality and other social functions.

BRANTON INTERNATIONAL
Imperial Way, Watford, Herts WD2 4DW
Tel: 0923 211211   Fax: 0923 53531

Branton manufacture and hire out their luxury, clear-span marquees which are of the latest modular design. The interiors have sumptuous ruched linings and can be curtain-walled or fitted with Georgian windows and outward opening or patio type doors. The solid wood floor panels can be carpeted in a choice of colours to match or co-ordinate with the furniture and table accessories. Branton could even organise the entire event through their party planning division.

CENTRAL MARQUEES & FURNITURE HIRE Unit 5, Fernfield Farm, Whaddon Road, Little Horwood, Milton Keynes, MK17 0AR
Tel: 0908 502727   Fax: 0908 504077

This family-run business hires out blue and white marquees, complete with flooring, linings, dance floors and a full range of furniture and crockery for any occasion.

HART & COMPANY 151 St. Leonards Road, Windsor, Berks SL4 3DW
Tel: 0753 864075   Fax: 0753 830251

Established in 1929, Hart & Company hires out marquees, frame tents, clear-span structures, awnings, doors, windows, flooring, dance floors, lighting and heating. Also specialised interior decor and all types of furniture.

JAZ MARQUEES 8 Snowbury Road, Fulham, SW6 2NR
Tel: 071-385 3020   Fax: 071-381 6252

Drawing on 40 years of experience, Jaz Marquees provide high quality marquees and equipment with that little bit extra. Interiors are tailored to individual requirements with specialist lighting, dance floors in a variety of colours and trellis work. Backdrops can be enhanced with imaginative exterior lighting.

JULIANA'S Unit 7, Farm Lane Trading Centre, SW6 1QJ
Tel: 071-937 1555   Fax: 071-381 3872

As well as being party organisers, Juliana's have their own modern frame tents ranging in size from 10 feet to 60 feet wide. The range of smart interior linings includes a specially designed 'night sky' - black ceiling lining studded with white lights. (See also Party Organisers and Discotheques.)

M & G MARQUEES 1053-1055 High Road, N20 0QA
Tel: 081-446 4115   Fax: 081-445 5204

M & G provide traditional poled marquees and framed structures which are enhanced with an extensive range of ruched ceiling and wall linings. Ancillary equipment includes lighting, flooring, dance floors, furniture, lean-to awnings and walkways.

Marquees

MAIDSTONE MARQUEE HIRE
Senacre Lane, Suton Road, Maidstone, Kent ME15 8HB
Tel: 0622 691392
Fax: 0622 682202

Versatile frame tents from Maidstone Marquee Hire can cover any size or shape space for special occasions throughout the U.K. You can bring your garden in or view it through orangery doors and windows. There are 12 stock colours of interior linings to choose from. Trellis panels and arches can enhance the overall effect and the fully equipped lighting department will help to achieve the perfect atmosphere. The furniture shown in the photograph is supplied by their sister company Maidstone Furniture Hire (see Catering Equipment Hire).

MARQUEES OVER LONDON 319 New King's Road, Fulham, SW6 4RH
Tel: 071-731 6660   Fax: 071-736 9078

The green and white stripped tents come in free-standing modular units so any shape and size can be created using a combination of modules. Yellow and white internal linings are provided and a wide range of furniture, lighting, and flooring, including dance floors and staging is available.

NEPTUNUS 5 Vigo Street, Piccadilly, W1X 1AH
Tel: 071-734 2578   Fax: 071-434 3465

In the business for over half a century, Neptunus are now one of the three largest tent hiring companies in the U.K. With clear-span frame tents exceeding 25,000 square metres, they could easily house a party for 2,500 guests. They have a creative team, headed by an interior designer, who will transform the tent into whatever environment you want. The company specialises in large scale major events, but is just as happy to supply a small oasis tent for 25 guests. Also furnishings, lighting, staging and sound equipment.

PIGGOTT BROTHERS 40 London Road, Stanford Rivers, Ongar, Essex CM5 9PI
Tel: 0277 363262   Fax: 0277 365162

Best known for supplying the tentage for the Chelsea Flower Show, Piggott Brothers has over 200 years' experience in the manufacture and hire of marquees, providing a comprehensive, high quality service. The range of associated items and services includes decorative linings available in over 40 colours, carpeting, lighting, orangery windows, furniture, polished parquet dance floors, mobile toilet facilities, floral displays and trellis work.

Portable Toilet Hire

AH-HA SOUTHERN MOBILE
53 School Lane, Bushey, Herts WD2 1BY
Tel: 081-950 5051   Fax: 081-950 4911

Up-market self-contained mobile toilet units can be supplied with an attendant if required. The units vary in size to cater from a whole range of events from a family wedding to the grandest ball.

DAISYLOO TOILET HIRE
Bishop Centre, Bath Road, Taplow, Nr Maidenhead, Bucks SL6 0NY
Tel: 0628 669466   Fax: 0628 660092

Daisyloo hire out unique yellow and white candy-stripe toilet units containing a flush WC, hand basin, vanity mirror and electric light. The meticulously maintained units are ideal to compliment marquee hire.

GLENBY'S TRAVELLING LOOS
68 Lessar Avenue, SW4 9HQ
Tel: 081-673 2035   Fax: 081-675 9386

Wherever these extremely smart travelling loos are stationed, a Glenby's attendant will be on hand to ensure it is kept clean and tidy and to replenish towels, soap and paper. The green and gold units are self-contained, carpeted and furnished with brass fittings and wall lights. Each unit is fitted to provide either ladies' and/or gentlemen's facilities.

Catering Equipment Hire _____

Denise Roe from HSS Event Hire explains the role of the hire company.

"When it comes to arranging a party, be it a formal event, private indoor dinner, garden party, business lunch or corporate entertainment, good planning is invaluable. Why perform juggling miracles behind your guests backs - clearing, cleaning and drying cutlery and china for use with the next course? A far simpler solution for your catering needs and peace of mind is to hire your catering equipment.

So consider the services offered by catering equipment hire specialists before finalising your guest list. No longer need the extent of your hospitality be limited by the quantity of your china, glassware and furniture.

If you are arranging a large event, perhaps for the first time and are uncertain as to your requirements, a simple telephone call to a catering equipment hire company will solve your queries. Discuss your event with them and request a copy of their catalogue. This will make you aware of all the products available that you had never considered to make your event a resounding success.

Hire firms can provide you with a vast selection of top quality products to compliment the biggest or the smallest event. Fine bone chinaware with matching tea services will grace any table setting. Cutlery can be requested in either stainless steel or EPNS silver. Crystal glasses add a touch of luxury your guests will remember. Stainless steel serving and banqueting dishes and platters are available for displaying your buffet foods.

If you are arranging an on-site function, you may require additional kitchenware to supplement existing facilities - hot cupboards, 6-ring burners and ovens, water boilers and larder refrigerators are available from many hire depots. If additional furniture is required, various styles of chairs and tables can be ordered to seat your guests.

Do not forget the summer months. When catering for a garden party - patio furniture, canopy awnings and barbecues, as well as china and glassware will make your party memorable.

Breakable items are securely packed away in easy-handled containers should you wish to pick up your order personally. Alternatively, many hire companies can arrange delivery and collection of your order for a small charge. Every single item from a tea spoon to a trestle table is thoroughly cleaned and checked before hire, so you should not have to worry about hygiene.

Bookings of orders can be made up to a year in advance, although most large hire companies can supply your order in just 24 hours. Remember, however, during the summer and Christmas seasons when many weddings and parties take place, it is advisable to book early! "

ANSON CATERING HIRE 137 Deans Lane, Edgware, Middx HA8 3NY
Tel: 081-959 1680

Anson supply a complete range of equipment for parties, all ready to place on the table and in large quantities if required. This includes china and porcelain in distinctive styles, silver plate and stainless steel cutlery, linens and glassware.

THE BARBECUE SHOP *(Right)*
Unit 7, Bramley Hedge Farm,
Redhill Road,
Cobham, Surrey KT11 1EQ
Tel: 0932 868522 Fax: 0932 860200

Everything for your barbecue party can be hired from here. There is a full range of large catering barbecues, either charcoal or gas operated. Also electrically driven pig/lamb spits, barbecue awnings, tables and chairs.

CASTLE CATERING SERVICES
57-66 King James Street, SE1 0DH Tel: 071-928 3242 Fax: 071-821 1703

You can hire anything from toothpicks to a giant barbecue with spit here. As they are also professional caterers, they know all about the equipment that you will need and are able to offer free advice.

HSS EVENT HIRE Brownlow House, Brownlow Road, West Ealing, W13 0SQ
Tel: 081-567 4124 Fax: 081-840 3285

HSS Event Hire is Britain's largest supplier of furniture, tableware and catering equipment for hire. They offer a very wide range of top quality products and massive stocks for any size of function, large or small. Whether you are organising an intimate occasion in your own home or a larger event out of doors, they can supply everything you need from chairs to crystal glasses, buffet tables to bars. They have distribution centres all over the country enabling them to deliver nationwide.

COUSINS CATERING HIRE 108 Ripon Way, Borehamwood, Herts WD6 2JA
Tel: 081-207 5566 Fax: 081-207 5567

Party equipment for hire includes tables, chairs, crockery, cutlery, glassware, silverware, coloured tablecloths and napery, ovens, hot cupboards and all kitchen cooking equipment.

Catering Equipment Hire

**JONGOR Martinbridge Trading Estate, Lincoln Road, Enfield, Middx EN11QL
Tel: 081-443 3333 Fax: 081-805 8710**

Only top quality equipment can be hired from Jongor, one of the largest hire companies in Europe. They hold enormous stocks of furniture and catering equipment including 46,000 chairs which come in white, gold or mahogany with a choice of seven different seats, and 15,000 tablecloths, in every size and shape and in seventeen different colours. They can supply real props for a variety of themes and everything that you might need for a garden party - giant sun umbrellas, garden furniture, garden lights, gazebos, even display fountains. All the equipment and furniture is kept in immaculate condition (seven qualified carpenters are employed to look after the furniture). Jongor (who's catch phrase is "when only the best will do") also has branches in Southampton, Bristol, Birmingham, Cambridge and Maidstone.

KOSHER CATERING HIRE 43a Old Hill Street, N16 6LR Tel: 081-806 4838

This is the only company specialising in hire of equipment for strictly kosher functions. They have an enormous supply of milk and meat catering equipment, cutlery, crockery, glassware, pop corn machines and linen in any size or colour.

MAIDSTONE FURNITURE HIRE Senacre Lane, Sutton Road,
Maidstone, Kent ME15 8HB Tel: 0622 691392 Fax: 0622 682202

Immaculately kept gilt, white and black banqueting chairs with five interchangeable colour seats can be hired here, along with an extensive range of catering tables to suit every need. They offer a friendly and reliable service and are the sister company of Maidstone Marquee Hire (see Marquees).

MAXINE'S 20 Russell Parade, NW11 9NN Tel: 081-458 3102

Disposable plates, serviettes, banqueting roll, cutlery and drinking glasses are just some of the hundreds of lines of disposable party items that can be found at Maxine's. There is a huge range of patterns and plains, suitable for office and private functions, plus lots of advice on quantities etc.

FOOD AND DRINK

Caterers

Personal recommendation has always been the best introduction to a caterer. Word of a good caterer travels fast so someone who has built up a glowing reputation should not be too difficult to find. If you have already decided where your party will be, your choice might be limited to those approved by the venue. Alternatively, your caterer might influence your choice of venue.

Experience, attention to detail, presentation and a background knowledge of your venue are all important qualities. Complete trust in your caterer is vital. They must inspire you with confidence and enthusiasm or the liaison will not gel. Tell them who the party is for, what the occasion is, where it will be and how many guests you are expecting. Do they have an implicit and sympathetic understanding of your requirements, essential in giving life to the party?

Trade on your caterer's experience to steer you through the arrangements. They can often contribute a lot, so why not get your money's worth? Their advice might even save you unnecessary expenditure. All caterers should be able to provide wines and a celebration cake, should you want them to. Most are able to organise the entire event for you or at least have contacts that they have worked with before and can justly recommend.

Make sure that any guests with special dietary needs will be catered for properly. They should be served a meal of equal quality to the other guests - after all, you are paying the same for their meal. As a general rule, vegetarians do not eat meat or fish and vegans eat no animal products at all. Religious dietary laws might also need to be considered, for example: Jewish - no meat or shell fish, Moslem - no beef or pork. Individual guests will usually indicate any dietary restrictions when they reply to your invitation.

Work out the menu together with the caterer and ask for an estimate with a detailed breakdown of charges. Check for hidden costs - what equipment is provided and is it of an acceptable quality? You might prefer to pay a little extra to have finer crockery or a different colour table linen. Are drinks offered at an all-in-one price or charged on consumption? Are staff costs included? Is the price of the venue included? Will children be charged the same as adults? You might want to obtain several estimates and compare like with like.

Finally, remember to include your toastmaster, photographer, band and any other entertainers who require a meal in your final numbers.

ALEXA 63 Church Way, Whetstone, N20 OJZ
Tel: 081-368 3587
An extremely versatile cook, Alexa can offer a variety of cuisines including continental, vegetarian, Tex-Mex, barbecues and kosher-style, all prepared to a very high standard and beautifully presented. Alexa will personally discuss menus with the client and is always open to an exchange of ideas. She will also organise staff, drinks, flowers and equipment hire.
Maximum Catering Capacity: 400

ALISON PRICE CATERING *(Right)*
Number Five, The Talina Centre,
Badley Lane, SW6 2BW
Tel: 071-371 5133   Fax: 071-371 5671
Alison Price Catering enjoys an outstanding reputation for consistently providing some of the most highly regarded food in London. They work very closely with their customers to design the menu especially for them, whether it be French, Italian, English, Japanese, Thai, Indian, Chinese or Mexican cuisine. Other party services include the provision

of drinks, staff, marquees, music, lighting, fireworks, valet parking, transportation and security.
Maximum Catering Capacity: 4000 (canapés), 900 (dinner), 2000 (buffet)

AM & PM 15-17 Ingate Place, SW8 3NS
Tel: 071-622 6229   Fax: 071-720 8157
All aspects of catering and party organising are handled with exceptional professionalism by AM & PM. They produce cuisine of all types and nationalities and excel with their decorative cold buffet. AM & PM offer a complete range of supplementary services - everything from venue finding and marquees to decoration and special effects.   Their own venue at Winchester House, Putney, SW15 can hold 100 seated or 250 in a marquee on the lawn overlooking the river.
Maximum Catering Capacity: Unlimited

ANNE-MARIE KIMBALL PRICE 8 Bywater Street, SW3 4XD
Tel: 071-584 9444
The business has been running for over seven years offering a carefully selected choice of menus and friendly and efficient service. The cuisine is mainly French and English, specialising in canapés and buffets. All types of party are undertaken, including weddings. Flowers, cakes and smart staff can also be supplied.
Maximum Catering Capacity: 500

ANNIE FRYER CATERING 143 Lots Road, SW10 0RJ
Tel: 071-351 4333 Fax: 071-351 5044
This long established company provides original and innovative food and a complete party planning service for corporate and private clients. International menus are designed to suit the individual client's taste and buget, and each event is superbly organised.
Maximum Catering Capacity: 500 (Dinner), 1000 (Reception)

BEETON RUMFORD Special Catering, PO Box 772, SW5 9TG
Tel: 071-368 9329   Fax: 071-370 8166
Part of the P & O Group, Beeton Rumford offers top quality food and service by professionals with no hidden extras - the price quoted is the price you pay. They will also provide a free venue finding service, flowers and butlers, and will cater anywhere, preferring the more prestigious London venues such as Banqueting House and the Livery Halls (see Venues).
Maximum Catering Capacity: Unlimited

BUFFS 42 Lavender Hill, Battersea, SW11 8TC
Tel: 071-228 0079   Fax: 071-585 0546
Buffs is a private catering service covering every possible occasion, whether for business or pleasure. The menu offers a good variety of international dishes to select from, some traditional and some with original combinations of flavours. Buffs will also supply fine wines and champagnes, all equipment, colour co-ordinated flowers, cakes (both novelty and traditional), entertainment and experienced staff.
Maximum Catering Capacity: 1000

BUTLERS CATERING 6 Holland Park Mansions, Holland Park Gardens, W14 8DY
Tel: 071-602 0390
Backed by professional, enthusiastic staff, Celia Butler provides good food cooked with flair. All the food is freshly cooked to order - never frozen. Menus are constantly changing with a new brochure every winter, summer and Christmas. Other services include organisation, decoration, lighting, marquees, discos and flowers. They are happy to cater anywhere - the more variety the better.
Maximum Catering Capacity: 1000

Caterers

BY WORD OF MOUTH 22 Glenville Mews, Kimber Road, SW18 4NJ
Tel: 081-871 9566   Fax: 081-871 3691

By Word of Mouth are far from being average caterers. They tend to be very different in the style in which they display and present themselves. Their food has gained them an enviable reputation, partly due to their insistence on using only top quality produce and constantly achieving the high standards that they set themselves. Using their creative skills to design original themes and ideas, they could plan and organise the entire event, co-ordinating the menu, design and entertainment. *Maximum Catering Capacity:* 1000

CAROLINE'S KITCHEN 52 Pembroke Road, W8 5QD
Tel: 071-229 4114

This is a small and exclusive company offering a very personalised service with an emphasis on quality rather than turnover. The proprietor, Sally Purvis, is the main chef and uses only the freshest ingredients to create individually tailored menus. They specialise in finger food of all shapes, sizes and tastes from around the world and are particularly strong on Oriental cuisine. If necessary, they could organise the whole party.
Maximum Catering Capacity: 500 (finger buffet), 300 (fork buffet or sit-down)

CARVED FORK BUFFETS Unit 50, Metrostore Centre, Townmead Road, SW6
Tel: 071-731 6802

Carved Fork Buffets were established in the summer of 1990 to provide traditional catering for parties and weddings, indoors or out. The meats are roasted freshly on the day, preferably on site, and are carved and served by uniformed chefs and waiting staff from decorative buffet tables.
Maximum Catering Capacity: 300

CAVELL'S CUISINE 160 Camberwell Grove, SE5 8RH
Tel: 071-274 2168

For the past twenty years, Bridget Stephens has run her own catering company, Cavelle's Cuisine, which specialises in buffet and cocktail parties but also caters for weddings, dinners and directors' lunches. The cuisine is a mixture of French and English. Waitresses, butlers, flowers, china, cutlery and linen can all be provided. *Maximum Catering Capacity:* 500

CHARIOTS OF FIRE Unit 50, Metrostore Centre, Townmead Road, SW6
Tel: 071-731 6802

Specialists in outdoor events, Chariots of Fire will prepare sizzling, top quality meats on their mobile barbecues and serve them with a range of fresh salads and baked potatoes. Spit roasted hogs and lambs have been added to their menu which already includes all the traditional barbecue favourites from prime steaks to gourmet sausages. The staff wear chef's whites and all the crockery, cutlery and napkins are included. Drinks and other requirements such as lighting and music could all be provided. *Maximum Catering Capacity:* 3000

CHESTER BOYD
Butchers Hall, 87 Bartholomew Close,
EC1A 7EB
Tel: 071-600 5777   Fax: 071-600 2777

A young, growing company based in the City with close ties to the financial sector and city corporation, Chester Boyd offers quality catering using only fresh produce - nothing tinned. They specialise in imaginative traditional English and classic French cuisine: baron of beef, foie gras, toffee pudding with dates, walnuts and toffee sauce. Their cellars stock over £50,000 worth of fine wines. Chester Boyd are the

sole caterers at Butchers Hall and Founders Hall (see Venues), and a will provide anything from audio-visual equipment to helicopters. *Maximum Catering Capacity:* 1000

CLASSIC CATERING SERVICE
Manor House, 71 High Street,
Beckenham, Kent BR3 1AW
Tel: 081 650 0624
Fax: 081-663 6416

This is an independent private catering company specialising in high quality banquet and party catering as well as themed events and barbecues. Floral arrangements, car hire, toastmasters and a full bar service are provided. Classic Catering Service will go anywhere in the Greater London and Kent area.
Maximum Catering Capacity: 800

COMPANY CUISINE 3 Cloth Street, EC1A 7LD
Tel: 071-600 3561   Fax: 071-0600 1059
Company Cuisine, pride themselves on being 'big enough to cope, small enough to care'. They already supply individually hand made canapés to Harrods and would be equally as happy to supply them to your home or venue of your choice. They offer a highly professional service run by experienced staff and using first class quality ingredients. Their Directors' Dining Room Service includes the provision of Wedgewood China, silver cutlery and cut crystal glasses. A complete event management service is available to take care of every aspect 'from invitations to inspirations'.
Maximum Catering Capacity: Unlimited

CONNOISSEUR CUISINE 2 Charlton King's Road, Kentish Town, NW5 2SA
Tel: 071-485 4840
The main aim of Connoisseur Cuisine is to please their customers, which they achieve by producing an exceptional standard of nouvelle and classical French cuisine. The staff have all trained at top hotels and the head chef/managing director, Simon Carpenter, himself has been chef at Duke's, Claridges and the Relais à Mougins in the South of France. They will also supply staff, music, flowers - almost anything.
Maximum Catering Capacity: 200

COPE'S CUISINE Camberwell Business Centre, 99-103 Lomond Grove, SE5 7HN
Tel: 071-701 1960   Fax: 071-703 4903
Simon Cope started his catering company in the early '80s and is brimming with creative ideas for all types of events both private and corporate. He provides an imaginative selection of international menus with separate suggestions for hampers, teas, barbecues and so on. Cope's Cuisine also offers a complete party planning service which could incorporate venue finding, equipment, staff, drinks, flowers, entertainment and marquees.
Maximum Catering Capacity: 800

CULINARY ARTS 67 Muswell Hill, N10 3PN
Tel: 081-883 3799   Fax: 081-883 3799
Nadine Abensur has been running Culinary Arts for more than five years providing up-market vegetarian catering. Her delicious, innovative recipes and menus have gained her a reputation for supplying some of the most imaginative vegetarian food in London. The cuisine is a combination of French and Mediterranean cuisines and is always beautifully presented, whether it be a four course dinner party or a wedding buffet. Vegan and special diets can be catered for and tableware, staff, wines and flowers provided.
Maximum Catering Capacity: Unlimited

Caterers

EATON CATERING   7 Willow Street, EC2A 4BH
Tel: 071-729 5447   Fax: 071-729 7199

As a city based catering company, Eaton Catering specialises in functions at the Livery Halls and other prestigious venues such as museums, historic houses and art galleries. With their free venue finding service, they will locate the perfect venue. Menus are individually designed to provide interesting, international cuisine as well as fine wines and excellent service by well trained staff. They also offer a complete party planning service. No strangers to organising functions for huge numbers, they are equally happy to cater much smaller parties at private homes and offices.
Maximum Catering Capacity: 4000

FOOD ON THE HILL 32 Woodberry Grove, N4 1SN
Tel: 081-802 7631

Run by Illona Hammans, Food on the Hill blends modern, healthy trends with the best of European cuisines and sophisticated presentation to provide a refreshingly individual style of catering. As both business and party caterers, they are equally at home preparing a boardroom lunch to a private cocktail party or cold buffet. If necessary, they will arrange everything from a marquee to flowers and entertainment. Wines and spirits are supplied on a sale or return basis.
Maximum Catering Capacity: Unlimited

GASTRONOMIQUE 25 Red Lion Street, WC1R 4PS
Tel: 071-242 9997

A fresh, imaginative and efficient service is provided by Gastronomique. They use the best fresh ingredients for traditional favourites as well as new and imaginative recipes designed for the individual client. Large buffets with their wide range of lovely salads are very popular. They also provide friendly staff, an enterprising list of venues, equipment, furniture, marquees, excellent wine and flowers. Gastronomique are recommended caterers for Banqueting House and Glaziers Hall (see Venues).
Maximum Catering Capacity: 750

GOODLOOKIN' COOKING   57 Rudolph Road, Bushey, Herts WD2 3DX
Tel: 081-907 6066   Fax: 081-907 0743

As the name implies, Goodlookin' Cooking pays a lot of attention to display and presentation. They can produce any type of cuisine including vegetarian and kosher, and specialise in cocktail receptions and attractive buffet spreads. All kinds of themes are undertaken and drinks, flowers and celebration cakes supplied.
Maximum Catering Capacity: 500

GORE CATERING SERVICES   45 Gwendwr Road, W14 9BG
Tel: 071-603 3733

Since its beginning in 1989, Gore Catering Services has matured into a small, successful company with a personal and professional attitude to service. The emphasis is on fresh, seasonal food tailored to meet their clients' desires. The style is simple and unfussy, taking in the best of Mediterranean, Californian and traditional English cooking. The presentation is elegant, original and often witty, depending on the occasion. They can supply staff, hire equipment, suggest appropriate venues and work closely with Kosie Turner Flowers (see Flowers).
Maximum Catering Capacity: Unlimited (reception), 250 (seated).

GORGEOUS GOURMETS Gresham Way, Wimbledon, SW19 8ED
Tel: 081-944 7771   Fax: 081-946 1639

Gorgeous Gourmets offer not only good food but a full hire service including catering equipment and mini marquees. They cater for a wide range of clients, both private and corporate, for all types of parties from business lunches to charity balls. Glaziers Hall and the Great Hall at St Bartholomew's Hospital (see Venues) are their preferred venues though they will cater anywhere in and around London.
Maximum Catering Capacity: 500

**GREAT BRITISH PANCAKE COMPANY 23 Lancaster Road,
Wimbledon Village, Wimbledon, SW19 Tel: 081-944 6345**
Sweet and savoury pancakes can be freshly prepared on griddles in front of your guests by the Great
British Pancake Company. There is a variety of fillings to choose from ranging from chicken and
sweetcorn to banana and rum. Savory pancakes are topped with grated cheese and sweet ones with
sugar and whipped cream. They are ideal for both indoor and outdoor events.
Maximum Catering Capacity: Unlimited

**HEAD CHEFS 2 St Nicholas Mansions, 6/8 Trinity Cresent, SW17 7AE
Tel: 081-767 5849   Fax: 071-493 6345**
Head Chefs is an exclusive company led by Jacqueline Pickles, a 3-star Michelin trained chef
with experience gained at Le Gavroche and at a Relais Château restaurant in France. All types of
cuisine can be produced including classical and modern French, Italian and English with a great
emphasis on style and presentation. They are able to organise the entire event if required.
Maximum Catering Capacity: 200 (sit-down), 1500 (cocktail)

**JOHN (PERSONAL SERVICES) 99d Talbot Road, W11 2AT
Tel: 071-792 1162**
The company was established in 1952 by Mr John who, now in his eighties, still oversees the
running of the business. They operate a traditional French kitchen producing no-nonsense Grand
French cuisine and excellent canapés. They keep a small cellar of vintage wines and port and will
also supply butlers, liveried footmen and waiting staff, even if they don't do the catering (see Party
Staff).
Maximum Catering Capacity: 500 (cocktails), 500 (sit-down)

**LEITH'S GOOD FOOD 86 Bondway, SW8 1SF
Tel: 071-735 6303   Fax: 071-735 1170**
Prue Leith started the company in 1961 to provide excellent, elegant yet unpretentious food for
any kind of party. Today, they can plan and manage the entire party from start to finish, although
the food is still considered the most important element. Leith's Good Food is the appointed caterer
to Leighton House, the Orangery and the Serpentine Restaurant (see Venues), and provides all
the food for the Orient Express. Other party services include venue finding, staff, equipment hire,
entertainment, flowers, ice carving and wines.
Maximum Catering Capacity: 800

**LEON LEWIS 132b London Road, Brentwood, Essex CM14 4NS
Tel: 0277 218661**
For gourmet vegetarian feasts, Leon Lewis is brimming with exciting ideas drawn from recipes
from all over the world. A crusader for vegetarianism, Leon is the author of "Vegetarian Dinner
Parties" which gives an idea of the dishes he can create. Because of the wide variety of dishes that
he loves to prepare, he prefers catering for buffet parties.
Maximum Catering Capacity: 5000

**LONDON CATERING SERVICES 11 Keswick Road, Putney, SW15 2HZ
Tel: 081-874 4234   Fax: 081-877 0280**
Specialist banqueting caterers, established in 1950, London Catering Services operate from a
number of production kitchens in London. They provide good, traditional English food and have
their own banqueting suite at the Royal Horticultural Halls in Victoria.
Maximum Catering Capacity: Unlimited

**LORNA WING Studio 21, The Talina Centre, Bagleys Lane, SW6 2BW
Tel: 071-731 5105   Fax: 071-731 7957**
Considered to be one of the most creative caterers in the UK, Lorna Wing has won an enviable
reputation for providing stylish food with inspired presentation. They will arrange the complete
event (including marquees, flowers, lighting and musicians) or are happy to just organise the
catering. Members of the Royal Family are among their many private clients and their corporate
clients include many high profile companies. The cuisine is extremely varied - from modern British

Caterers

Lorna Wing Continued....

to classic French and from rustic Mediterranean to authentic Oriental. The presentation is always simple and uncluttered. Canapés are Lorna Wing's speciality. The company created the idea of canapés based on miniature meals from around the world and such classics as one-bite sized hot dogs, hamburgers and fish and chips in miniature Financial Times cones.
Maximum Catering Capacity: 2000 (cocktails), 700 (sit-down)

MARTHA FISHER Unit A3, Connaught Business Centre, Hyde Estate Road, NW9 6JP
Tel: 081-200 9303   Fax: 081-200 9303
Martha Fisher's catering company produces tailor-made food to suit a discerning clientele. They can provide all types of cuisine, always exquisitely presented and using only the finest, freshest ingredients. As complete party planners, they can also organise music, themes, photography, video, flowers and lighting.
Maximum Catering Capacity: 500

MICHAEL JAY THE FREELANCE CHEF 13 Tottenham Street, W1P 9PB
Tel: 071-580 5090
Michael Jay and his team provide complete catering with a personal bias, offering an à la carte service at homes, businesses, marquees, galleries and so on, and at an exclusive function room in Kensington. All types of parties are catered for, dinner parties, cocktail parties and weddings being his forte. Wine, staff, equipment hire and marquees can all be supplied.
Maximum Catering Capacity: 500

MOSIMANN'S 11 Elbaston Place, SW7 5QG
Tel: 071-823 9992   Fax: 071-584 2467
The outside party catering service is an off shoot of Anton Mosimann's private dining club. Its services are offered not only to the club's 2000 members but also to the general public. Mossimann's specialise in cuisine naturelle and can cater in any environment, be it a private home or the Royal Academy.
Maximum Catering Capacity: Unlimited

MOVEABLE FEASTS 83-85 Holloway Road, N7 8LT
Tel: 071-607 1178   Fax: 071-607 1555
Moveable Feasts started in 1967 and enjoys a good reputation in the City and throughout London. They cater for most types of party, especially buffets and weddings receptions, but also banquets, City lunches and barbecues. Although they will cater at any venue, they are happiest at the client's home or marquee. They will provide all the necessary equipment, staff and flowers.
Maximum Catering Capacity: 800

MOVING VENUE 14 Calico House, Plantation Wharf, Battersea, SW11 3TN
Tel: 071-924 2444   Fax: 071-978 5178
The extensive range of cuisine that Moving Venue have been asked to prepare includes English, French, Italian, Russian, American, Chinese and Scottish. They specialise in themed cuisine such as the Horrific Feasts that they present at The London Dungeon where they are the sole caterers (see Venues). Although the emphasis is always on superb food, The Moving Venue offers a complete range of services such as drinks, marquees, staff, equipment, flowers, entertainment, lighting, photographers, toastmasters, security, and some unusual venues. Packages are created to suit the client's preferred location, budget and particular requirements. Their name appears on recommended lists at such venues as the Natural History Museum, Science Museum, London Transport Museum, Baltic Exchange, Le Palais and The Sanctuary (see Venues).
Maximum Catering Capacity: 2000

MUSTARD CATERING 1-3 Brixton Road, Kennington, SW9 6DE
Tel: 071-582 8511   Fax: 071-793 1024
Mustard regularly caters at London's top venues and at a large amount of private events in marquees in the country. They generally provide very English food, but it is no problem for them to match the

Mustard Catering Continued....

food to a theme, say Japanese or Thai. They pride themselves on being very flexible and tailoring each party to the personality and requirements of each individual client. That way, every party is different but hallmarked by their distinctive quality of food, service and attention to detail. As well as providing the catering, they will also help with finding the right venue or marquee, florist, musicians, security, choosing themes and colour schemes and of course the menu and wines.
Maximum Catering Capacity: 600 (dinner), 1500 (canapés)

NEWINGTONS 40 Yoakley Road, N16 0BA
Tel: 081-802 8810
This small, well established company prepares traditional English and French cuisine for canapés, buffet luncheons and dinner parties. Presentation, reliability and client satisfaction are their main aims. They also provide butlers, waitresses, music, equipment hire, marquees and flowers.
Maximum Catering Capacity: 400

NEW QUEBEC CUISINE 13 New Quebec Street, W1H 7DD
Tel: 071-402 0476
The highly professional team, headed by Sharon Davy, has a creative, flexible and skilful approach to catering. New Quebec Cuisine creates modern, traditional, theme and seasonal menus with a personal touch and unlimited imagination. They specialise in using the best quality produce - organically grown vegetables and naturally reared meat, poultry and eggs. They love working in unusual venues, but also have the ability to transform any ordinary location into a venue of wonder.
Maximum Catering Capacity: Thousands

PAELLA PARTIES *(Right)*
Unit 50, Metrostore Centre, Townmead Road, SW6
Tel: 071-731 6802
Traditional Spanish paellas and tapas are prepared in front of your guests, preferably in the open air. 150 people can be served at a time or up to 1000 if service is staggered - it takes about 20 minutes to prepare the next paella. There is a choice of three paellas - fish, chicken and 'The Paella' combining seafood, fish and chicken - all served with Spanish salad. Tapas can either be served from a decorated buffet table or by staff wearing traditional Spanish costume.
Maximum Catering Capacity: 1000

PARTY INGREDIENTS
Unit 1a, Tideway Industrial Estate, Kirtling Street,
SW8 5BP
Tel: 071-627 3800   Fax: 071-720 6249

With more than 15 years of experience, Party Ingredients offer personal involvement, inspired cooking and a command for detail. The cuisine ranges from traditional to the more imaginative to suit the client's requirements. They specialise in formal banqueting and theme parties and can help organise all aspects of the event. They are recommended caterers at many of London's leading galleries, museums and livery halls. Party Ingredients are also independent wine importers and a catering equipment hire service.
Maximum Catering Capacity: 2000

Caterers

PAYNE & GUNTER   Mayfair House, Belvue Road, Northolt, Middx UB5 5QJ
Tel: 081-842 2224 Fax: 0818452319

Baltic Exchange

Toy Museum

Kew Gardens

Marquee

Established in 1786, Payne & Gunter is the largest privately owned outside catering company in the country. With an enviable reputation for innovative catering, they specialise in historical banquets and themed evenings as well as large corporate hospitality events. They will take care of the entire party, from finding the venue to organising the theming, decoration and entertainment together with superb food, drink and service, all within a pre-arranged budget.
Maximum Catering Capacity: 5000

THE PIE MAN FOOD COMPANY 16 Cale Street, Chelsea Green, SW3
Tel: 071-627 5232
This is a small, well established company with two retail outlets and a catering service to both private and corporate clients. They make a variety of dishes from around the world, working closely with each client to achieve exactly what is wanted. Cocktail canapés and directors' lunches are their fortes.
Maximum Catering Capacity: 1000

RICHARD GROVES CATERING COMPANY Unit 4, The Swan Centre,
Riverside Road, SW1 0LD
Tel: 081-947 1213   Fax: 081-944 1895
Apart from catering, the company specialises in event and party management providing set design, discotheques and light shows, marquees and a venue finding service. A high standard of international cuisine and themed food is presented. Richard Groves has catered at events in such prestigious venues as the Victoria and Albert Museum and Queen's House, Greenwich (see Venues).
Maximum Catering Capacity: 1000

SCOTTY GRAHAM 10 Thurloe Square, SW7 2TA
Tel: 071-584 6761   Fax: 0737 843242
Scotty Graham is an enthusiastic catering and party planning company. Specialising in canapés and buffets, they provide a fast and professional service, even for last minute parties. They will also supply hampers, freezer food, vintage wines, bands, magicians and videos.
Maximum Catering Capacity: 750

SEARCY'S 124 Bolingbroke Grove, SW11 1DA
Tel: 071-585 0505   Fax: 071-223 4599
150 years after the company was founded, Searcy's now caters for 1000 parties a year worldwide. A complete party management and advisory service is provided with a reputation for meticulous attention to detail. The highly trained and experienced waiting staff and butlers work solely for Searcy's and have been much admired. Searcy's appear on the recommended list at many top London venues - museums, galleries, Livery Halls - and cater exclusively at their own Georgian townhouse at 30 Pavilion Road, Knightsbridge (see Venues).
Maximum Catering Capacity: 4000

SOPHIE BATCHELOR 157 Lower Richmond Road, Mortlake, SW14 7HX
Tel: 081-878 6431
The business is only five years old yet Sophie's regular clients include a list of well known West-End advertising agencies and property companies. She caters both private and business cocktail parties, buffets and barbecues as well as directors' lunches. Drinks, flowers, marquees and entertainers can also be provided.
Maximum Catering Capacity: 300

SPATS   47 Kendal Street, W2 2BH
Tel: 0836 201216   Fax: 0491 575914
Spats aim to provide the highest quality food from the finest available fresh ingredients. James Forbes, the proprietor and head chef, tailors his menus to the clients' requirements and enjoys fitting menus to themes. You could choose hot raw beef pasta salad, barbecued butterflied leg of lamb with four pepper marinade and blueberry bread and butter pudding. Their mobile kitchen has massive fridge space and allows them to cater anywhere. A full party planning service is available as well as their own jazz discotheque. *Maximum Catering Capacity:* 300

TAZ COOKS 12 Wilberforce Road, Finsbury Park, N4 2SW
Tel: 071-359 9580
This is a small specialised caterer working in the areas of art and imagery with a love of detail and a belief in quality. Exotic dishes are created by Tamasin Marsh who's food sculptures are a feast to the eyes and her cocktail canapés and buffet tables unforgettable. Food can be themed to suit any event or occasion. *Maximum Catering Capacity:* 350

Caterers

SQUIRE'S   Unit 13, Canonbury Yard, 190 New North Road, N1 7BJ
Tel: 071-359 8741   Fax: 071-354 0858
A relatively young and very flexible catering company, Squire's has a bias towards innovative and spicy dishes. They specialise mainly in cold buffets with a good fish and vegetarian content, and spectacular seafood displays. They are mainly involved with corporate business, but are building up their list of private clients. Among the other services provided are staff (their own team), drinks, flowers, entertainment, costumes, fireworks, lighting, backdrops and venues which include the London Transport Museum and Glaziers Hall (see Venues).
Maximum Catering Capacity: 700

TEMPTATION CATERING 16 Keslake Road, Queens Park, NW6 6PL
Tel: 081-969 0903
Sarah Hamilton has built up a notable clientele for her company by combining good, friendly service with exciting presentation and unusual flavours in her dishes. A very versatile cook, she can prepare all types of cuisine but specialises in food for drinks parties. She can organise a pianist, butler and waitresses and will provide drinks and flower arrangements.
Maximum Catering Capacity: 300 (drinks party), 400 (buffet)

20TH CENTURY FOOD 1 Alma Place, NW10 5NX
Tel: 081-960 3119
This is a small, innovative firm of a New York designer and London chef who offer flexibility, a creative approach to composing menus and striking styling. They can produce all types of cuisine from around the world and specialise in vegetarian, fish and game dishes. 20th Century Food will also organise staff, equipment hire, flowers and drinks.
Maximum Catering Capacity: 500

UNCOMMON COOKS 50 Hardy Road, Blackheath, SE3 7NN
Tel: 081-469 0651
Fax: 081-692 3555
Uncommon Cooks is a hospitality company offering distinctive and imaginative food to private and corporate clients. The partnership was established in 1979 and from the early days has been consistent in providing a highly professional standard of flexible and attentive service. Specialising in themed cuisine, they also provide innovative contemporary, traditional and vegetarian food. They are always happy to design an event to suit the client's budget and requirements offering a complete package to include venue

finding, invitation and menu design, equipment hire, floral decoration, entertainment and staff.
Maximum Catering Capacity: 1000

You don't have to be Jewish to enjoy kosher catering. You can expect a very high standard of cuisine but without forbidden food groups such as pork products and shellfish. Dairy foods cannot be served during the same meal as meat or poultry in accordance with the strict dietary laws.

The following Caterers are not under Rabbinical supervision unless expressly stated.

CATERING BY LORAINE 13 Napier Drive, Bushey, WD2 2JH
Tel: 0923 38867

Loraine Myers specialises in weddings and barmitzvahs with a reputation for friendly staff and good home cooking on a large scale. Among her many specialities are hot spicy meat buffets, salmon buffets, barbecues, canapés and outstanding desserts - especially the Crêpes Suzettes.
Maximum Catering Capacity: 200

CREATIVE CATERING 46 Rotherwick Road, NW11 7DB
Tel: 081-455 0096/081-346 5274

A complete professional service is provided by Creative Catering which is expertly run by Judith Shaerf and Nicole Schlagman. They specialise in fish and vegetarian dishes for cocktail parties and buffets, though they can handle an intimate dinner for two or a dinner dance for two hundred equally well. Waitresses, flowers and equipment hire can all be provided.
Maximum Catering Capacity: Unlimited

FAY SCHNEIDER 85b Crowland Road, N15 6UP
Tel: 071-435 4223   Fax: 081-802 1760

Shirley Davidson now runs the catering company that was started by her mother more than 20 years ago. Under Kadassia supervision, Fay Schneider produces exquisite French cuisine, both traditional and nouvelle, as well as dishes from all around the world. Venues include the Royal Garden Hotel and the Royal Lancaster Hotel (see Venues) where they are the sole kosher caterers. They are also happy to cater at your home, marquee or business premises.
Maximum Catering Capacity: 1000 plus

M & M KOSHER CATERERS 58 Portland Avenue, Stamford Hill, N16 6EA
Tel: 081-800 1058   Fax: 081-802 1760

M & M and Fay Schneider are affiliated companies which share the same kitchen and offer similar services under Kadassia supervision. In addition to a complete party service, which includes flowers, wines, cakes, equipment and staff, M & M also provide a party take-away service where food is prepared and presented on disposable platters ready to serve. Venues include the New Connaught Rooms (see Venues), the London Press and Conference Centre and any venue of the client's choice.
Maximum Catering Capacity: 1000 plus

M. OBERLANDER 1A Cecil Road, Colindale, NW9 5EL
Tel: 081-205 5994

This family run company has been involved in kosher catering since 1895 and now cater for both corporate hospitality and private functions, supervised by the London Beth Din.. Their deluxe style of catering varies from traditional to unusual and themed food. The Guildhall, Langham Hilton, London Hilton and London Marriott are just some of the venues where Oberlander cater.
Maximum Catering Capacity: 1000 (sit-down), 2000 (reception).

RAQUEL & MARK'S KOSHER CUISINE 28 Elmstead Avenue, Wembley, HA9 8NX
Tel: 081-908 3025 / 081-958 5870

Under the supervision of the London Beth Din, Raquel and Mark provide a fully comprehensive catering service. A typical menu would consist of reception canapés followed by a four course meal with evening tea served later on. Whole dressed salmons, ice cream gateaux and swan meringues filled with exotic fruits are some of their specialities. Table linen (any colour), flower arrangements and table wines are all included.

Maximum Catering Capacity: 300

V. SCHAVERIEN 132 Great Cumberland Place, W1H 7DJ
Tel: 071-723 7933   Fax: 071-402 0399

Schaverien's expertise and professionalism have lead them to gain exclusive arrangements to provide kosher catering (supervised by the Beth Din) at The Dorchester, St James Court, May Fair Inter-continental, Hyatt Carlton Tower and Grosvenor House, and they are sole caterers for the popular King David Suite (see Venues). Under the guiding hand of Tony Page, they will design and organise the entire event - they've done dozens of different themes - or just handle the catering anywhere and for any number of guests. Each event is created around the clients' individual requirements, so they do not just present set menus to choose from. Schaverien's services have been required at Buckingham Palace, Windsor Castle, and at virtually every five-star hotel in London.

Maximum Catering Capacity: Unlimited

SPIELSINGER & ABRAHAMS The Kinloss Suite, Kinloss Gardens, N3 3DU
Tel: 081-346 5450   Fax: 081-349 0391

Spielsinger and Abrahams have been established for 60 years. Their cuisine, however, has certainly moved with the times to produce nouvelle cuisine under the supervision of the London Beth Din. They combine superb food with imaginative decor and ideas to create some memorable themes, and take care of every detail. They are the exclusive kosher caterers at the Cumberland Hotel, Holiday Inn Swiss Cottage and the Kinloss Suite in Finchley, and are happy to caterer in a marquee or the venue of your choice.

Maximum Catering Capacity: 1200

SUPERCOOKS 10 Longwood Gardens, Clayhall, Ilford, IG5 0BA
Tel: 081-550 6930

Supercooks is a small, personal kosher catering business run by head cook Maureen Sharpstone who caters each function as if it were her own. All the food is freshly prepared by the company who are opposed to convenience food. Their 'pièce de resistance' has to be their spectacular dessert buffets. Other party services provided include drinks, balloons and flowers.

Maximum Catering Capacity: 300

THELMA KOORLAND 27 Springfield Avenue, Muswell Hill, N10 3SU
Tel: 081-883 1049

Thelma Koorland has the highest reputation for unique catering and exquisite presentation. Thelma creates not just food, but a rather special experience with her individual style of kosher, vegetarian, vegan and macrobiotic cooking. The complete service includes decorations, music and staff.

Maximum Catering Capacity: Unlimited

"You can't have a party without a cake," according to **Jane Asher of Jane Asher Party Cakes**, "particularly if the party is celebrating a wedding, christening, anniversary or birthday. A cake has become much more than just part of the food; it forms the centrepiece for the gathering, a glorious symbol of the festivities and of course the essential excuse for the singing of Happy Birthday or the ceremonial cutting of the wedding cake.

If you are going to take the trouble to make or buy someone a very special cake, it's far more pleasing that it should be obviously designed and planned especially for them. I believe that cakes should be personal and unusual, often bringing humour into the designs, and always taking into account the hobbies or tastes of the person they are made for. There are few greater pleasures than seeing the delight in a child's face when presented with a cake the shape of a beloved toy, or an elderly lady being given a beautiful cake covered in her favourite flowers recreated in sugar.

There are a few basic rules when planning the cake for your special event: if you're choosing a sponge, don't have it too big. It would be a pity to have too much left over as a good sponge won't keep fresh for more than a few days. Otherwise, a rich fruit is usually popular - especially at Christmas time. Little slices can be boxed up and sent to absent friends and will keep perfectly well for months. Or you can make the cake part of the pudding and choose something like a rich, boozy chocolate Sacher filled with cream and strawberries. Almost anything can be decorated appropriately.

If you're not making the cake yourself - and it's lovely to have that burden taken off you when there's so much else to do - remember to order it in plenty of time and to discuss it with the shop so that you get exactly what you want. Don't ever be palmed off with a standard line or unwillingness to try something exciting - it's your special party and the cake has to look so fabulous that it will always be remembered. Whether it's an enormous wedding feast or just a few friends round for a 'welcome home', your cake has got to make them all say...WOW!"

**ANNE FAYRER CAKES & FLOWERS   66 Lower Sloane Street, SW1W 8BP
Tel: 071-730 6277**

High class novelty and celebration cakes are baked, modelled and decorated in front of your eyes at this exclusive cake shop, just a stone's throw from Sloane Square. Established for over 10 years,

Party Cakes _____

Anne Fayrer Cakes & Flowers will make anything from a champagne bottle to a model of your home. Wedding cakes can be traditionally decorated or hand painted. Whether a car, newspaper or cigar, they all taste as good as they look. Each cake is individually crafted to the customer's exact requirements, however simple or demanding, and as nothing is sold off the shelf, freshness and quality can be guaranteed.

CRUMBS OF LONDON *(Right)*
12 Methuen Park, Muswell Hill, N10 2JS
Tel: 081-444 0393

Run by 'edible artists' Greg Robinson and Max Schofield, Crumbs of London specialises fantasy cakes for birthdays, weddings and celebrations of any sort. Designs range from a wedding cake in a gale to a cleaning bucket complete with scrubbing brush and bottles of cleaning fluid - all edible. Greg and Max will create to the customer's specifications or design exactly the right cake for the people and the occasion. The cakes can be made in any flavour and tast as spectacular as they look.

FINAL TOUCH Studios E & F, Canada House,
Blackburn Road, NW6 1RZ
Tel: 071-625 9617 Fax: 071-372 0729

Final Touch produces quality decorated cakes for weddings, birthdays, christenings, anniversaries and corporate occasions. All the cakes are individually designed and produced with as much emphasis on taste as design.

JANE ASHER PARTY CAKES 24 Cale Street, SW3 3QU
Tel: 071-584 6177 Fax: 071-584 6179

Even before the shop was opened in 1990, Jane Asher was well known for her spectacular party cakes. Now these beautiful and extraordinary cakes are available either to order or immediately from stock, including a 'cake of the month' recording a current event. Every one is designed by Jane and baked fresh on the premises. They vary from tiny personalised cakes for a few pounds to sensational wedding cakes or launch centrepieces for a few hundred, and cover every possible subject - including the kitchen sink!

SLATTER'S BAKERY 111 Sydenham Road, SE26 5EZ
Tel: 081-778 4705

Winner of 34 medals, Slatter's specialises in decorated cakes of all kinds from elaborate wedding cakes to personalised centre pieces for corporate functions, either selected from the catalogue or individually designed. Slatters also supplies baked goods for the catering trade.

STEPHEN HAUDÉ 109 Midhurst Road, Ealing, W13 9TJ
Tel: 081-567 1081

Stephen Haudé supplies top West End hotels with wedding and celebration cakes. The retail shop supplies the public with these fine cakes as well as every tool, colouring, book, ribbon, cake board and ornament, plus icings in all colours, marzipan and edible decorations. They also offer a cake tin hire service for tins in all shapes and sizes.

The amount of wine and champagne that you will need will vary according to the type of party you are giving. As a rough guide, for a sit down meal, allow for one bottle of wine per person, half to three quarters of a bottle per person for a cocktail party. If you are serving champagne or champagne-based cocktails such as Buck's Fizz or Kir Royale at a reception, half a bottle per person should be enough. You will be best advised by your caterer or wine merchant on how much to purchase, but always have extra bottles in reserve, especially if you are buying on a sale or return basis. You will also need plenty of soft drinks - mineral water, fruit juices and fizzy drinks. If there is dancing at your function, the soft drinks will disappear very quickly. A jug of iced fruit cup on each table will be appreciated by hot, thirsty dancers.

David Hinmers of Balls Brothers offers this advice on selecting the wines for your party...

"Wine merchants are frequently asked to recommend a good 'party' wine. Usually what is meant by the enquiry is 'what have you got in the way of downright cheap, nasty plonk, which can be drunk by the bucketful?' A good wine merchant will not have what is wanted here but he will have a range of wines to fulfil certain expectations.

The prime criteria is cost. There are plenty of good inexpensive wines. A reputable merchant will have a selection and you can taste and find enough wine to slake the thirst of your invited hordes. But how to be selective? The procedure is to firstly work out your budget. Ask assistance from your wine merchant. Make a selection with regards to whether your guests will be drinking wine on its own or whether food will be served. You will quickly narrow down the selection to three or four wines which will do. Try them, discuss them and you will end up with the best available.

What you have done is allowed yourself the necessary time to make best use of the sort of service that an independent wine merchant will give you. His knowledge of his own stock and his judgement of suitable wines will save you both hours and money. Only beware of arriving when the doors are closing and the staff are ready to go home. The advice you receive may not be quite what you expected!

The independent wine merchant will offer a unique and exclusive range of wines. He will know their origins, the differences between vintages and their suitability for various functions. He can guide you to shelves filled with bottles of wine with telephone number prices attached, starting with three figures. He will also take you to the middle range where worthy wines are lined up. He will listen to what you want and select a few for you. It is his ability, skill and knowledge that you obtain and a merchant's selection of wine will grace your party and ensure a convivial time is had by all."

If you are still in doubt about what to serve your guests, consider the words of Brilliant Savarin.... "Burgundy makes you think of mischief, Bordeaux makes you talk of mischief But Champagne makes you get up to mischief."

AD HOC WORLD OF WINES 363 Clapham Road, SW9 9BT
Tel: 071-247 7433   Fax: 071-737 7420
Winner of the 'Which Wine?' Wine Warehouse of the Year award, Ad Hoc is reputedly the largest wine warehouse in Europe with over 1100 wines, selling by the single bottle. Also glass hire, ice and free delivery in London of orders over one case.

BALLS BROTHERS OF LONDON 309-317 Cambridge Heath Road, E2 9LQ
Tel: 071-739 6466   Fax: 071-729 0258
Balls Brothers is a family run City wine merchant dating back over 150 years, specialising in wines and spirits. The extensive range of wines is personally tasted and selected by the partners of Balls Brothers. There is a wholesale division and retail service offering delivery service to a home or office address or alternatively you can collect from their Wine Centre at Bethnal Green. Balls Brothers also operates several wine bars in the City which are suitable for parties including the recently restored Hop Cellars (see Venues).

BORDEAUX DIRECT 144 High Street, Bushey, Herts WD2 3DH
Tel: 081-950 0747   Fax: 0734 461493

Specialist wine merchant, Bordeaux Direct is noted for quality wines from all over the world, especially France and Chile. All their wines are single estate and direct from the vineyard. Any quantity can be catered for. They offer free delivery for orders over £50, sale or return, glass hire, discounts for party orders (over 36 bottles) and you can taste before you buy.

CORNEY AND BARROW 12 Helmet Row, EC1V 3QJ
Tel: 071-251 4051   Fax: 071-608 1373

Established in 1780, Corney and Barrow is an independent wine merchant with a national and international mailing list. Honest advice and an outstanding range of House wines are offered along with free delivery, sale or return, free glass hire and a complete personal service.

DOMAINE DIRECT 29 Wilmington Square, WC1X 0EG
Tel: 071-837 1142   Fax: 071-837 8605

Domaine Direct are specialist importers of high quality Domaine-bottled Burgundy and excellent value New World wines. As wholesalers, they supply many of the top London restaurants and corporate bodies. Glass hire and delivery within Central London is free with a minimum purchase of one case.

GRAPE IDEAS 2a Canfield Gardens, NW6 3BS
Tel: 071-328 7317

Large stocks of claret, Burgundy and port can be found here. Grape Ideas ship approximately 80% of wines direct from the vineyards, with an emphasis on areas such as the Loire and South America. The knowledgable and helpful staff have all attended wine courses. There are discounts for cases and free deliveries in the area. Other branches are in Oxford and Liverpool.

HAIR OF THE DOG 401 North End Road, SW6 1NR
Tel: 071-385 5483

As both a wholesale and a retail wine store, Hair of the Dog stocks over 600 wines as well as champagnes, beers, spirits and liqueurs. They offer glass hire and a delivery service.

LIQUID I.D. Maritime House, Clapham Old Town, SW4 0JP
Tel: 071-622 4452   Fax: 071-498 0458

Liquid I.D. is a champagne importer and wholesaler specialising in small, lesser known Champagnes. The main business is personalised champagnes for companies, special events, anniversaries and weddings.

LONDON WINE Chelsea Wharf, 15 Lots Road, SW10 0QF
Tel: 071-351 6856   Fax: 071-351 0030

This cash and carry wine warehouse has been offering first class service and advice to the public and catering trade for over 10 years. Over 200 lines are stocked covering wines from around the world, spirits, beers, mixers, champagnes, sherries and ports. Plus free local delivery, sale or return, free glass and bin loan, and ice.

VINTAGE HOUSE 42 Old Compton Street, W1V 6LR
Tel: 071-437 2592

Vintage House carries a complete range of wines, beers, champagnes, cigars and spirits including ports dating back to 1955, clarets to 1949 and over 170 different malt whiskies.

WINE CELLARS 153-155 Wandsworth High Street, SW18 4JB
Tel: 081-871 2668   Fax: 081-874 8380

Independent Wine Merchant of the Year 1991 (Wine Magazine/Sunday Telegraph), Wine Cellars are England's leading Italian specialists with an extensive range of wines from Tuscany and Piemonte, French country wines and Burgundies - over 600 wines in all. Three masters of wine are among the experienced, knowledgable warehouse staff. Tutored tastings are available, plus sale or return, free glass loan and free delivery within the M25.

DECORATION

Decoration

DUNCAN HAMILTON
ICE SCULPTOR
14 Tideswell Road,
SW15 6LJ
Tel: 081-785 9192
Fax: 081-780 0291

Duncan Hamilton is London's leading ice sculptor. His highly artistic designs, produced from in Wimbledon studio from unique crystal ice, are famous throughout London's leading hotels and party venues. His work is used as a focal point for product launches, major sporting events, weddings and all private occasions. Almost any subject can be re-created in ice, from swans to company logo's. The sculptures are at their best two hours after going on display and will last for about seven hours. Duncan has worked extensively in advertising and made many personal appearances on television. He personally presents his work with lighting and specially produced perspex drainage trays, creating the ultimate talking point.

FISHER LIGHTING *(Right)*
Unit 1, Heliport Industrial Estate,
Lombard Road, SW11 3SS
Tel: 071-228 6979   Fax: 071-924 2328

Specialist lighting for marquees, hotels and banqueting venues is provided by Fisher Lighting, as well as power distribution for outside caterers. They are the recommended lighting contractors for the Natural History Museum, Imperial War Museum, Baltic Exchange and the Victoria and Albert Museum.

LASER CREATIONS
55 Merthyr Terrace, Barnes, SW13 9DL
Tel: 081-741 5747 Fax: 081-748 9879

Laser Creations hire out laser systems complete with
operators to provide spectacular laser effects and graphics to enhance any special event.

LAURENCE CORNER 126-130 Drummond Street, NW1 2NV
Tel: 071-388 6811   Fax: 071-383 0334

A huge range of props is available for hire for almost any theme - the selection of horror props is enough to give you nightmares. You can also hire nets, backdrops, flags of the world and costumes (see Dress Hire).

MOSTLY LIGHTING 7 Greenock Road, W3
Tel: 081-993 7227   Fax: 081-993 4637

Effective period lighting, chandeliers, Victorian street lamps and posts, and gas and oil lamps can all be hired from Mostly Lighting.

NICOL & MOON 5 Hardwicks Way, Wandsworth, SW18 4AW
Tel: 081-874 2022   Fax: 081-874 8415

N & M will screenprint a multi-coloured birthday or wedding bannergram onto a durable sign cloth which is then finished by hand.

STARLIGHT Unit 5, Gateway Trading Estate, Hythe Road, NW10 6RJ
Tel: 081-960 6078   Fax: 081-960 7991

Starlight was originally a lighting company, specialising in providing unique, spectacular and innovative lighting for parties. The company has now expanded to include a set design and build service with an unrivalled stock of different themes, and a fireworks division specialising in electronically detonated shows accurately synchronised to music.

THEME TRADERS 16 North Square, NW11 7AD
Tel: 081-458 3253 Fax: 081-458 2462

Whatever the theme or era, Theme Traders can supply and install props and decorations for themed parties. They can also provide costumed performers with props for all occasions, such as a period news vendor and stand, flower seller and cart, onion seller and trike, even a living statue - human art on a pedestal. There is a range of period style indoor stalls for hire for fairground activity evenings. Theme Traders also specialise in costume hire (see Dress Hire).

WATER SCULPTURES St George's Studio, St George's Quay, Lancaster, LA1 5QJ
Tel: 0524 64430   Fax: 0524 60642

Specialists in the design of water features for one-off events, Water Sculptures supply everything from small portable fountains to cascading waterfalls with a complete service from design to installation in your chosen venue.

WESTWAY EVENTS 90 Cambridge Gardens, W10 6HS
Tel: 081-968 0736

Lucy Smail and Jayne Buswell can together design and produce functions that will fulfil your wildest dreams. They have the ability to organise the entire event, but their strength is in set design, construction and lighting for unique and imaginative special events.

WISE PRODUCTIONS 22 Pensbury Street, SW8 4TJ
Tel: 071-978 1223

A complete technical support service is supplied by Wise Productions. Their services include internal and external lighting, lasers and decor for themed events.

Flowers _____

Large venues and marquees have a tendency to 'swallow up' flowers, but if you are going to do it, then do it properly. Let your imagination run wild. Obviously, the time of year will influence the type of flowers you go for. In winter, when the choice is limited, you might consider using silk flowers, hiring plants, or combining fresh flowers with foliage, fruit, vegetables, berries, nuts, ribbons, feathers, balloons or anything that might tie in with your theme or colour scheme. Your choice of containers can add an original dimension to your flower arrangements, so look around for ideas. As a basic rule, if it doesn't leak, you can use it!

Sonja Waites of Pulbrook & Gould suggests how you can expect the best from your chosen florist:

"Flowers are an important part of any function. They can create the required atmosphere and bring the feeling of life into an otherwise cold area.

Once the type of function you are planning has been decided upon and the date and venue booked, the next task is to decide the theme or style that you wish to create. You should at this stage call in your chosen florist to discuss how best this can be achieved.

The florist will ask questions and, if necessary, arrange to meet you at the venue. Look for focal points. Don't be tempted to dot flowers about - it is much more important to have one large receiving group than three small ones. Ask about colours, type of flowers and foliage available. Look at photographs of previous work, show fabric samples where possible and advise on how many guests will be attending. The florist should then be able to give you an estimate of the cost.

Do not leave the ordering of the flowers until the last minute. If you want something beautiful and perfect on the day, it needs thought and time to order. The more time the florist is given, the better the result will be."

**ALEXANDER REYNE FLOWERS 200 Battersea Park Road, SW11 4ND
Tel: 071-622 1023**

Specialists in high quality floral services, Alexander Reyne was voted by House and Garden as one of the top ten florists in London. It is part of the Plantation Landscaping Group which is owned by P & O.

**AZAGURY FLEURS 38 Knightsbridge, SW1X 7JN
Tel: 071-259 5141   Fax: 071-259 5319**

Azagury Fleurs specialises in the design and supply of flowers, both fresh and dried, for all types of special occasions.

**BILL & BEN'S GREENHOUSE Chesterfield House, 385 Euston Road, NW1 3AU
Tel: 071-387 0007   Fax: 071-388 4491**

Floral decorations for large and small functions are regularly provided by Bill and Ben's Greenhouse. This may involve something that they make and the client collects or, on a larger scale, something their team of designers will arrange on site. They also operate a tropical plant hire service.

**BLOOMING MARVELLOUS 40 Battersea Rise, SW11 1EE
Tel: 071-223 9099**

Debra Smith-Symmonds and Pat Wong met at Pulbrook and Gould where they both trained and gained their skills. They formed Blooming Marvellous in 1985. It quickly earned the reputation for being an adventurous company whose fresh ideas and use of unusual materials has attracted commissions to decorate various prestigious luncheons and dinners, glamorous P.R. receptions and all types of parties and functions.

CAROLINE EVANS   9 Mendora Road, SW6 7ND
Tel: 071-384 1566

Being a small company, Caroline Evans is able to offer a very personal service. The style is always natural, mostly using fresh garden flowers and foliage, occasionally dried and silk flowers, but ribbons and lace are definitely not their style.

EDWARD GOODYEAR 45 Brook Street, W1Y 2JQ
Tel: 071-629 1508   Fax: 071-495 0524

From their three flower shops in central London, much of Edward Goodyear's work is done for parties, weddings and receptions in some of the top hotels. They provided the floral arrangements for the wedding party of The Prince and Princess of Wales. Established in 1880, Edward Goodyear, Court Florist, holds four Royal Warrants, one of only twelve companies to do so. No function is too big or too small for them to handle.

THE FLOWERSMITH 34 Shelton Street, Covent Garden, WC2H 9PH
Tel: 071-240 6688   Fax: 071-836 8395

This unusual flower shop in Covent Garden offers rare and exotic blooms co-ordinated with woodland findings - bark, fungi, wriggly willow and blossom. They have provided flowers for some spectacular occasions. Clients include the Hayward, National and Portrait Galleries, the Royal Opera House and several famous musicians and singers.

GARDEN VISIONS 60 Mowbray Parade, Edgware Way, Middx HA8 8JS
Tel: 081-958 7447

Garden Visions provides fresh and silk flower arrangements for special occasions and all kinds of balloon structure and decoration. They can combine flowers and balloons to create gorgeous table decorations.

JANE PACKER 56 St James Street, W1M 5HS
Tel: 071-935 2673   Fax: 071-486 5097

Jane Packer is a florist very much in demand, especially since she was responsible for the sensational floral displays at Westminster Abbey and Buckingham Palace for the wedding of The Duke and Duchess of York. Jane is full of creative ideas and loves to work to a theme or concept, using her favourite flowers which differ according to the time of the year and the occasion.

JANET ROSENTHAL
43 Lyndale Avenue, NW2 2QB
Tel: 071-431 4192
Fax: 081-446 9317

Janet avoids overheads by working from home and so is able to offer a very personal service and excellent value for money. She works mainly with fresh flowers, producing traditional floral arrangements to suit the specific requirements of each client.

Flowers

KOSIE TURNER FLOWERS
Unit B247, Riverside Business Centre,
Bendon Valley, Haldane Place,
SW18 4LZ
Tel: 081-877 9288 Mobile: 0831 384531

This young and exciting company provides innovative floral arrangements to an eclectic clientele. Work undertaken can vary from a traditional country wedding to bedecking a Christmas Tree in Times Square. Kosie Turner Flowers specialise in creating a visual feel, whether it be the traditional rich and voluptuous English look or a way out party with an original theme using a variety of props. They often work in conjunction with Gore Catering Services (see Caterers) to provide a complete party service.

LAURELS FLORIST
61b Judd Street, WC1H 9QT
Tel: 071-387 6200
Fax: 071-383 3501

Laurels deal in only the best and unusual flowers, which their customers have come to appreciate. They have impressed several London venues with their work and as a result now have the contract for The Brewery where they supply their arrangements for the eight function rooms. They are also one of the recommended florists for Spencer House and have provided the floral decorations for functions at the Serpentine Gallery and the Roof Gardens (see Venues).

MARY ADAMS FLOWER DESIGN STUDIO 4 Kinnerton Place South, SW1X 8EH
Tel: 071-235 7117

Country flowers, foliage and herbs are used by Mary Adams in her natural style of arrangements for parties, often combined with lace, ribbons or tulle for weddings. Her book "Natural Flower Arranging" will give you an indication of her style and expertise. Mary has been teaching and arranging from her delightful Belgravia studio since 1964, having gained seventeen years of experience with Pulbrook and Gould.

MOYSES STEVENS   6 Bruton Street, W1X 7AG Tel: 071-493 8171   Fax: 071-493 0618
and 157-158 Sloane Street, SW1 Tel: 071-259 9303   Fax: 071-259 9279

Established in 1876, Moyses Stevens has been one of London's leading florists for over a hundred years. The company was granted a Royal Warrant by The Queen Mother in 1940 and continues to supply several members of the Royal Family. The two shops offer arrangements for all sorts of private functions, favouring a country style of floral decoration.

PAULA PRYKE 20 Penton Street, N1 9PS
Tel: 071-837 7336

With probably the largest selection of flowers anywhere in the capital, Paula Pryke specialises in wild and countryish flowers from all over the world. She loves to create an atmosphere and set the scene for parties.

POT POURRI 255 Chiswick High Road, W4 4PU Tel: 081-994 2404

This flower shop specialises in unusual and interesting flowers and decorations for parties, weddings and receptions.

PULBROOK & GOULD Liscartan House, 127 Sloane Street, SW1X 9AS
Tel: 071-730 0030 Fax: 071-730 0722

Internationally renowned, Pulbrook and Gould is probably the finest flower shop in London. This is where many of the top florists learned their skills and gained experience before branching out on their own. They will supply all types of arrangements and displays, traditional or modern, specialising in country flowers and foliage.

SARAH WATERKEYN 29 Lambs Conduit Street, WC1N 3NG Tel: 071-430 2287

Sarah Waterkeyn has a great team of experienced designers with lots of imagination and flair who love a challenge, small or large. They enjoy using different objects, fabrics, fruits and vegetables, combining colour, texture and form to create different atmospheres and themes to stunning visual effect.

SILK FLOWER AND PLANT HOUSE 66 Burnfoot Avenue, SW6 5EA
Tel: 071-736 7861

One way to ensure that your floral decorations won't wilt before the evening is over is to go for the eternally fresh looking artificial arrangements from the Silk Flower and Plant House. Countess Beatrice Hochberg has been running her business for fifteen years and will make up table centres and posies to suit your colour scheme. Another advantage is that you can use these arrangements time after time, occasionally popping them back to the Countess for maintenance.

SOPHIE HANNA FLOWERS Arch 49, New Covent Garden, Vauxhall, SW8 5PP
Tel: 071-720 0841 Fax: 071-720 1756

This small private company, based in the centre of the flower trade, specialises in floral decorations for all types of social functions - theme parties and everything from society weddings to barmitzvahs. They are full of original design ideas and provide a very personal and discreet service, hence their impressive client list. Sophie Hanna will also organise the entire party.

VASE 10 Clifton Road, W9 1SS
Tel: 071-286 2535 Fax: 071-266 2427

Vase supplies superb, stylish floral displays and plants for all functions. Themed and mixed material decorative work is a speciality. With over forty trained staff, six vehicles and five senior designers, large scale or out of town projects are no problem to them.

HIRE

PLANT PEOPLE Unit A2, Cumberland Park, Scrubs Lane, NW10
Tel: 081-960 8303 Fax: 081-960 4389

You can hire exotic tropical plants in various sizes from the Plant People for all occasions. A design and creation service is available for special theme parties and events.

STROUDS OF LONDON Rochester Square, NW1 9SD
Tel: 071-485 5514 Fax: 071-267 2166

Palm trees and tropical plants, water effects, lightweight statues, columns, catwalks, lampposts, gazebos, urns and containers, cut trees, foliage and forests can all be hired from Strouds of London. They also supply fresh flowers and floral decorations.

Balloons

It is a long time since balloons were only associated with children's parties. Their growing popularity at 'grown-up' events is explained by **Barbara Jago of The Balloon Factory:**

"In the ten years that I have been in the balloon business I have seen it grow from a few inventive companies, delivering gorgeous big bunches of balloons to individual clients, to a business that turns over millions of pounds a year.

So why this phenomena in balloons? People will tell you it is the age old fascination with things that fly or the beautiful colours that balloons come in and they would be right but there is another aspect - practicality. How else could you achieve a wonderful visual effect for your functions at such reasonable costs? Todays balloon artists can create the most stunning effects. Balloons can be swagged and swirled and bunched into order. There is no social divide with balloons. In our time we have catered for major companies and minor companies, princesses, pop stars and thousands of average families who all have something in common - they want to create a wonderful magical effect which is also great fun for either their family and friends of their employees.

Tens of thousands of balloons are printed every year bearing brand names or company logos. This is because of the incredible success of the balloon as a promotional tool. Who ever heard of someone throwing a balloon in the bin? Many companies go for a balloon release, launching their products in a spectacular way. The world record balloon release of one and a half million is held by the Americans but one day a British company out there somewhere will take up their challenge and create world news.

Some balloon companies, like ourselves, have been in the business for a long time and reputations have grown from being able to come up with what the customer wants in the most effective and cost productive way. To ensure you get the best results, I would recommend that when you order you get clear quotations with no hidden costs and a definite plan of what the balloon artists will do for the budget you have given them. Even ask for references of work done in the past. A good balloon artist will be happy to let you talk to previous employers. Cover these things and I am sure that you will finish with a terrific result. Remember, balloons add a touch of magic to any occasion."

BALLOON FACTORY 6 Sutherland Avenue, Maida Vale, W9 2HQ
Tel: 071-289 7455   Fax: 071-266 3166

The Balloon Factory can do wonderful things with balloons, theming them to match any occasion. They will decorate large and small venues for banqueting and special events and supply unusual table centres. They have worked at all the top London hotels are reputedly one of the country's premier balloon services.

BALLOONLAND   44 Warwick Lodge, Shoot-Up Hill, NW2 3PE
Tel: 081-452 1587   Fax: 081-450 6357

A very personal service is offered by Balloonland. They provide the finest quality latex balloons for helium or air filled decorations including balloon flowers, hot air balloon decorations and 40 inch paddles.

BALLOONMANIA 13 Spaniards End, NW3
Tel: 081-421 0670

This small, enthusiastic company specialises in the individual requirements of each client. They can make absolutely anything with balloons from company logos to Christmas trees and table decorations.

BALLOON PRINTERY 5a Washington Road, E18 2JZ
Tel: 081-530 5055

Large and small quantities of latex and metallic balloons, either plain or with personalised printing can be supplied by The Balloon Printery. They also do bannergrams and hall decorations, and offer a helium filling service.

BALLOONS & PARTIES TODAY 2/20 Crediton Hill, West Hampstead, NW6 1HP
Tel: 071-431 5528   Fax: 071-431 5528

The experienced team of decorators at Balloons & Parties Today will use fabrics and props with their balloons to create the right atmosphere or theme for any type of party. The company can also organise the event entirely and supply a complete range of party goods.

BUBBLES In Shops, The Maltings, St Albans, Herts AL1 3HF
Tel: 0727 43025

Sandra and Barbara, who run Bubbles, regularly attend seminars and balloon academies to keep up to date with all aspects of balloon decorating. They do balloon bouquets, sculptures, arches, drops and table centres for all occasions, plus gift wrapping in a balloon.

INDEPENDENT BALLOON COMPANY Unit 1, Carew Street, SE5 9DF
Tel: 071-274 1388   Fax: 071-326 1084

Specialists in party decoration, the Independent Balloon Company can deliver and set up balloon drops, table decorations, arches, swirls and so on throughout London and the South East.

JUST BALLOONS 127 Wilton Road, Victoria, SW1
Tel: 071-434 3039

Just Balloons offer a huge variety of promotional and gift balloons ranging from the balloon in a box to 10,000 balloon releases like the one they did for Disney. For parties they offer a full decorating service or will supply the balloons already inflated or with the helium or air pumps for you to inflate them yourself. A novel idea is to send invitations or thank you messages printed on a balloon in a red and white presentation box, which can be delivered to anywhere in the U.K.

KITE & BALLOON COMPANY 613 Garratt Lane, SW18 4SU
Tel: 081-946 5962   Fax: 081-944 0027

With fifteen years of experience behind them, the Kite and Balloon Company can offer everything that is currently available in the balloon industry, from both here and abroad. The complete balloon decorating service includes balloon gas, inflated balloons, exploding balloons, table centre displays and party supplies.

PARTY PARAGON   Chelsea Farmers Market, 125 Sydney Street, SW3 6NR
Tel: 071-351 5771   Fax: 071-373 2582

Party Paragon has decorated parties and events all over the world with their balloon sculptures. The shop was first opened in 1987 and remains open seven days a week for balloons and a full range of party goods. They also hold classes on party decorating.

WORLD OF BALLOONS & DECORATIONS 90 Cardinal Avenue,
Kingston, Surrey KT2 5SA Tel: 081-549 5999

Proprietor Ann Cowling-Last offers a personalised wedding and party decorating service - with or without balloons. For theme evenings, she is full of exciting and imaginative ideas. Silk flowers are available for hire.

Table Gifts and Novelties _____

Presenting your guests, or at least the ladies, with a small gift is now an accepted part of any celebration. Bonbonieres, also known as 'favours' are traditionally given to wedding guests, but are also becoming a popular gift at christenings and other celebrations. The five sugared almonds, or chocolate dragees, symbolising health, wealth, happiness, fertility and long life, are most often wrapped in tulle and decorated, but can also be presented within another gift, such as a lace hanky or small trinket box. Two or three hand-made chocolates or truffles also make a very acceptable gift. These can be presented in little coloured boxes, tied with ribbons and decorated with tiny flowers, all of which could be co-ordinated with your colour scheme.

Beautiful hand-made crackers are becoming increasingly popular as a way of 'gift wrapping' your choice of gift, and not just for Christmas parties.

Gifts can be presented to your guests in many different ways. They can be used to decorate the place setting, displayed in the wine glass or arranged in baskets on the tables. Alternatively, they can be handed out individually by the hostess or her helpers, such as the bridesmaids, during the reception.

Novelties distributed among your guests will involve them in your theme or 'set' during the evening. Masks, hats, flags, parasols, canes, grass skirts and leis, fans and noisemakers can be taken home as a memento of a fun evening.

ABSOLUTELY CRACKERS 9 Walkers Green, Marden, Hereford HR1 3DN
Tel: 0432 72352

Absolutely Crackers produces top quality hand-made crackers for all occasions. They can decorate crackers to specific themes, such as with pearls and ostrich feathers for the ladies and bow ties for the men at a 20's party. They have an exciting standard range of crackers or can design one-off specials. They can contain all sorts of gifts which can be chosen from a large selection including miniature bottles of whisky, perfume or after-shave, hand-painted silk scarves (silk evening scarves for men), or something relevant to your theme. Alternatively, you can provide your own gifts.

ALL OCCASIONS 1 Redbridge Lane East, Redbridge, Essex IG4 5ET
Tel: 081-550 4030

A delightful selection of party goods can be found at All Occasions, such as wedding favours, English and American invitations, Belgian chocolate table gifts, perfumed gifts and exquisite champagne and chocolate presentations. They also offer a helium balloon decoration service.

ANONA'S 13 Highgate High Street, N6 5JT
Tel: 081-348 5213

Here you will find a wonderful selection of imported hand-made chocolates. Anona will make up gift boxes for your guests or fill sweet dishes for the tables. There is also an attractive selection of dried flower arrangements and fresh flowers.

A TASTE OF HONEY 11 Finchley Lane, NW4 1BN
Tel: 081-203 1080 Fax: 081-203 0044

This specialist company offers kosher chocolates from Belgium, France and Israel, bonbonerie, petits fours, balloons and table gifts for weddings, barmitzvahs and all occasions.

NOVELTIES GALORE 8 Aldenham Road, Watford, Herts WD1 4AA
Tel: 0923 51011

Balloons, decorations, party hats, crackers, garlands, streamers, party poppers, blowouts,
parasols, and a large selection of noisemakers can all be found at Novelties Galore. They specialise
in party themes such as Hawaiian, French, American, Irish, Halloween and special requests. They
also offer loads of advice to help you plan your function.

SWEET FAVOURS of LONDON 69 Green Lane, Edgware, Middx HA8 7PZ
Tel: 081-958 1225 Fax: 0727 47218

Their bonbonieres are beautifully presented in white or coloured net or lace, decorated with tiny
flowers, pearls, miniature hats or padded satin hearts. The stem designs are trimmed with ribbons
and have the five sugared almonds individually wrapped in net 'petals' to resemble flower buds.
Containers include padded satin heart-shaped boxes, tuxedo boxes with wing collars (for the men),
and various coloured mini boxes trimmed with ribbons and flowers. For special gifts, there is a
selection of crystal and ceramic trinket boxes containing the favours.

THE PERFECT TOUCH by DECORPRINT 4 Northwold Road, N16 7HR
Tel: 071-254 1083 Fax: 071-254 5077

A selection of gifts and novelties is among the wide range of party requirements available from The
Perfect Touch. These include bonbonieres (with either sugared almonds, chocolate dragees or
pot-pourri for a change), mini 'choc' boxes, cake boxes, book matches, 'book match' gifts, key
fobs, crackers, pens, fans, noisemakers, balloons, decorations, wedding accessories and stationery
(see Stationery & Printing). Most of the items can be printed with a personalised message, a choice
of motifs or your own design.

VILLAGE FAYRE 369 Uxbridge Road, Hatch End, Pinner Middx HA5 4JN
Tel: 081-421 0363 Fax: 081-421 2671

Village Fayre is renowned for innovative confectionery presentation. They specialise in creating
chocolate thins embossed with names or logos with personalised ribbon and boxes which they can
deliver nationwide. They have designed a range of hand-finished chocolates which they import
from Belgium and make their own sensational liqueur chocolates, petits fours and chocolate
novelties.

ENTERTAINMENT

Entertainment Agencies ———————————————

This expert advice is from **Andrew Chance of Chance Entertainment.**

"Your choice of entertainment will set the tone of the evening and will be remembered by your guests as amazing, alright or perhaps even awful. So, how do you ensure that your evening is truly amazing, that the entertainment is flawless and, above all, fun?

You have chosen your venue, your menu, the invitations have been sent and now for the entertainment. Whether you are organising an intimate dinner for twelve or a spectacular gala evening, the entertainment will make or break the evening. It must be able to hold the attention of your guests, but at the same time, change the mood or set the atmosphere without being intrusive or noisy. It is important to decide what effect you are trying to achieve. Are you aiming to dazzle your guests with an international star? Relax them with chamber music? Amuse them with a witty after-dinner speaker? Encourage them to dance until the early hours of the morning? Or perhaps a combination of all these and more would suit your particular needs. Having decided upon the desired effect, what do you do next?

That jazz band that Aunt Margaret booked never arrived for the dance, the dance band that Harold organised for his evening could not be heard above the level of conversation, and as for the after-dinner speaker last Christmas...well, the less said about him the better! How do you avoid these situations? Our advice is to consult a professional organisation. The world of entertainment is a jungle and you need someone to help you bypass the pitfalls and save your time and energy. They will know what fee to offer that international pop star, whether he will need a piano and where to get it. They may be able to suggest ideas that you had not even thought of and advise you on what sort of entertainment would work best in your particular venue. These are things that you cannot possibly be expected to know.

What do you spend? You can spend tens of thousands of pounds if you wish but the small gesture can be equally as effective. This is where clear priorities and planning, together with skilled entertainment specialists come into play. The top operators should have the ability to deliver the goods without throwing money around.

It must be right on the night so get advice and make sure your evening goes with a swing."

**ABLE ARTISTES 32 Manor Road, Wallington, Surrey SM6 0AA
Tel: 081-647 4783**

The best British dance and cabaret bands can be booked through Able Artists including Andy Ross Band & Singers, Johnny Howard Orchestras, Ray McVay Band & Singers, Jack Hawkins Showband, Kenny Ball Jazzmen, Miller Magic, West One Sound and Latin American band Carlos Romanos. They will also find you entertainment for theme nights such as Italian, Spanish, French and German.

**ANGUS GIBSON MUSIC 117 Stephendale Road, SW6 2PS
Tel: 071-384 2270   Fax: 071-731 1580**

Drawing on contacts made during his many years in the business, Angus Gibson provides bands pooling musicians from top rock and jazz groups instead of just dance bands. Angus also does party planning and supplies discos (see Discotheques).

**APSLEY ENTERTAINMENTS 116 Belswains Lane, Hemel Hempstead, Herts HP3 9PP
Tel: 0442 256856**

Apsley provides jazz, rock 'n' roll, rhythm and blues, dance and cocktail bands, as well as dancers and speciality acts. They are sole managers of Happy Feets - the national Dixieland squad that offers from 1 to 14 musicians, and are agents for 'The Roaring Twenties' show.

THE BARN DANCE AGENCY/FOLK ENTERTAINMENTS
62 Beechwood Road, South Croydon, Surrey CR2 0AA Tel: 081-657 2813 Fax: 081-651 6080

The Barn Dance Agency will organise a complete event, theming it around barn dancing, or just supply one of the 700 bands available nationwide. They will also organise country dancing, square dancing, hoedowns and ceilidhs. Through their sister company, Folk Entertainments, they are also able to offer many other forms of entertainment - all types of bands, discos, cabarets, fund raisers and theme evenings.

BRAITHWAITE'S THEATRICAL AGENCY
8 Brookshill Avenue, Harrow Weald, Middx HA3 6RZ Tel: 081-954 5638

All types of entertainment is supplied by Braithwaites - bands, variety acts, comedians, vocalists - though their speciality is their long list of circus-type acts which includes acrobats, jugglers, stilt-walkers, unicyclists, clowns and fire-eaters.

CHANCE ENTERTAINMENT 321 Fulham Road, SW10 9QL
Tel: 071-376 5995 Fax: 071-376 3598

With years of experience in the business, Chance Entertainment have organised everything from jazz bands to jugglers, marching bands to magicians and rock stars to roller-skating waiters. As specialist entertainment organisers, they are able to provide any act or entertainer you can think of. Bands include the Chance Band, Oliver Twist, Mike d'Abo and his Mighty Quintet, and The Gramophones, playing music from the swing era. Cabaret and side acts include illusionists, circus-type acts, caricaturists, mime artistes, belly dancers, lookalikes, after-dinner speakers - even a bucking bronco. Chance Entertainment also specialises in theming, lighting and decoration.

CLASSIC ENTERTAINMENT 78 Hatherley Road, Walthamstow, E17 6SB
Tel: 081-521 6250 Fax: 081-509 3038

Classic Entertainment is an agency specialising in live musical entertainment for private and corporate functions. You can choose from over 150 varied combinations, from soloists to big bands and orchestras, from medieval, classical and light to jazz, dance and cabaret.

CROWD PULLERS 158 Old Woolwich Road, Greenwich, SE10 9PR
Tel: 081-305 0074 Fax: 081-858 9045

A very specialised agency, Crowd Pullers can book the best of all kinds of street performers - bands, clowns, illusionists, stunt performers, jugglers, unicylists, fire-eaters, stilt-walkers, wire-walkers, balancing acts and more.

CROWN ENTERTAINMENTS 103 Bromley Common, Bromley, Kent BR2 9RN
Tel: 081-464 0454 Fax: 081-290 4038

Crown Entertainments has been providing entertainment for all types of functions for over 10 years. Their range includes television personalities, after-dinner speakers, cabaret, bands, groups and discos, with an emphasis on bands for dinner-dance functions.

DARK BLUES MANAGEMENT 30 Stamford Brook Road, W6 0XH
Tel: 081-743 3292 Fax: 081-740 5520

For more than 25 years, Dark Blues Management has been supplying a variety of acts for private and corporate functions. The emphasis is on live music - dance bands and background music. They handle some of the U.K.'s top party bands such as The Dark Blues (see Bands & Musicians), The Wallace Collection, The Phil Allen Sound and Runcible Spoon. But they also have an extensive range of discotheques, humorists, magicians, speakers and all sorts of cabaret performers and novelty acts.

Entertainment Agencies

DENNY WISE ORGANISATION & ORCHESTRAS
65 Shawley Way, Epsom Downs, Surrey KT18 5PD
Tel: 0737 361077 Fax: 0737 363186

As well as The Denny Wise Orchestras (The D.W. Band & Singers, The D.W. Connection, The D.W. Premiers, The D.W. Swinging Affair and The D.W. Renaissance), this organisation can provide all types of bands, string quartets, lookalikes, international cabaret artistes and discos with light shows. They also offer a complete party planning service and music custom written specifically for your event.

ENTERPROL The Folly, Pinner Hill Road, Pinner, Middx HA5 3YQ
Tel: 081-429 3737   Fax: 081-868 6497

A general entertainment planning service, Enterprol is able to provide all kinds of live entertainment and discotheques. They have some imaginative suggestions to offer with advice and assistance in booking top quality bands, musicians, cabaret, celebrities, speciality bands and more unusual entertainers to suit private parties and corporate events.

EXPRESS ENTERTAINMENTS
The Coach House, 12 Popes Grove, Strawberry Hill, Twickenham, Middx TW1 4JZ
Tel: 081-744 442

Musicians Eleanor Keenan and Chris Dean created Express Entertainments to provide a wide range of musical entertainment for all types of functions. They will find you anything from a solo pianist to 22 piece orchestra. All forms of music are represented from rock 'n' roll to country and western.

GIANTPATCH 36 Eastcastle Street, W1N 7PE
Tel: 071-436 8277   Fax: 071-436 2519

Giantpatch is Europe's only Black Gospel agent featuring English and American groups, such as The Edwin Hawkins Singers. They will also find you Flamenco groups and celebrities.

JOLLY GOOD PRODUCTIONS 71 St George's Square, SW1V 3QN
Tel: 071-630 5302   Fax: 071-630 8454

All forms of musical entertainment can be found through Jolly Good Productions. The Piccadilly Dance Orchestra, Bellacappella (a female a cappella trio) and Rupert Parker (electric harp) are just three selected from a long list of musical acts covering classical, jazz, pop, dance and specialist musicians and groups. For something completely different, they offer 'Give it a Whirl', the hilarious company gameshow (see Participation Events).

LAWSON ROSS MANAGEMENT 116 Finchley Lane, Hendon, NW4 1DB
Tel: 081-203 0626

Lawson Ross supplies general entertainments, specialising in European and Ethnic musical and theatrical acts. Varying from a Russian folk ensemble to a German Oompah band, these acts offer the perfect entertainment for your themed event.

LONDON MUSIC AGENCY 17b Woodford Avenue, Gants Hill, Ilford, Essex IG2 6UF
Tel: 081-550 6673

Everything in entertainment can be supplied by the London Music Agency from a cocktail pianist to a full orchestra and including jazz bands, string quartets, dance bands, discos, karaoke, celebrities, and every type of cabaret act. They can also co-ordinate a whole range of theme nights, from a complete evening of World War II entertainment to a South Sea Island night with Hawaiian music, hula girls and a tropical buffet.

McKEAN'S MUSIC 6 Gunter Grove, SW10 OUT
Tel: 071-352 8806   Fax: 071-352 2428

Jenni McKean specialises in finding the right music for the right venue at the right price and is highly selective in who she sends out. All forms of music from a piper to a 40 piece orchestra can be provided, including her own singing talents.

MERLIN ENTERTAINMENTS 29 Norwood Drive, Harrow, Middx HA2 7PF
Tel: 081-866 6327

Although Merlin Entertainments is the largest specialist agency in the U.K. for supplying children's entertainers, they also supply adult magicians for cabaret and table hopping, and clowns for circus themed events.

MIKE MALLEY ENTERTAINMENTS 10 Holly Park Gardens, Finchley, N3 3NJ
Tel: 081-346 4109   Fax: 081-346 1104

Not just an agency, but party entertainment organisers, they can provide all types of entertainment from top rock bands and cabaret artistes to fairground equipment. Discos, dance bands, Beatles lookalikes, comedians, dancers and drag artistes can all be supplied by Mike Mally Entertainments, who's motto is " If you can think of it, we can get it!"

MUSIC MANAGEMENT PO Box 1105, SW1V 2DE
Tel: 071-976 6262   Fax: 071-584 7944

High calibre musicians and bands are supplied by this music consultancy for corporate and private entertainment. Music Management has the ability to match the right musician or band to any type of event from concerts to dances. There is a wide range of styles covering all types of music from classical to jazz for background, dancing or cabaret.

MUSIC SERVICES AGENCY 75 Clarmont Road, Tunbridge Wells, Kent TN1 1TE
Tel: 0892 27970

All kinds of music for special occasions can be supplied - from Palm Court trio to full orchestra and from harpist to barbershop. Music and performers are matched to any subject or historical theme, or can be specially arranged and written for specific events.

NDS MANAGEMENT SERVICES 52 Haliburton Rd, Twickenham, Middx TW1 1PF
Tel: 081-891 5551   Fax: 081-892 9344

Specialists in live music, theme party decor and general entertainment, NDS can supply dance, jazz and rock and roll bands, discos, casinos, fair ground attractions and so on. They also have a range of theme packages which include Caribbean, French, USA, 20's, Hollywood, Italian and Russian evenings.

NIC PICOT AGENCY 79 Anglesmede Crescent, Pinner, Middx HA5 5ST
Tel: 081-863 2522   Fax: 081-427 5253

Nic Picot, himself a talented magician (see Magic and Novelty Acts), formed his agency in 1986 to supply magic and novelty acts for private and corporate functions throughout the U.K. While still specialising in magic (with over 200 performing magicians on the books), the agency has expanded to include all types of entertainment from mix and mingle entertainers to cabaret and function bands. They will provide you with absolutely any kind of artiste including caricaturists, fortune-tellers, jugglers, lookalikes, mime artistes, robots, silhouette cutters and sword swallowers.

Entertainment Agencies

NORMAN PHILLIPS AGENCY 2 Hartopp Road, Sutton Coldfield, West Midlands B74 2RH
Tel: 021-308 1267   Fax: 021-308 5191

For over 30 years, Norman Phillips has been supplying every form of top quality entertainment to the corporate and private markets, at venues throughout the U.K. Specialities include 'Casino Royale' - a highly successful mobile fun casino, and 'A Question of Murder' - a brand new murder mystery quiz.

PACE Flames Studio, Galena Road, W6 0LT
Tel: 081-977 1115   Fax: 081-977 1171

PACE (which stands for Performer and Choreographic Enterprises) have a register of 2,000 artistes covering all aspects of entertainment, mainly for the corporate market. They can supply cabaret, speciality and disco acts, dance acts and international dance reviews, all types of bands and musicians, comedians and after-dinner speakers.

PRIME PERFORMERS The Studio, 5 Kidderpore Avenue, NW3 7SX
Tel: 071-431 0211   Fax: 071-431 3813

As entertainment consultants rather than agents, Prime Performers, headed by Barbara Kelly and Bernard Braden, have over 1000 contacts in a variety of fields covering bands, musicians, cabaret artistes, magicians, comedians, circus performers, personalities and after-dinner speakers. Not only will they locate the performers, but also instruct them in tailoring their acts to suit the event.

SONG AND SUPPER PRESENTATIONS 43 St Marks Road, Maidenhead, Berks SL6 6DP
Tel: 0628 27163   Fax: 0628 777413

Song and Supper is a consultancy and production company offering high quality entertainment in various themed settings. These include Elizabethan banquets, fun casinos, Wild West barn dances, and their speciality 'Good Old Days' music hall and cockney pub evenings with pearly kings and queens, honkey tonk piano and buskers.

SPECTRUM ENTERTAINMENT 32 Berridale House, Kingsway,
Hove, East Sussex BN3 4HD Tel: 0273 206569

Discotheques, pop groups and cabaret artistes can be supplied by Spectrum Entertainment. They specialise in large and small discos, some with big screen video and laser extravaganzas, and ex-chart groups and names from the 60's and 70's such as The Tornados, Hedgehoppers Anonymous and The Applejacks.

SPLITTING IMAGES 3 Cedric Chambers, Northwick Close, NW8 8JH
Tel: 071-286 8300

All types of lookalikes can be supplied by Splitting Images for personal appearances at a variety of special occasions. Formed three years ago, they now have over 170 lookalikes on their books ranging from Prince Charles to Michael Jackson and from Marilyn Monroe to Tina Turner.

STAGE TWO ENTERTAINMENTS Unit 1, Penfold Trading Estate, Imperial Way,
Watford, Herts WD2 4YY   Tel: 0923 30789   Fax: 0923 55048

More than just and entertainment agency, Stage Two will also plan and co-ordinate your function. They will supply bands, cabaret, after-dinner speakers and speciality acts as well as staging, dance floors, sound and lighting equipment.

124

In case you haven't heard them perform before, bands and musicians will quite often be able to send you a short demonstration tape. These are usually recorded in a studio so are not an accurate reproduction of the live sound but nevertheless serve a valuable purpose and should give you an idea of whether this is the sound and repertoire you are after. If tapes are not available, it is occasionally possible to arrange to eavesdrop on a function where the band or musician is playing, but make sure that you have the hosts' permission first (some will object to this intrusion and they have every right to do so). If its acceptable, check when would be the most convenient time to turn up so as to be as unobtrusive as possible and not have to hang around while the band takes a break.

A single musician, such as a guitarist or harpist, can help to relax the first guests to arrive, while there are not yet enough people for the party to get going. As more guests turn up, the musician might only be heard by those on the same side of the room, but this is more desirable than a musician who can't be talked over.

During dinner, a pianist sets a leisurely mood and a string trio or quartet adds a touch of elegance. Strolling musicians, perhaps in costume, could be perfect for a theme party.

A dance band can also supply background music, usually just instrumental or with soft vocals. If there is to be dancing between courses, it is the responsibility of the band leader to make sure that guests return to their tables when the next course is served, so he needs to have a good rapport with the caterer. Expect the meal to take much longer to complete at a dinner dance than at a dinner and ball. If leaving the dancing until after dinner, the band leader should be able to judge the mood of the party (and the energy levels of the guests) and adjust the tempo accordingly. The band leader will also be able to judge when is the best time to wind up the party. If people are beginning to file out half an hour before the evening is due to end, he might suggest bringing the finale forward. Alternatively, if the party is still in full swing, it might be possible to go on a bit longer, but this is not always advisable. It's better to end on a high, but if your guests are dropping from exhaustion, you've gone on too long!

It is important that you discuss with the band beforehand the type of music you want played. If you have a favourite song, let them know. If you feel that Viva Espana! or The Birdie Song will have your guests running for their coats, it is vital that the band are fore-warned (though they probably wouldn't have dreamed of playing them anyway!). Also, it would be helpful for the band to know whether you would like some sort of audience participation such as a conga or The Locomotion. If national dance music is wanted, such as Scottish or Israeli, check that the band's repertoire includes some of the more well known tunes (or give them time to learn them). The band should be aware of any theme or set that you might have in mind. They might even oblige by dressing accordingly, even if it just means changing the colour of their bow ties!

Dance Bands

BACK TO BACK 1a Alandale Drive, Pinner, Middx HA5 3UP
Tel: 081-868 4831

Back to Back is a five piece dance band experienced in promoting a party atmosphere for all age groups. Their repertoire ranges from jazz standards to jump jive, rock 'n' roll, Tamla Motown, party favourites and contemporary pop songs.

DANCING BEAR 17a South Villas, NW1 9BS
Tel: 071-267 9793

This is a very versatile, multi-instrumental band specialising in barn dances and ceilidhs. The band is made up of three musicians and a caller who, between them, play mandolin, violin, concertina, bass, guitar and Northumberland pipes and a vast repertoire of tunes to dance to.

Bands and Musicians

THE DARK BLUES 30 Stamford Brook Road, W6 0XH
Tel: 081-743 3292   Fax: 081-740 5520

With over 25 years of experience and more than 3000 performances to their credit, The Dark Blues have earned the reputation of being Britain's leading dance band. No wonder, then, that they have played at some of the very best parties including the 40th birthday party held at Buckingham Palace for His Royal Highness Prince Charles, having previously played there at his 21st.

ENIGMA 17 Brook Way,
Chigwell, Essex IG7 6AW
Tel: 081-500 2849   Fax: 081-501 3717

Originally formed back in 1980, Enigma are rapidly becoming one of the top function bands in London and the south of England. They have had two top twenty hit singles as Enigma and have been behind several more recent hits under different names. Enigma are basically a six piece band augmenting up to an eight piece, catering for all ages and tastes. They specialise in 60's and 70's music and current party favourites. One of their talents is the ability to 'read' their audience, customising their programme to keep the party swinging to the very end and ensure its success.

F.B.I. c/o Mayfair Music Management, 15 Parkhill, Clapham Common, SW4 9NS
Tel: 071-622 1614

The Federal Blues Investigation, known as F.B.I. is an exciting rhythm and blues outfit covering music ranging from The Blues Brothers to James Brown. The band has an impressive record of successful gigs around London, Oxbridge balls and the university circuit.

MAYFAIR RADIO ORCHESTRA c/o Mayfair Music Management,
15 Parkhill, Clapham Common, SW4 9NS Tel: 081-622 1614

An authentic reminder of a bygone era, The Mayfair Radio Orchestra recreate the big band sound of the 20's, 30's and 40's. This stylish, enthusiastic 12 piece band, featuring chirpy vocalist Sandra Barker, is perfect for tea dances and theme parties.

MICK URRY ORCHESTRA &
SINGERS 15 Eastport Lane,
Lewes, Sussex BN7 1TL
Tel: 0273 472931

Having completed ten years, including six world cruises, aboard the prestigious liner Queen Elizabeth II, Mick Urry is now back in the U.K. with his exciting Orchestra and Singers and is available for private functions and special events. Experience and enthusiasm contributed to the popularity of the Orchestra whose great mix of music, from the big bands, to 60's, to present day chart material, will suit all tastes. This 12 piece orchestra can be reduced to a 9 piece and augmented to an 18 piece.

MODERN SYNCOPATED ORCHESTRA
Ardenlea, Cinder Path, Hook Heath, Woking, Surrey GU22 0ER
Tel: 0483 763231   Fax: 0483 724916

Resident at the Waldorf Hotel tea-dances, The Modern Syncopated Orchestra are available for private functions. The 16 piece orchestra, complete with wing collars and bow ties, play authentic music of the 1920's to 1940's.

ONE NIGHT STAND *(Right)*
The Coach House, 12 Popes Grove, Strawberry Hill,
Twickenham, Middx TW1 4JZ Tel: 081-891 3071

The versatility of One Night Stand makes them one of the most sought after bands on the party scene. Under the leadership of Chris Dean, the band has played at most of the top London venues, at prestigious private parties, charity balls and society weddings. Depending on the clients' requirements or the size of the party, the band is available from a quartet up to a 22 piece orchestra and the repertoire contains a complete cross section of music to suit any age group.

PASADENA ROOF ORCHESTRA
Priors, Tye Green, Elsenham, Bishops Stortford,
Herts CM22 6DY
Tel: 0279 813240   Fax: 0279 815895

This renowned and highly acclaimed 11 piece dance orchestra, including a singer, presents a full programme of 20's and 30's popular sings and hot dance music.

THE RIO TRIO 26 Harold Road, E11 4QY
Tel: 081-539 5229   Fax: 081-556 9545

Music from the 1920's, 30's and 40's is played by 'the smallest big band in the world'. The Rio Trio provide music for dancing, dining and cabaret at corporate events, weddings and parties. They are also available as Mick Wilson and The Rio Trio playing classic pop from the 50's and 60's.

SKYLINE 29 Oakley Gardens, SW3 5QH
Tel: 071-351 2875   Fax: 071-376 8187

From the Lord Colwyn stable, this extremely versatile band perform a wide range of music. Skyline has played at many society parties and other prestigious events all over the country. The band is full of life and energy and knows how to really get (and keep) a party swinging. The line up can be changed to suit, from a quartet to a full 20 piece dance orchestra when required, though they seem most comfortable as a 6 piece.

TILLY PLUMP 4 Chiltern Street, Aylesbury, Bucks HP21 8BT
Tel: 0296 21134

This is a lively 5 piece band playing English, Irish and Scottish folk music and specialising in barn dances. The band comprises two fiddles, guitar, bass and drums and is fronted by Mick Brooks - an experienced barn dance caller and folk singer. Mick is also half of Caffy O Lait - a melodeon and hurdy-gurdy duo providing a very French atmosphere, ideal for a theme party.

Bands and Musicians

Background Music

THE AMELIA STRING QUARTET 2 Maltings Place, Fulham, SW6 2BT
Tel: 071-731 0376

This stylish string quartet comprises two violins, a viola and a cello. They play a wide repertoire which includes all the standard classical works, songs from the shows, 20's and 30's arrangements through to the music of The Beatles and Phil Collins. Programmes are carefully structured according to individual requirements be it a business function, dinner party or cocktail reception.

THE CAROLIAN STRING TRIO
60 South Croxted Road,
West Dulwich, SE21 8BD Tel: 081-761 8131

The three classically trained musicians that make up The Carolian String Trio cater for all musical tasks, whether it be baroque, classical, light music or show numbers. They are happy to take centre stage or blend discreetly into the background and perform at a wide range of functions from parties and balls to corporate events, cruises and weddings.

FREWER STRING QUARTET 3 Vyner Court, Rossington Street, E5 8SF
Tel: 081-806 1229

Formed eleven years ago, The Frewer String Quartet play classical and light popular music from an extensive repertoire for all kinds of functions. They usually appear in white dinner jackets, but can also dress in tails, black dinner jackets or lounge suits to suit the occasion.

HOLLAND PARK PLAYERS 3a Penzance Place, W11 4PE
Tel: 071-229 7392

Founded by cellist John Franca, a former pupil of Pablo Casals, The Holland Park Players are a palm-court group of a piano trio or string quartet. Their repertoire includes classical, musical comedy and light music.

JEANETTE CORDERY 43 Hogarth Hill, Hamstead Garden Suburb, NW11 6AY
Tel: 081-455 0719

Jeanette is a solo harpist and half of The Savoy Harp Duo.

JULIE ALLIS 123 Ashmore Grove, Welling, Kent DA16 2SA
Tel: 081-856 9651

Professional harpist, Julie Allis provides beautiful, well presented music that will add a touch of class to any occasion. She is fully experienced in adapting to any situation with a repertoire that includes well-known classical music, folk tunes, standards, film and show medleys and popular music.

LESLEY DUKE DUO 1a Alandale Drive, Pinner, Middx HA5 3UP
Tel: 081-868 4831

Lesley sings the songs of many eras, moods and genres with inspiring and lively accompaniment from Peter Churchill, providing background music and atmosphere for special functions. Leslie also fronts Back to Back - no pun intended! (see Dance Bands).

NOISE OF MINSTRELS 94 High Street, Tring, Herts HP23 4AF
Tel: 044282 5191

Noise of Minstrels specialises in the performance of early and traditional music. The repertoire consists of Medieval, 16th and 17th century dances, tunes and songs as well as 18th and 19th century material, all played in a lively manner on authentic reproduction instruments including hurdy-gurdy, English bagpipes, vielle, violin, citole, lute and percussion. The group, comprising 2 to 6 musicians, will appear in period costume where required and can play loudly or quietly as may be appropriate.

OMEGA 43 Nightingale Lane, Hornsey, N8 7RA
Tel: 081-341 9739

Omega is a Greek bouzouki band with a Greek and International repertoire, performing as a four piece band or as a duo.

PATRICIA SPERO *(Right)*
Oaks Farm, Vicarage Lane, Chigwell, Essex IG7 6LT
Tel: 081-500 6112

Harpist Patricia Spero specialises in playing cocktail or dinner background music. She also has a harp and flute duo.

SEICENTO 1 Bourne Road, N8 9JH
Tel: 081-341 5404

Seicento is a 5 piece band offering a repertoire of Elizabethan and Jacobean chamber music for played on cornet, sackbut, dulcian, flute, lute and harpsichord.

Cabaret

CABINET SHUFFLE 3 Hall Place Gardens, St Albans, Herts AL1 3SB
Tel: 0727 57841   Fax: 0727 45772

Vocal entertainment is provided by six young singers who have taken the world of corporate and private hospitality by storm. They sing - totally unaccompanied - anything from a 16th century grace to a current number one hit. They will compose and perform an original song especially written to contain amusing references to you and your guests.

GROVE OPERA 8 Skeena Hill, Southfields, SW18 5PL
Tel: 071-788 7582

In 1987, a group of singers with a wide range of vocal and musical experience came together to form Grove Opera. The group comprises a soprano, tenor, baritone and accompanist who introduces and sets the scene for each item in the programme.

STREET SOUNDS 201 Lonsdale Road, Stevenage, Herts SG1 5DH
Tel: 0438 364427

Shaky Jake's one man band and his performing dog, Busker, or Spike and his barrel organ will entertain your guests as they arrive at your event and/or the one man band will perform a hilarious cabaret spot during the evening.

Discotheques

The case for the travelling discotheque is enthusiastically put by **Jonathan Seaward of Joffin's.**

"So often, clients say to me 'I can't afford both - which should I have, a band or a discotheque?' A difficult choice. A good live band is fabulous entertainment, will definitely appeal to the older generation but is costly and may require a number of extras - stage, piano, dressing room etc. A discotheque can certainly play every kind of music, takes up less space, will charge less but isn't some of the magic missing? Not always.

The term 'mobile discotheque' tends to conjure up the image of young men playing their favourite records at deafening volume, blinding the guests with stroboscopes and jabbering into a microphone.

In reality this is rarely the case. Of course the operators are young, the music vibrant and the lights coloured and flashing, but how many people realise just how much care and attention has gone into each performance? How much time and money has been invested in the selection of the sound and lighting equipment and the record collection? How many hours of practice and thought go to make a good operator?

A professional discotheque can cost a great deal to buy. Add to that the cost of painstakingly putting together a record collection - a collection which must span every musical era and appeal to every musical taste and it soon becomes apparent that running a travelling discotheque is a serious commitment for a dedicated few.

Equipment costing this much needs to be safely transported in expensive flight cases in expensive vans. It is rarely a one man job and setting up can take hours. All the while, the operator is running through the evening in his mind, guessing at the sort of music he's going to play, how he's going to pace himself through a long night, using his experience to assess his surroundings, the likely background and tastes of the guests.

And now he has to start the dancing. An audience will get up when a live band strikes up. They feel obliged, even if they don't like the music. There is nothing worse than a band playing to an empty floor. But a discotheque? No-one is going to offend the sensibilities of a mere record! The person behind the console is the only driver - he's as unconcerned as you are. He'll get it going later on. But he is concerned, his entire day, week possibly, has been geared to this moment, he's thought of little else. This is his moment and the choice of record is vital. He's cracked it! The dance floor is packed, faces alight, arms and legs flying in every direction. There's the magic!"

**ANGUS GIBSON DISCOTHEQUES 117 Stephendale Road, SW6 2PS
Tel: 071-384 2270   Fax: 071-731 1580**

Angus Gibson has been in the disco business since 1972. He spent five years with Juliana's and now provides discotheques using top quality equipment and outstanding DJs who only play excellent music.

**BANANA SPLIT 19 Station Parade, Whitchurch Lane, Edgware, Middx HA8 6RW
Tel: 081-951 1515 Fax: 081-200 1121**

There are three styles of travelling discotheque to choose from. The basic or main show is most suitable for homes or smaller halls. The superior show has a star cloth frontage and backdrop, posts for lighting and effects and better quality sound and effects. The mobile discotheque is just as it sounds, with a trussing erected over the dance floor for all sorts of effects including strobes, neon and lasers and a facility for quadraphonic sound. Banana Split Discotheques are backed up by a fully comprehensive technical hire department and comprehensive party planning service (see Party Organisers).

BOJOLLY'S Unit 14, Brentford Business Centre,
Commerce Road, Brentford, Middx TW8 8LE
Tel: 081-568 6447 Fax: 081-569 9355

Bojolly's offers clear sound at the right volume, effective and atmospheric lighting to match but, most importantly, the music you want to hear. With eight years experience in discotheques, Bojolly's can boast over 2000 parties completed. From their basic units to the 'lighting rig' discotheque, they are able to cater to most clients needs and will plan the entire party if required (see Party Organisers).

CLOUD 9 DISCOTHEQUES 25 Monkfirth Way, Southgate, N14 5LY
Tel: 081-368 7447/081-366 0432

Cloud 9 provides a quality professional service for up to five discotheques a night, including sound, lighting and special effects. A complete party package could be incorporated, if required, covering all facilities and additional entertainment.

EUPHORIA 40 Carlton Road, East Sheen, SW14 7RJ
Tel: 081-878 5188

Four years ago, six independent professional disc jockeys joined together to form Euphoria. They have a library of over 20,000 records covering music of the 50's right up to the latest hits. Programmes for each event are worked out on a computer, taking into account the age range of the guests and specific musical tastes. The DJs are always correctly attired and well versed in procedures for all types of functions.

JOFFIN'S DISCOTHEQUES Joffin Music, Unit 1, Heliport Estate, Lombard Road, SW11 3SS
Tel: 071-350 0033 Fax: 071-228 6213

Established in 1979, Joffin's quickly took their place alongside the market leaders gaining a reputation for professional sound and lighting equipment, excellent presentation and that magic ingredient - the ability to play exactly the right music to suit the mood of the party. Chosen for eleven consecutive years to entertain 3000 guests at the prestigious Berkeley Square Ball, Joffin's is equally at home at a private dance in the country, a company party in the City or with 50 friends in a wine bar. A wide selection of superb music is carried with every unit. Joffin's is the sister company to The Jonathan Seaward Organisation (see Party Planners).

JULIANA'S TRAVELLING DISCOTHEQUE Unit 7, Farm Lane Trading Estate, SW6 1QJ
Tel: 071-937 1555 Fax: 071-381 3872

With over 25 years experience, Juliana's is the longest running mobile discotheque in the U.K. They cater for any size party, from 10 to 10,000 guests, with no time limit attached. Smart, well presented, fully trained disc jockeys will gauge the mood of the party and play the appropriate music - a top quality service, backed up by Juliana's party planning and marquee hire (see Party Planners and Marquees).

NIGHT MOVES 22 Pensbury Street, SW8 4TL
Tel: 071-978 1223

Night Moves provides a complete disco show with excellent technical back up from their sister company Wise Productions, they can even provide the dance floor.

RAFFLES AND CHANCE DISCOTHEQUES 321 Fulham Road, SW10 9QL
Tel: 071-376 5995 Fax: 071-376 3598
Part of Chance Entertainment, Raffles and Chance are two very professional discotheques with more than 25 years' experience between them. The latest technology is used to produce the highest quality sound, lighting and special effects. Taking the disco one step further, the Chance Video

Discotheques

Raffles and Chance Discotheques Continued....

Wall consists of a bank of 16 screens showing the latest pop videos or live images of your guests stretched over the 8 feet wide wall, changing to 16 small images or a combination of both.

STEVE ST JOHN DISCOTHEQUES   15 Gladswood Road, Belvedere, Kent DA17 6DB Tel: 03224 35808

Steve will provide a lively, exciting and professional disco service complete with full light show, smoke machine, confetti bombs and thunder flashes. Over the last ten years, he has catered for an impressive list of corporate and private parties and fashion shows. He uses top class equipment to play a huge selection of compact discs suitable for any age group, covering everything from opera to reggae. Steve also offers a combined disco and karaoke evening.

TRAVELLING GRAMOPHONE DISCOTHEQUES
Unit J, Penfold Trading Estate, Imperial Way, Watford, Herts WD3 4YY
Tel: 0923 30789   Fax: 0923 55048

A wide range of discotheques is available to suit all occasions, especially black tie functions. Staging, dance floors, speciality sound and lighting equipment, karaoke systems and operators are supplied.

YOUNG'S DISCOTHEQUES & EQUIPMENT HIRE   20 Malden Road, NW5 3HN
Tel: 071-485 1115   Fax: 071-267 6769

Young's provides experienced, fun personality DJs, equipment and lighting with a variety of music ranging from the 50's through to the 90's to suit all occasions, age groups and tastes in music. Young's also hires out an extensive range of do-it-yourself disco equipment, lighting and special effects.

Equipment Hire

COMMERCIAL LIGHT AND SOUND SYSTEMS 837 Garratt Lane, Wimbledon, SW17 0PG
Tel: 081-944 1400   Fax: 081-944 0141

C.L.A.S.S. is a specialist sound and lighting company offering a variety of services including a comprehensive range of hire equipment: from a simple light show for a small party to a massive sound rig and laser show.

JUKEBOX JUNCTION 90 Charlton Street, Euston, NW1 0HJ
Tel: 071-388 1512

Jukebox Junction buys, sells and hires jukeboxes from the 1930's to the 1990's. For parties, they have a catalogue of over 3000 records for the hirer to choose from.

RAINBOW INTERNATIONAL 448 Uxbridge Road, Shepherds Bush, W12 0NS
Tel: 081-743 9999

Hire disco sound and lighting equipment and background music systems or book mobile discotheques and professional disc jockeys. Rainbow's entertainment agency can also supply live music, comedians and cabaret acts.

WING SOUND & LIGHT 354-356 Purley Way, Croydon, Surrey CR0 4NY
Tel: 081-688 0440   Fax: 081-681 0479

You can hire (or buy) disco equipment complete with stage pyrotechnics, smoke machines and dry ice effects from Wing Sound & Light. Sound systems range from small combined units to large concert P.A.s, specialist radio microphone applications and laser karaoke packages.

Magic and Novelty Acts _____

Magicians

If you are thinking of booking a magician for your function, **Mark Lee of Marks Magic** suggests you consider the following points before making your choice.

"Are you looking for a cabaret performance, a stage show or a close-up magician? Consider the range of ages of the audience and their attention span. For instance, a 'once in a blue moon' family gathering may not be the ideal occasion for a cabaret spot. This might be seen merely as an unwelcome intrusion for your guests trying to catch up on family gossip. On the other hand, it may prove a useful talking point if the family have little else in common! A close-up magician might be a suitable compromise on such occasions. Everyone gets to see something but those deep in conversation can choose not to be interrupted.

A close-up magician can perform during receptions and is a perfect ice-breaker for all sorts of parties. During the meal, he will only perform between courses. This can be ideal for sit-down buffet-style meals, but do remember that the close-up magician, by definition, only entertains a small number of guests at a time. Guests waiting their turn at the buffet will not all be able to watch the magician at the same time. It is important, particularly in private homes, restaurants and marquees, that there is adequate space between the tables for the magician to move around.

If the party itself or just the entertainment is a special surprise for anyone in particular, such as at a birthday or anniversary party, make sure that the entertainer can recognise the guest of honour. Are there any other specific guests that you want your entertainer to pay particular attention to or to avoid at all costs? Cabaret performers will often use 'volunteers' from the audience and may ask you to point out 'fun' people with whom they can interact and also who they should leave alone.

Many performers will have a specific act which is performed regardless. A 'patter act' (a term which would include all close-up magicians) will often be able to make reference to your special party theme and/or dress appropriately, particularly if given sufficient advance notice.

Close-up magicians cannot compete with a disco or band playing dance music (as opposed to background music). Similarly, if you intend the lights to be turned down for dancing, then that is probably the time for your close-up magician to pack up and go.

As a rough rule of thumb, for functions with more than 150 to 180 guests, it is preferable to engage more than one close-up magician. They will need to interact and liaise to ensure that they aim to provide entertainment to all of your guests.

Generally speaking, you should expect to pay for experience. Find out how long your entertainer has been performing at parties. Is he or she a youngster, middle-aged or retired? Sophisticated audiences may not respond well to a particularly youthful close-up performer, for instance.

Finally, do not forget to advise your entertainer of any relevant changes in the party arrangements. He or she may be a magician or a novelty act, but will rarely be a mind reader as well!"

**ALAN SHAXON 7 River Mount, Walton-on-Thames, Surrey KT12 2PW
Tel: 0932 228796**

Cabaret magician and illusionist Alan Shaxon incorporates a touch of class in his style of entertainment. He is a Gold Star Member of the Inner Magic Circle and has appeared on TV more than 50 times, entertained on luxury cruise liners and four times at Buckingham Palace. For parties his act is usually 35 minutes of close-up magic, using only little in the way of props and lots of audience participation and for larger occasions, he has a number of original illusions including his own 'Fishing in Mid-Air' - catching live goldfish on a line cast over the audience.

BRIAN CASWELL 54 Brighton Avenue, E17 7NE
Tel: 081-521 8846

The talents of Brian Caswell cover three very different types of act. Primarily, Brian is a mentalist, performing magic of the mind producing effect very close to a demonstration of the impossible. His comedy magic act is where he becomes magic's answer to Basil Fawlty. For his other unusual comedy act, Brian uses slides and performs comedy revue sketches.

DARRYL I. ROSE 6 Leaf Grove, West Norwood, SE27 0SF
Tel: 081-769 2737

Darryl's unique creativity and delightful style of close-up magic has earned him the prestigious Silver Star award as an associate member of the Inner Magic Circle. Darryl can perform close-up or in cabaret, either as himself or in character to fit in with your theme.

DENNIS PATTEN 14 The Crest, Goffs Oak, Herts EN7 5NP
Tel: 0707 873262

Known as 'The Wandering Wizard', Dennis performs close-up magic at dinners and banquets anywhere.

HOWARD POSENER The Penthouse, 2 Kiddipore Avenue, NW3 7SP
Tel: 071-794 7523

Acknowledged as one of the most entertaining close-up, cabaret and stage performers, Howard has a unique brand of magic applicable to any occasion, whether for business or pleasure. He has produced custom made illusions for many major product launches throughout the world and has performed at Loewes, Monte Carlo and at the Berkeley Square Ball. Howard has frequently appeared on major national TV shows and is a member of the Magic Circle.

JOHN RICHARD Oakwood, Ambleside Gardens, Hullbridge, Essex SS5 6ES
Tel: 0702 230253

John performs unbelievable close-up magic for all sorts of functions, large and small. He has worked at many of the top venues in London and has entertained at private parties for a number of well known personalities including Michael Jackson. His hilarious cabaret act features audience participation, comedy, magic and mentalism.

JON VINE (Renfield the Butler) 19 St James Park, Tonbridge Wells, Kent TN1 2LG
Tel: 0892 23123 Fax: 0892 36735

Renfield, Jon's butler and 'front man' will have your guests in hysterics with his amazing repartee and his wicked wit. Looking almost the part of a respectable butler - greasy centre parting, fingerless woollen gloves - Renfield dabbles in magic and recitations as he serves and casually insults your guests. Jon's cabaret act includes comedy mime, eccentric dancing and general clowning around. He does impersonations ranging from Tina Turner and Freddy Mercury to Charlie Chaplin and Dracula.

LEN BELMONT PRODUCTIONS 48 Morland Estate, E8 3EJ
Tel: 071-254 8300

A very experienced versatile entertainer, Len Belmont performs patter magic, novelty ventriloquism and light comedy for all ages. His 20 to 30 minute variety act can be arranged to suit any occasion.

Magic and Novelty Acts

MARKS MAGIC 68 Grimsdyke Road, Hatch End, Middx HA5 4PW
Tel: 081-428 5789

Mark Lee presents close-up magical entertainment with his own exciting and enthusiastic style. He performs to a few people at a time while mingling with guests during the reception, table hopping during dinner or at any stage during the function.

MARTIN NICHOLLS Albany House, Albany Crescent, Claygate, Esher, Surrey KT10 0PF
Tel: 0372 68022 Fax: 0372 472057

A highly entertaining and humorous after dinner speaker, Martin Nicholls is internationally experienced and has written a book on the subject entitled 'After Dinner Speeches'.

NIC PICOT 79 Anglesmede Crescent, Pinner, Middx HA5 5ST
Tel: 081-863 2522 Fax: 081-427 5253

Nic's relaxed manner fits comfortably into any type of function. He will perform close-up or cabaret magic presenting special effects and illusions with his own unique style. (A word of advice - keep an eye on your watch while he's around!) Nic also runs his own entertainment agency which specialises in magic acts (see Entertainment Agencies).

RODEO DAVE 19 Temple Road, Croydon, Surrey CRO 1HU
Tel: 081-681 0998 / 081-313 3751

Show jumper turned trail boss, Dave Charnley performs a thrilling ten minute show of Western trick riding and shooting on the dance floor - don't worry, the horses will be wearing rubber shoes so the floor will be quite safe (though you will be advised to have someone with a bucket and shovel standing by, just in case!). For out-door events, Dave includes a young bull in the act.

The aim of the following companies is to ensure that your guests are enjoying themselves by involving them in the activities. Some will rely on a certain amount of 'snooping', but it is never the intention to embarrass your guests. Sensitively handled, these events are great fun and guarantee a memorable evening.

ACCIDENTAL PRODUCTIONS 76, Enfield Cloisters, Fanshaw Street, N1 6LD
Tel: 071-739 3582 Fax: 071-700 4304

Murder by Accident evenings and weekends feature brightly coloured, larger-than-life characters. Scripts are adapted to suit the audience and will contain some personalized touches. Guests can choose whether to join in the fun or just be entertained without getting involved. Accidental Productions also organise Ghost Weekends where guests arrive at the hotel already dead, are issued with death certificates and enjoy the games, videos, ghost hunt and horror themed party as ghosts.

GIVE IT A WHIRL Jolly Good Productions, 71 St George's Square, SW1V 3QN
Tel: 071-630 5302 Fax: 071-630 8454

The ultimate game show, Give It A Whirl, provides a whole evening of hilarious entertainment tailor-made to suit the event. The show's host, Dickie Divine, ably assisted by his friendly hostesses, will encourage the audience to participate. The show can be adapted from a quiz show for 100 using squeaky toys for buzzers and questions combining in-house gossip, business and general knowledge, to a full-blown stage show for 300 with booby prizes and the Give It A Whirl wheel, all done with lots of tongue-in-cheek humour.

INITIATIVE UNLIMITED 24 Blacklands Drive, Hayes, Middx UB4 8EX
Tel: 081-573 8829 Fax: 0895 431984

Dixon Jones, who runs Initiative Unlimited, writes, organises and runs Murder Mystery evenings for corporate and private groups. Each of the guests becomes a character in the plot, having been primed before the event, so everyone is involved. The evenings can be arrange for between 10 and 100 guests. Prices are charged per head. Initiative Unlimited will provide the evening's food, entertainment and mayhem, and can also arrange the drinks and location if required.

"MURDER, MY LORD?" Britannia House, 1-11 Glenthorne Road, W6 0LF
Tel: 081-846 9491 Fax: 081-748 4250

Hire these contract killers and they'll murder your managing director for cash - anytime, anywhere. "Murder, My Lord?" specialises in researching into your company and writing an original and hilarious mystery play, based on all the gossip and scandal that really exists in your company. Each event is tailor made to the clients requirements. They will infiltrate the party with professional actors and one of them will become the victim before very long. All the guests become suspects and the detective will select those who he considers game for a laugh to interrogate. Clues will have been hidden around the venue and there are prizes for the most amusing solutions to the murder.

SPYBUSTERS Jolly Good Productions, 71 St George's Square, SW1V 3QN
Tel: 071-630 5302 Fax: 071-630 8454

How better to deal with industrial espionage than to call in the Spybusters? Special agents Buttock and Cramp, cunningly disguised as foreign waiters, will interrogate guests to flush out the mole in your company. Needless to say, everyone is suspect and clues are dotted around just waiting to be discovered. Each event is tailor-made incorporating interesting and amusing facts uncovered during research into your company.

Fireworks

Providing you have a suitable clear space, a firework display can be a spectacular interlude or finale to a special event. Except possibly for Guy Fawkes Night, it is difficult to keep your guests enthralled for longer than about ten minutes, especially on a chilly evening, so go for quality rather than quantity. If you are firing the display yourself, follow the firework code implicitly.

FANTASTIC FIREWORKS Rocket House, Redbourn, Herts AL3 7RH
Tel: 058-279 2436 Fax: 058 279 3741
Fantastic Fireworks produce beautiful displays for parties, weddings and corporate hospitality. Special effects include fireworks on balloons, exploding pianos and the breakfast special - a potent pyrotechnic mix of eggs, bacon, beans and gunpowder!

THE FIREWORK COMPANY Shine House, High Street, Uffculme, Devon EX15 3AB
Tel: 0884 840504 Fax: 0884 841142
Based in the West Country, this family run business sells fireworks nationwide to a variety of customers from party organisers to pop stars. They specialise in firework spectaculars and can provide displays for indoors or out, in daylight or at night. In addition to operator-fired shows, their firework packs can be fired by their clients using the comprehensive safety information supplied.

FIREWORKS INTERNATIONAL Yeoman House, 16 The Green, Aston-on-Trent,
Derby DE7 2AA
Tel: 0332 792666 Fax: 0332 799248
Fireworks International believe that fireworks represent one of the finest forms of visual entertainment available. They provide operator-fired displays and self-firing display packs with loads of special effects.

KIMBOLTON FIREWORKS 7 High Street, Kimbolton, Huntingdon, Cambs PE18 0HB
Tel: 0480 860988 Fax: 0480 861277
This company has provided spectacular displays for the Henley Regatta and Festival, Thames Day, and the Battle of Britain celebration. They will also supply a variety of self-fired packs.

NATIONWIDE FIREWORKS
Building 240, Hurn Airport, Christchurch, Dorset BH23 6DT
Tel: 0202 579442 Fax: 0202 581592
Since it was formed in 1976, Nationwide has been supplying firework and pyrotechnic spectaculars of all sizes anywhere in the U.K. As well as displays operated by their full-time professional firers, they also offer DIY kits such as their Aerial Kits or the value for money Rocket and Shell Packs.

PHOENIX FIREWORK DISPLAYS Pinden End Farm, Pinden, Nr Dartford, Kent DA2 8EA
Tel: 0474 72956 Fax: 0474 74017
Phoenix are pioneers in the art of creating dramatic and spectacular fireworks displays. They specialise in the design and execution of a wide range of firework shows for every type of event, from weddings and parties to mammoth extravaganzas. If you want to do it yourself, they offer a wide range of packs and a useful instructional video to help you identify each type of firework and how to set them up and fire them.

SHELL SHOCK FIREWORK COMPANY South Manor Farm, Bramfield,
Halesworth, Suffolk IP19 9AQ
Tel: 098 684 469 Fax: 098 684 582
Specialists in professional aerial firework displays, Shell Shock are well known for their energetic firing and spectacular effects. Each display is designed to suit the occasion and the site, using only their own imported material for both day and night time displays.

VULCAN FIREWORKS 52 North Street, Carshalton, Surrey SM5 2HH
Tel: 081-669 4178 Fax: 081-773 0305
Vulcan design breathtaking displays and have a reputation for delivering the right show for the occasion. Effigies, 30 feet high larger - than - life models erupting into a fabulous pyrotechnic display - are unique to this company. They claim that almost anything can be reproduced.

138

Fun Casinos

BLACKTIE PROMOTIONS 77 Copthorne Road, Leatherhead, Surrey KT22 7EE
Tel: 0372 373519

Up to 400 guests can enjoy all the fun, exhilaration and glamour of an international casino knowing that they can't lose. Each guest is given a predetermined number of chips to play with or to surrender during the evening in exchange for prize points. There are no cash gains but prizes are awarded on the clients behalf to the highest scorers. Blacktie Promotions use only experienced professional croupiers and the highest standard gaming tables and equipment.

WHEELS 151 Hurst Road, Sidcup, Kent DA15 9AH
Tel: 081-309 1630

Wheels have had years of experience in the world of gaming and supply authentic gaming tables for American Roulette, Black Jack, Craps, Punto Banco, Roulette Dice, Joker Seven and Roller Dice. Their professional croupiers are willing to teach guests the rules of the games and come dressed to suit the occasion in formal wear or a choice of fun costumes. The fun casinos can be used as a form of fund raising, at charity balls for example, by asking guests to purchase 'funny money' to play the tables, which cannot be redeemed, but prizes can be awarded for the highest scores. Alternatively, guests could be charged a nominal fee for each bet placed.

Karaoke

ECCENTRIC KARAOKE Jolly Good Productions, 71 St Georges Square, SW1V 3QN
Tel: 071-630 5302 Fax: 071-630 8454

If you've ever dreamed of singing with a live band, Eccentric Karaoke can offer you the chance. The live karaoke machine comes with over 150 word sheets, but the band's repertoire includes any other song that might be requested. The show can take on different formats, ranging from singalong to competitive game show style with audience voting and prizes, each individually tailored to suit the circumstances. The show usually lasts between 45 minutes to an hour but the band can also provide dance music after the show for a complete evening's entertainment.

KARAOKE MOVING MUSIC COMPANY 24 Pooles Lane, SW10 0RH
Tel: 071-352 1230 Fax: 071-351 4860

This entertainment company supplies a karaoke show including a presenter and camera operator with an optional disco. The presenters are all professional singers, actors or actresses. They incorporate a video camera as part of the show so that the person who is singing can not only be heard but seen on all three TV monitors, generating a terrific party atmosphere.

KARAOKE SOUND MACHINE 16 Liverpool Road, Islington, N1 0PU
Tel: 071-226 0912

The aim of Karaoke Sound Machine is to plan and organise karaoke parties professionally and provide the music and video shows using the latest technology.

KARAOKE QUEEN 79a Canrobert Street, E2 6PX
Tel: 071-729 4319

Karaoke Queen is a video music and laser entertainments company. Their karaoke nights include video filming and a presenter providing a complete evening's entertainment.

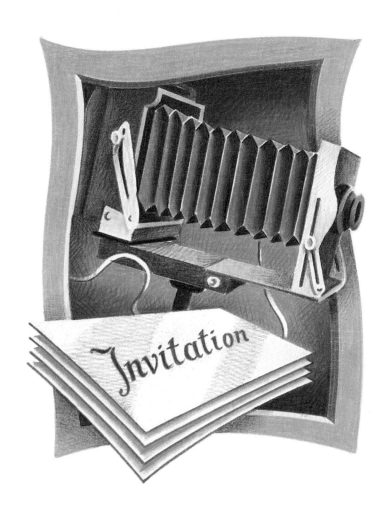

STATIONERY, PRINTING,
PHOTOGRAPHY AND VIDEO

Stationery and Printing

The invitation can say a lot about the type of function you are planning, not only by the wording but also by the quality of the card and the printing. Various methods of printing produce different effects - lithography or letter-press gives a plain, flat finish while thermography or 'imitation engraving' gives a raised, shiny effect. But copperplate engraving is the only method for 'proper' invitations according to **Andrew Ross of Aquila Press.** He explains why:

"Why go to the expense of copperplate invitation cards for your party? Why pay all that money for a simple article of stationery? After all, you only need a means of imparting information.

You could write letters to your guests; you could visit the newsagent and buy invitation 'blanks' possibly with balloons and popping champagne corks; you could even get your local instant print shop to job something up for you to send to your friends or, hopefully, you could order bespoke invitation cards printed from a hand engraved copperplate: Why?

The reason is excellence, being in possession of and handling a top-class product, together with the confidence that those receiving such fine stationery will appreciate you having taken the trouble.

From the moment you make contact with a copperplate printer or stationer and give him your 'copy', the job will be laid out according to your requirements and his experience. It will be checked for accuracy; names, titles, places, social form, protocol etc. The final copy then goes to the engraver who will 'lay-up' and start to engrave the plate in the style you have chosen. This may be Script, Roman, Italic, Old English or perhaps a shaded face.

The engraver looks at the job 'as a whole' and is not restricted by type size or printing measures:- hand engraving means that the plate is peculiar to the customer. Consequently, the engraver provides the necessary measure of emphasis, an originality and specific 'touch' unobtainable in any other form of printing.

The copperplate, once engraved, is checked for printing, or a 'rubbing' from it is submitted to the customer for proofing. When it is passed, the printer takes over.

He mounts the plate on the press and, after adjustments, the cards are printed off one by one and laid out to dry. The invitations are then inspected, trimmed, tissued and packed. Of course all these processes are carried out by hand.

The job is delivered and the invitations are issued, the guests are gratified to receive them and you, the customer, are pleased to know that you have instigated a production process just as skilful and individual as, say, the manufacture of a Bristol motor car or Purdey gun. In short - excellence!"

AQUILA PRESS 37 Bury Street, St James's, SW1Y 6AU
Tel: 071-839 4910 Fax: 071-839 5409

This old-established company offers a complete range of bespoke stationery. Invitation cards are all hand engraved on copperplate. They stick to the traditional style, steering well away from the popping corks type of design. They offer a prompt, courteous and discrete service to clients all over the world.

DECORPRINT 4 Northwold Road, N16 7HR
Tel: 071-254 1083 Fax: 071-254 5077

Decorprint is a long established specialist printer and supplier of a wide range of party requirements (see Table Gifts & Novelties). They have hundreds of different designs and styles in The Perfect Touch range, or they will create a unique design to suit your theme or colour scheme. You will need to make an appointment to visit the studio where you will be able to view the many sample books and discuss your requirements in detail.

FRANK SMYTHSON 44 New Bond Street, W1Y 0DE
Tel: 071-629 8558 Fax: 071-495 6111

Frank Smythson invitations are printed from hand engraved copper plates. These are complimented with exclusive menus and place cards. Expert staff are always available to advise on protocol and stationery etiquette, as has been the case since the company was founded in 1887.

GEE BROTHERS 221 Saint John's Hill, Spencer Park, SW11 1TH Tel: 071-228 4081

Gee Brothers is a small firm of ten staff working both letterpress and lithographic presses as well as engraving and type-setting. They are able to supply a complete range of stationery from invitations to table plans and are always ready to guide the customer with advice gleaned from many years of experience and contacts.

HAND SCRIPTED PRODUCTIONS 13 Calton Road, New Barnet, Herts EN5 1BY
Tel: 081-440 2582 Fax: 081-449 9266

This hand lettering and design company operates from a North London studio under the personal supervision of Melvyn Sharpe, a fully trained calligrapher. Specialities include calligraphic and/ or photoset artwork for custom made invitations and monogram artwork prepared for blind embossing. Hand Scripted Productions will co-ordinate invitations, menus, seating plans and place cards, and do all the hand lettering including addressing the envelopes.

INVITATION 2000 30 Church Street, NW8 83U Tel: 071-224 8820 Fax: 071-224 8801

Invitation 2000 carries a full range of English invitations for all occasions, the same cards as can found in the high street shops but at discounted prices. For something extra special, they also carry a range of American and Italian invitations, plus colour co-ordinated accessories including personalised place cards, serviettes, matchboxes and menus, as well as exclusive, illuminating cake ornaments, Italian bombonierie and gifts.

LONSDALE ENGRAVING   28 New Kings Road, SW6 4ST
Tel: 071-736 9520 Fax: 071-736 6232

Lonsdale Engraving print only 'proper' traditional copperplate engraved stationery, with an emphasis on weddings - they do about 250 weddings a year. Their invitations tend to be formal in style, using copperplate script and traditional wording. They use top quality card and a variety of coloured inks for different occasions, for example, red ink for a ruby wedding invitation.

SOVEREIGN INVITATIONS S Frankel Ltd, 7 & 9 Old Nichol Street, E2 7HR
Tel: 071-739 1367 Fax: 071-739 6547

Sovereign have been established in the East End since 1919. Their invitations are printed on the highest quality card which has been cut and fashioned by hand, and their specialities include gold and silver foiling and embossing. Sovereign print in all languages and scripts which is one of the reasons why their invitations are in demand to notable clients all over the world. In special circumstances, orders can be completed in 36 hours.

VALERIE DUGAN
"Brooklands", The Avenue, Worcester Park, Surrey KT4 7HH Tel: 081-330 1051

Beautiful hand lettered party and wedding stationery in italic or copperplate script can be specially designed by professional calligrapher, Valerie Dugan. She will letter the original artwork, then have the invitations, menus and anything else printed to your requirements in black or coloured ink on a variety of cards ranging from white with a gold leaf edge to embossed and parchment cards in many colours. Valerie can also design monograms and drawings of flowers to enhance the stationery, and hand write the invitations, envelopes, place cards and table plan.

Photography and Video _____

Good photographers become booked up months in advance so it is advisable to start looking around early. Be wary if the photographer you want cannot guarantee that he or she will personally attend your function. They might send a less experienced colleague instead if a more lucrative engagement comes along.

Philip D. Durell of Aardvark Photography explains the importance of employing a professional photographer.

"Everyone enjoys looking through the party photographs. Photographs of people fascinate. 'Look at that hat!', 'What on earth was she wearing?!', 'He hasn't changed a bit.'

Planning a party for a special occasion takes a lot of thought, hard work and a considerable amount of money. Having a photographic record of your investment will give you lasting pleasure long after the event has faded in the memory.

Having decided on photographic coverage, do hire a professional. So many times I've heard sad tales of the enthusiastic uncle or the friend who attends evening classes offering their services - even at weddings. This can sometimes be successful, though too often, after a few drinks and various attractions, together with a lack of experience, will lead to disappointing results. I find it a positive advantage, when photographing a party or wedding, being a stranger to most of the guests. I can circulate freely without being cornered into long conversations giving me time to observe and photograph people uninterrupted. It's important to maintain a certain level of concentration to achieve really good results.

All professional photographers have their own way of approaching a job - their personal style. When selecting a photographer, find out about their ideas for you party photographs, how they suggest it could be best covered - after all, they should be drawing from years of experience. Look through some samples of their work and you will discover particular strengths or weaknesses. Personally, I prefer a more informal, spontaneous approach to photographing people at parties, corporate functions perhaps being the exception. I like to take many shots capturing people engrossed in conversations unaware of my presence. I find that I get more natural, interesting and amusing results this way, rather than being presented with someone's 'Oh no, I hate being photographed' face when you politely ask them to smile at the camera, though VIPs usually react to this with ease.

Also, you will have to consider how you will want the party covered. For instance, do you want a portrait record of every guest arriving which can occupy the photographer for up to an hour or would you rather have the emphasis more on guests chatting? Are there any particular events during the party that should be singled out for special attention, such as a speech, a presentation, or some entertainments? Are there any special guests that you want the photographer to concentrate on? If possible, provide a schedule for the proceedings and a good idea of the coverage you want, or perhaps you may be happy to pass the responsibility over to the photographer entirely to cover the party freely in his or her own style. Either way, do make it clear.

The pricing of the photographer's services is another important point. Obviously, you'll want to get an idea of what it will all cost. This can be somewhat confusing as every photographer seems to have their own different pricing system. Be sure to check what the price quoted actually includes. For example, does it include individual finished photographs or merely a set of contact proofs from which you would then have to order enlargements at a considerable additional expense? How many photographs would you get? Is VAT included in the price? What is the cost of ordering re-prints? and so on. What may, at first sight, seem a reasonable price could end up being expensive when you add up the extra charges. Ask for an estimate tailored to your requirements.

So finally, the party's over, the guests have all gone home, that's it until next year......I can't wait to see the party photos!"

AARDVARK PHOTOGRAPHY *(Right)*
3 Stockwell Terrace, SW9 0QD
Tel: 071-735 8901

Philip D. Durell specialises in complete wedding coverage, parties, receptions and high quality still life work. He covers all aspects of the party and is particularly strong on capturing the interior decor.

BELGRAVE & PORTMAN PRESS BUREAU
7 West Halkin Street,
Belgrave Square, SW1X 8JD
Tel: 071-235 3227

Specialising in society weddings, The Belgrave & Portman Press Bureau has covered more than 100,000 weddings since it was founded over 60 years ago. They rely on a traditional style of photography not going in for gimmicks, and they are always reliable and unobtrusive.

CHARLES GREEN PHOTOGRAPHY *(Right)*
309 Hale Lane, Station Road,
Edgware, Middx HA8 7AX
Tel 081-958 3183   Fax: 081-958 1947

Outstanding wedding and portrait photography and video are captured by Charles Green FBIPP, FMPA, FRPS, FRSA. He combines artistic excellence with a relaxed and natural style. Charles Green's very personal, friendly and reliable service has made his one of the leading studios in the country.

GAVIN WILLIAMS PHOTOGRAPHY
43 Rutland Walk, Catford, SE6 4LG
Tel: 081-291 0129

Gavin Williams Photography offers a personal service at your home or venue, for social functions of all kinds including weddings and family portraiture.

JANE LEGATE PHOTOGRAPHY 7 Mercier Road, Putney, SW15 2AW
Tel: 081-789 1173

As a specialist in people photography, Jane Legate covers weddings, christenings, parties and portraits.

JEROME YEATES 34 Barton Court, Barons Court Road, W14 9EH
Tel: 071-385 3121 Fax: 071-385 5770 Mobile: 0860 503873

Top quality photography for private and commercial clients is provided by Jerome Yeats. Specialising in portraiture and weddings, he was recently awarded a certificate of merit by Kodak. He brings a portable studio flash to receptions for extra flattering lighting.

Photography and Video

NICOLA HOLLINS 67 Redston Road, Priory Park, N8 7HL
Tel: 081-341 2080 Fax: 081-348 4895

A full time photographer since 1978, Nicola Hollins specialises in informal photographs which capture the people, events and atmosphere of a function, working as unobtrusively as possible. She is also able to organise large groups if required. She will attend private and corporate functions and has often worked for well-known families and individuals to whom trust in, and discretion by their photographer is essential.

PAMELA GIBBS 27 Hendon Avenue, Finchley, N3 1UJ
Tel: 081-346 8496

Effective and powerful professional photography is provided by Rena Pearl for P.R., corporate events and private functions. The service is creative, comprehensive, competitive and efficient.

VIDEO

HOMEVIEW VIDEO PRODUCTIONS 1a Merry Hill Mount, Bushey, Herts WD2 1DJ
Tel: 081-950 9473

Founded in 1985, Homeview provides quality video programmes for all kinds of social events including weddings and parties. The services include video production for domestic and professional users, multiple tape duplication, editing, and the transfer of film, slide and photographic materials to video.

GOLDEN VIDEO PRODUCTIONS 69 Lake View, Edgware, Middx HA8 7SA
Tel: 081-958 7850 Fax: 081-958 7850

Videos are shot on SVHS by a professional TV cameraman. Special effects are their speciality.

LES COVERDALE 46 St Johns Street, Colchester, Essex CO2 7AD
Tel: 0206-767339 Fax: 0206 36971

Les Coverdale comes highly recommended. He specialises in weddings and social events, using professional equipment to produce excellent quality pictures. He is discrete and unobtrusive in the way he operates and avoids using bright lighting.

MAGICBOX PICTURES 27 Meadow Walk, Ewell, Epsom, Surrey KT17 2EF
Tel: 081-393 8511

A professional, unobtrusive video coverage can be provided for any function by Magicbox Pictures. The same level of care will go into a five minute speech as a one hour programme.

RAINBOW VIDEO FILMING 90 Duke Road, Chiswick, W4 2DE
Tel: 081-994 3678

Rainbow uses semi broadcast equipment and caters for weddings, parties and all types of function.

TAKE ONE VIDEO 116 Richmond Park Road, Kingston-upon-Thames, Surrey KT2 6AJ
Tel: 081-549 0652

Take One provide a broadcast quality service recording society weddings, parties and promotional events. They are noted for the clarity of their pictures and the stability of their camera work, while remaining unobtrusive. They have worked in most of the major London hotels and venues for a broad spectrum of clients.

TRANSPORT

Transport

A chauffeur-driven car or horse-drawn carriage is a fundamental part of any wedding. However, it is worth considering hiring transport for other events, not only for the host and hostess but also for principal guests and VIPs. Where the venue might be difficult for guests to find or further away than some guests care to drive, a coach or mini bus might be the answer.

Apart from the obvious prestige of arriving in style, the advantages of hiring chauffeured transport are many. The spaciousness of the interior of a limousine prevents ball gowns from getting crushed and is easy to get in and out of elegantly. You won't have to walk through the rain in your finery from where you managed to find a parking space - streets away from the party, or walk back in the early hours to where you think you left the car. Providing it hasn't been towed away or acquired a yellow boot, will you really be in a fit state to drive? Drinking and driving takes on a whole new meaning when you are sitting back in your chauffeur driven limousine sipping champagne.

Theme parties provide the opportunity to really go to town. You can hire a pink Cadillac for a 50's evening, an authentic New York Yellowcab for an American theme, a vintage Rolls Royce for a 20's party or a horse-drawn carriage for a Victorian themed event. Vintage cars and horse-drawn carriages, though, are only suitable for shorter distances and plenty of time should be allowed for the journey. Open top cars and carriages are only for the brave as you are likely to get very windblown and arrive dishevelled unless you travel at a snail's pace.

Some venues, such as London Zoo, HMS Belfast, Hays Galleria and Cottons Atrium, can be reached by boat. Ask the venues to help with the arrangements for this. Some would say that the only way to really make an impression is to arrive by air. Helicopters, however, do need a suitable landing place such as a lawn or a car park, but cannot land in the centre of London except at designated helipads.

Car Hire

AMERICAN 50'S 45 Lucerne Walk, Shotgate, Wickford, Essex SS11 8PZ
Tel: 0268 735914

If you fancy arriving in a 1959 pink Cadillac, American 50's has the car for you. Their collection of late 50's Cadillacs includes pink, red and white convertibles, and blue, pink and white hard tops.

BRENTS LUXURY LIMOUSINE & COACH HIRE 485 Park Avenue,
Bushey, Watford, Herts WD2 2BN Tel: 0923 210039 Fax: 0923 245842

Specialising in travel arrangements for small groups and individuals, Brents has mini-coaches ranging from 12 to 30 seaters and chauffeur driven Mercedes saloons and Lincoln limousines.

DREAM CARS 8-10 Ingate Place, SW8 3NS
Tel: 071-627 5775

Specialists in classic 1950's American cars, Dream Cars has coupés, convertibles and limousines for sale or hire, all with big fins and lots of chrome.

EUROPCAR Chauffeur Drive Division, Davis House, 129 Wilton Road, SW1V 1JZ
Tel: 071-834 6701 Fax: 071-233 5193

Europcar not only hire out chauffeur driven Rolls Royces, limousines and saloons, but also chauffeur driven mini buses and coaches.

GOLDEN WEST CHAUFFEUR HIRE 5th Floor, 29-30 Warwick Street, W1R 5RD
Tel: 0800 181 521 (Freephone) FAX: 081-564 8252

Uniformed chauffeur driven limousines and luxury mini coaches can be hired from Golden West for any occasion.

HUXLEY CAR HIRE 10 Whitchurch Lane, Edgware, Middx HA8 6JZ
Tel: 081-952 5555 Fax: 081-903 5075

Huxley hires out all types of chauffeur driven luxury saloons, limousines and Rolls Royces as well as minibuses and coaches.

LEXHAM CARS & LIMOUSINES 4 Lexham Garden Mews, W8 5JQ
Tel: 071-373 9533 Fax: 071-373 8928

Choose from Rolls Royces, 7-seater Daimlers, Eagle Crest Limousines, Mercedes and Ford luxury saloons, and a 12-seater executive minibus. All the cars are equipped with telephones. Lexham Cars has been trading in Kensington for more than 20 years.

RED CARPET CARS 19 Lingfield Close, Northwood, Middx. HA6 2FP
Tel: 09274 27616

Red Carpet Cars offers a very high standard of chauffeur driven cars, specialising in weddings. There is a a choice of white, blue or red Rolls Royce Silver Shadows.

TEN TENTHS 106 Gifford Street, N1 0DF
Tel: 071-607 4887 Fax: 071-609 8124

Whatever form of transport you're looking for, from jet-skis to a luxury liner, Ten Tenths will find it for you. They hire out specialist cars, bikes, boats and aeroplanes of any era, usually for films or photographic shoots.

V-12 55 Chelsham Road, SW4 6NN
Tel: 071-738 8228 Fax: 071-738 8220

V-12 specialises in vintage and modern motor cars, aeroplanes and motorbikes. They actually own over 50 cars, 8 planes and many bikes but have a further 3,000 vehicles on their books and can supply almost any vehicle, however unusual. They can also arrange air displays.

WHITE CARS 243 Acton Lane, Park Royal, NW10 7NR
Tel: 081-453 1212 Fax: 081-453 1195

Chauffeur driven modern and vintage Rolls Royce, Daimler and Mercedes limousines and luxury saloon cars can be hired from this family-run business specialising in weddings and other special occasions.

YELLOWCABS Rake Service Station, London Road, Rake, Liss, Hants GU33 7JH
Tel: 0730 893285 Fax: 0730 893822

Yellowcabs is a specialist vehicle hire company supplying classic and modern vehicles for parties, promotions and filming. They have two New York Checker cabs, a 1961 pink Cadillac convertible, a 1964 white Cadillac limousine and a 1966 white Lincoln four-door convertible among their vehicles available for hire.

Horse Drawn Carriages

LONDON CARRIAGE COMPANY 100 Gifford Street, N1 0DF
Tel: 071-609 9462

Single horse drawn enclosed or open Victorian carriages can be hired with liveried drivers. The London Carriage Company operates in a ten mile radius of Central London and has three carriages to choose from.

Transport

SANDERS CARRIAGE COMPANY 32 Latchmere Lane,
Kingston-upon-Thames, Surrey KT2 5PD Tel: 081-549 6267

Sanders hire out horse drawn carriages for all social occasions, though weddings are their speciality. They offer reductions for Sunday or weekday weddings.

Coaches

LONDON COACHES Wandsworth Garage, Jews Row, Wandsworth, SW18 1TB
Tel: 081-877 1722 Fax: 081-877 1968

London's leading bus and coach company can provide a variety of vehicles including vintage buses from the early 1900's which they are able to borrow from The London Transport Museum. They have luxury 53 seater coaches, 30-seater executive coaches and closed or open-top double decker buses.

Aircraft

AIR LONDON INTERNATIONAL Mack House, Aviation Court, Gatwick Road,
Crawley RH10 2GG Tel: 0293 549544

Air London is a charter brokerage company that will find you any aircraft from a helicopter to a Boeing 747 anywhere in the world. They could arrange for a Dakota to fly your guests across the Channel on the Beaujolais Run or organise a supersonic party aboard Concorde.

CB HELICOPTERS The Blue Hangar, Biggin Hill Airfield, Kent TN16 3BN
Tel: 071-228 3232 Fax: 0959 76478

You can charter a helicopter or executive jet from the CB Group. They can also provide a chauffeur driven car to meet your flight.

Hot Air Balloons

BALLOON SAFARIS 27 Rosefield Road, Staines, Middx TW18 4NB
Tel: 0784 451007

Float away from your wedding or event in a hot air balloon hired from one of the longest established passenger carrying companies. Vouchers for their champagne balloon flights make exciting and unusual gifts.

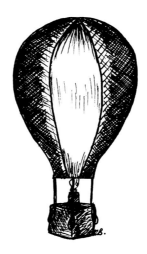

COUNTRY WIDE PARKING LTD   69 Summer Road, East Molesey, Surrey KT8 9LX
Tel: 081-398 4590 Fax: 071-630 9857

C.W.P. Ltd offers a specialised highly sophisticated valet parking service. The strictly vetted team comprises a number of well qualified men and women with clean driving licences and are the only team to be fully insured on private and public roads. Valet parking can be provided for the largest wedding, banquet, conference or office opening, to the smallest dinner party at your home or even outside your favourite restaurant. The staff come suitably attired either in American style bomber jackets or in tuxedos for formal events.

Other services offered by C.W.P. Ltd include chauffeur driven executive cars, concierge/doormen and a range of security staff from highly trained former army and police personnel. Also complete event management from traffic control and parking to crowd and admission control at larger events. All staff are extremely professional and discreet.

PARTY PROFESSIONALS

Party Planners

If organising the party, seems too much for you to handle on your own (even with the help of The Good Party Guide), or if you simply do not have the time (and it is always a very time consuming business), consider seeking help from experts. **Valli Watson of Party Professionals** explains how party planners can organise the whole event or just part of it.

"Every year, there seem to be more party organisers in the back of the glossies. One thing to realise is that not all the organisers advertise and if they do, you end up paying for it. There are a few who rely on getting clients by word of mouth and personal recommendations. These generally offer the greater personal service, so it is worth asking your friends.

In the main, there are two types of party organisers. Some firms have fallen into party planning as a by-product of their main business, e.g. party shops, discotheques or caterers. Their recommendations may appear independent, but often reflect formal business connections with various suppliers. They have less in-house facilities devoted entirely to planning and you often end up speaking directly to a variety of sub-contractors rather than one co-ordinator. On the night, they tend to concentrate more on the main part of their business than on the party as a whole.

The independent party planners, on the other hand, do nothing but organise parties and give a greater degree of unbiased, objective advice. They have a far better range of contacts, and are more likely to offer a higher degree of supervision and back-up, with a much more personalised service. You will find that you generally deal with one person throughout. The catch is that they often charge consultation fees for so doing, which may appear expensive. However, you can be sure that companies that do not charge fees make their money somewhere else.

The advantage of using party organisers are many. Few people realise until they are in the middle of arranging a party, exactly how much time, effort and running around it takes. Planners can advise you where to economise and where not to, offer ideas and take the headache out of organisation. More importantly, you can really enjoy your party on the night. There is nothing worse than worrying whether the band will turn up or not, or whether the food will be edible.

The other major advantage is that you should know exactly how much your party is costing before the event and instead of writing out a multiple of cheques, you are presented with one comprehensive quotation before the party and one bill afterwards. This is especially useful at weddings when 'Daddy' is paying and where business-like quotations are very reassuring.

Things to look out for:- Make sure that you get the right party planner by finding out what sort of parties they do and who their clients are. A good sign is if they know and are enthusiastic about food - if so, you are half way there. The last thing one wants for a private party is a corporate style party planner... typed menus are a no-no! Insist that they do what you want and not what they think is easiest because they have done it millions of times before. Parties must reflect their hosts and not the organisers, so make sure that they are producing something that fits in with your character and not an 'off the peg' party. Make sure you are aware of all the costs you are liable for - the best companies will provide you with up to date summaries of costings, so there should be no nasty shocks at the end.

Lastly, if you do go to a party organiser, choose one in whom you have complete confidence and then let them get on with it."

THE ADMIRABLE CRICHTON
6 Camberwell Trading Estate,
Denmark Road, SE5 9LB
Tel: 071-733 8113   Fax: 071-733 7289

The Admirable Crichton specialises in designing, organising and catering for weddings, dances, dinners and drinks parties for both private and corporate clients. Every aspect of the event, from start to finish, is handled with creative flair, individuality and professionalism. Staff is supplied through The Admirable Crichton Staff Bureau (see Party Staff).

ALEXANDER'S ENTERTAINMENT 7 Crableigh Mews, Cabul Road, Battersea, SW11 3LX
Tel: 071-738 0644   Fax: 071-738 0602

From supplying a single discotheque to arranging and co-ordinating complete functions, Alexander's will do as much or as little as required for corporate and private occasions. They can theme events and supply all the necessary lighting.

AT THE STROKE OF MIDNIGHT The Arches, Grosvenor Terrace, SE5 ONP
Tel: 071-703 0011   Fax: 071-703 8123

From concept to presentation, At the Stroke of Midnight's youthful and original flair will ensure the visual success of any occasion and at any venue. They will organise all the decor, lighting and special effects as well as unusual requests and one-off surprises.

BANANA SPLIT 11 Carlisle Road, NW9 0HD
Tel: 081-200 1234   Fax: 081-200 1121

Banana Split is a very professional party design company and entertainment agency incorporating a fully comprehensive technical hire department for sound and lighting and their renowned Banana Split travelling discotheques (see Discotheques). They will theme your event, decorate the venue with flowers and balloons (for which they have an enviable reputation), provide the cabaret and musical entertainment and organise all the printing requirements and catering.

BENTLEY'S ENTERTAINMENT 26a Winders Road, SW11 3HB
Tel: 071-223 7900   Fax: 071-978 4062

Party planners and organisers, Bentley's Entertainment have full production facilities in-house. They are specialists in lighting, decoration, marquees, catering, staging, dance floors and special effects and can supply all forms of entertainment. They have organised some very prestigious occasions such as Her Royal Highness the Princess Royal's 40th birthday party, the Red October Ball and the opening party and launch for Miss Saigon.

BOJOLLY'S Unit 4, Brentford Business Centre, Commerce Road, Middx TW8 8LE
Tel: 081-568 6447   Fax: 081-569 9355

Bojolly's has now become one of London's foremost party design and production services, using carefully controlled in-house production. They provide a complete, experienced and original design service with great attention paid to detail. They will organise the entire event, if required, from finding the venue to supplying the entertainment, which might include their own Bojolly's discotheque (see Discotheques).

Party Planners

CHANCE ORGANISATION 321 Fulham Road, SW10 9QL
Tel: 071-376 5995   Fax: 071-376 3598

When Andrew Chance formed Chance Entertainment in 1981, he already had several years of experience in the entertainment industry. Specialists in imaginative theming, spectacular lighting and sensational decoration, Chance Organisation will design and arrange any type of event, both private and corporate. They provide marquees which they refer to as their 'portable palaces', international cuisine and wines, and any form of entertainment you can imagine.

FAIT ACCOMPLI 32b Queensgate Mews, SW7 5QN
Tel: 071-581 0384   Fax: 071-581 3216

With a wealth of experience behind them, Fait Acompli has built up a reputation for efficient organisation of everything from small dinner parties at home to lavish balls. Every aspect is expertly co-ordinated.

FÊTES
Southcote, Huntingdon House Drive,
Hindhead, Surrey GU26 6BG
Tel: 0428 604989   Fax: 0428 604989

Fêtes provides a total personalised service that specialises in the planning and administration of special occasions anywhere in the world. All forms of private and corporate hospitality events are tailor-made and catered for from start to finish. Advice is given on the most suitable arrangements and no obligation quotations are supplied.

THE FINISHING TOUCH 19 Warren Avenue, Richmond, Surrey TW10 5D2
Tel: 081-878 7555   Fax: 081-878 8444

As a hospitality and entertainment company, The Finishing Touch specialise in designing, organising and managing events for the corporate market. They offer an outstanding selection of unique and unusual venues, excellent entertainments including fun casinos, karaoke and discotheques, plus a full range of novel activity days. They are specialists in imaginative themes and lighting.

FUNCTION SERVICES The Folly, Pinner Hill Road, Pinner, Middx HA5 3YQ
Tel: 081-429 3000   Fax: 081-868 6497

This company specialises in theme parties and provision of technical support facilities as well as complete marquee packages and event management. All the necessary elements for a successful theme party are supplied including entertainment, novelties, advice on costumes, decor, backcloths, props, lighting, sound and staging.

GENERAL FACTOTUM 80 Eccles Road, SW11 1LX
Tel: 071-223 0342   Fax: SW11 1LX

Kim Anderson started her company over three years ago to offer a wide service to both private and corporate clients. General Factotum, as its name suggests, is prepared to tackle a very wide range of projects from a birthday party for a three year old to a spectacular Christmas dinner at the Natural History Museum. The emphasis, though, is on weddings for which General Factotum can organise every aspect. On occasion, they have even organised the bride and groom's wedding night, packed their wedding clothes, collected their wedding presents and had them delivered to their house on their return from honeymoon.

IVOR SPENCER ENTERPRISES   12 Little Bornes, Dulwich, SE21 8SE
Tel: 081-670 5585/8424   Fax: 081-670 0055

Famous toastmaster Ivor Spencer is acknowledged to be an expert on entertainment. He is able to organise a banquet, luncheon, wedding reception, conference, in fact, any event. He will arrange every detail in excellent taste and to the highest standard, including the catering, cabaret, bands, discos, marquees, lighting, sound and after-dinner speakers. (See Toastmasters).

THE JONATHAN SEAWARD
ORGANISATION
2 Heliport Estate, Lombard Road,
SW11 3SS
Tel: 071-350 0033   Fax: 071-228 6213

Stunning decor, excellent food and brilliant entertainment are the hallmarks of a JSO event. Having started out as Joffin's Discotheques (see Discotheques) in 1979, the company quickly built a reputation for imaginative yet realistically priced parties and the very best music and lighting. As a total event organisation, they also have their own marquees, caterers, florist, dance floors and equipment. A recent client commented "I cannot get over your attention to detail - you are complete stars."

JONGLEURS EVENT PLANNING 49 Lavender Gardens, SW11 4DJ
Tel: 081-780 1028   Fax: 081-780 1479

Jongleurs offers creative excellence in the organisation and supply of corporate and private entertainments. They provide a venue finding service, exquisite catering, all manner of entertainment including the best cabaret and speciality acts, exceptional interior design, sound, lighting, flowers, staff, pyrotechnics and anything else needed or desired for creating unusual and memorable events. Murder mysteries, treasure hunts and theatrical parties are their current specialities.

JULIANA'S PARTY ORGANISING Unit 7, Farm Lane Trading Estate, SW6 1QJ
Tel: 071-937 1555   Fax: 071-381 3872

A complete party organising service is offered by this long established company. They have their own marquees, discotheques, lighting and dance floors so don't charge such high commission as some who have to sub-contract. Juliana's will organise every aspect for any number of guests and to suit any budget. Their impressive list of prestigious clients is an indication that they provide a very professional service. (See Marquees and Discotheques)

MARY KAVANAGH & ASSOCIATES 98 Esmond Road, W4 1JF
Tel: 081-747 0272   Fax: 081-994 2562

Every aspect of both private and corporate parties is covered by the services of Mary Kavanagh - venues, menus, decor, music, transport, gifts, invitations and photographers as well as a complete information service for those who wish to arrange their own parties.

MASK ENTERTAINMENTS 26 Queen's Mews, W2 4BY
Tel: 071-792 1462   Fax: 071-792 2623

Party planning with imagination and flair is only part of what Mask Entertainments can offer. They also run their own mobile discotheque, entertainment agency, catering company and firework service. They have some novel ideas and props for theme parties including giant Scalextric.

157

Party Planners ———————————————————

NICKI COLWYN ASSOCIATES 29 Oakley Garden, SW3 5QH
Tel: 071-351 2875   Fax: 071-376 8187

Lady Colwyn started her company in 1976 to organise and co-ordinate social and business occasions with aptitude and style. Specialising in one-off special events such as gala dinners or themed events, the company will supply all musical requirements from discotheques to choirs and all types and sizes of dance bands.

PARTY PLANNERS 56 Ladbroke Grove, W11 2PB
Tel: 071-229 9666   Fax: 071-727 6001

Lady Elizabeth Anson has been running her successful company for over 30 years and has built up a wealth of experience to impart to her clients. Lady Elizabeth and her assistants are able to specifically design a party for a client, whether it be an intimate dinner for two, a charity ball or a corporate dinner dance. Alternatively, they will simply book a band or provide the champagne from their very competitively priced list. Party Planners is the best-known of all such companies and has an impeccable reputation for being, according to Harpers, quite simply 'the best'.

PARTY PROFESSIONALS 26 Holland Villas Road, W14 8DH
Tel: 071-602 0123   Fax: 071-603 0865

Run by Valli Watson, who gained some of her vast experience while working for Lady Elizabeth Anson, Party Professionals are now seen as a younger, more imaginative version of Party Planners. They plan all sorts of parties, from weddings and christenings to company centenaries and product launches. They are valued by their clients for their independent advice, personal service and discretion - very important when dealing with high profile clients. Not only do they design, organise and run the actual event, but also provide a comprehensive and very specialised back-up, from writing and sending out invitations to handling guest lists and replies, and placements at dinners.

PENGUIN'S Hatton Lodge, Snow's Ride, Windlesham, Surrey GU20 6LA
Tel: 0628 777791   Fax: 0628 34689

Serving the private and corporate markets, Penguin's provide entertainment, catering, venues, decoration and party organisation to the highest level. They entertain all ages at all styles of parties from 18th to 50th birthday parties, school balls to weddings, employing the finest quality services and entertainments.

THE PRESENTATION FACTOR 39-41 North Road, Islington, N7 9DP
Tel: 071-607 5322   Fax: 071-700 5645

The Presentation Factor designs, organises and manages entertainment and business events that are innovative, exciting and memorable. Whatever is needed for a successful party - they will supply it. It is their creativity and presentation that sets them apart.

RSVP 12 South Molton Street, W1Y 1DF
Tel: 071-491 0109   Fax: 071-499 0841

With creative imagination and a sharp eye for detail, RSVP design and organise spectacular one-off themed events. The secret to their success is that every aspect of the party is thoroughly checked to ensure that everything runs smoothly.

SAVOIR FAIRE ENTERTAINMENTS 94 Gordon Road, Ealing, W13 9NR
Tel: 081-567 4995   Fax: 081-566 7670

Founded in 1984, Savoir Faire have built up a reputation for having an acute eye for detail. They offer a personal service coupled with a determined price to please policy. They specialise in all

158

aspects of event organisation from sophisticated travelling discotheques to complete party packages.

SCENES ORIGINAL Little Grove, Grove Lane, Orchard Leigh, Nr Cheshire, HP5 3LQ
Tel: 0494 778163

As theme-party specialists, Scenes Original will design a unique theme and co-ordinate every detail from invitation cards to costumes and make-up. They will transform the venue of your choice then transport you back in time or ahead to the future with appropriate music, cuisine, cabaret and costumed staff. Headed by thespian Carol Burns, Scenes Original has the experience and ability to temporarily make your dreams come true.

SWANSFLIGHT PRODUCTIONS 48 Uxbridge Road, Hampton Hill, Middx TW12 3AD
Tel: 081-941 1595   Fax: 081-783 1366

Swansflight's 'World of Fantasy' creates themed events such as a banquet with Henry VIII and his Royal Court, complete with costumed artistes, Medieval crockery and room decor. Or they could take the theme further by incorporating archery, jousting or even a Tudor fair. Another popular theme is a pirate fantasy.

THEMES FOR DREAMS 4 Square Rigger Row, Plantation Wharf, SW11 3TZ
Tel: 071-978 5422   Fax: 071-738 0956

Director Sandra Simpson's vivid imagination and drive has stage managed hosts of glittering events for her company. In addition to grand scale corporate and charity balls, her team also themes large or small 'fun' parties, dream weddings and formal or intimate dinners with colour, originality, sparkle and style.

UNIQUE ENTERTAINMENT Designer Liner, Becketts Wharf,
Hampton Wick, Surrey KT1 4ER
Tel: 081-997 8889   Fax: 081-977 8893

Themed parties and corporate events are written and produced to a brief by Unique Entertainment. Set design, room dressing, entertainment, sound and lighting are all provided.

VENUE & CATERING ADVISORY BUREAU 45 Chartfield Avenue, SW15 6HP
Tel: 081-788 5353   Fax: 081-789 9230

VCAB offers a unique service throughout the U.K. to guide the corporate and private client through the labyrinth of the hospitality world. They can select and advise you on the choice of venues and locations, cooks and caterers from their continuously up-dated research.

WHITE TIE Kingsgate House, 536 King's Road, SW10 0TE
Tel: 071-973 8001   Fax: 071-351 4207

Formerly with Lady Elizabeth Anson's Party Planners, Diana Christie Miller and Lizzie Grant founded White Tie in 1988. Their success lies in their belief that every party must be different, excellent and fun. White Tie will organise as much or as little as the client wishes, though they are happiest when responsible for conceiving, planning and organising every detail, from initial concepts to the end result.

Party Planners

WILLIAM BARTHOLOMEW PARTY ORGANISING
18 Talina Centre, Bagleys Lane, SW6 2BW Tel: 071-731 8328   Fax: 071-384 1807

William Bartholomew has been organising parties since 1976. His company can plan, design and co-ordinate your party, and provide the most elegant marquees, unusual venues, superb caterers, beautiful decor, exciting lighting, and top class entertainment including his famous discotheque (see Discotheques). With impressive experience of planning parties for top private and corporate clients, William Bartholomew Party Organising will ensure that you have a resounding success.

Your caterer should be able to supply waiting staff for your party. But if you are not employing a caterer, or if you want extra or more specialised party help, a reputable agency will be able to provide reliable staff.

When you contact an agency, be very specific about your requirements. Make certain the staff know how to get to the venue, what time you would like them there and for how long, and what there duties will be. The ratio of staff to guests varies according to the type of party it will be and the expertise of the staff.

Writing from experience, **Kate Herbert-Hunting of Universal Aunts** offers these observations:

"The engagement of staff for your party is intended to provide expert attention to the needs and comfort of your guests, while host and hostess relax and enjoy their company. For the arrangement to operate at it's best, there needs to have been good co-operation between the agency and the hostess, it's client. The agency should enquire as to, and the hostess provide, the exact party plan and requirements.

If one can afford a party, in comparison to the overall cost of the food, drink and flowers, the hiring of staff is not out of proportion. The well trained butler and waitress are proud of their highly skilled expertise and give of their best whatever level of social entertaining they serve.

The resulting elegance of a relaxed host and hostess, smooth service, and the saving on drink consumption when handled by an expert, is well worth concluding 'why spoil the ship....?"

**ABLE MINDERS 10 Barley Mow Passage, Chiswick, W4 4PH
Tel: 081-994 1440 Fax: 081-742 1462**

Able Minders can supply capable, experience party helpers for anything from bar work and silver service to cleaning up afterwards. All staff are interviewed by the agency and two references are taken up and verbally checked.

**THE ADMIRABLE CRICHTON STAFF BUREAU 6 Camberwell Trading Estate,
Denmark Road, SE5 9LB Tel: 071-733 8113 Fax: 071-733 7289**

All types domestic staff from plongeurs to dog-walkers can be supplied by The Admirable Crichton Staff Bureau, a subsidiary of the party planning company (see Party Planners). For parties they can provide waiters and waitresses, butlers, valet parking and security.

**BUSY BEES BUREAU 144 Merton Hall Road, Wimbledon, SW19 3PZ
Tel: 081-542 0926**

Well vetted waitresses, cleaners and general party help are supplied by Busy Bees to the South London area.

**CINDERELLA HOME SERVICES 323 Kirkdale, Sydenham, SE26 4QB
Tel: 081-676 0917 Fax: 081-778 6906**

For more than 10 years, Cinderella has been providing staff for parties including caterers and waitresses, cleaners for before and after, and babysitters while parents are at the party. They operate in North and South London.

**JOHN (PERSONAL SERVICES) 99d Talbot Road, W11 2AT
Tel: 071-792 1162**

These old fashioned grand caterers will supply all party staff, including liveried footmen and butlers, with or without their catering services.

Party Staff

SOLVE YOUR PROBLEM 5 Vale Road North, Surbiton, Surrey KT6 5AG
Tel: 081-974 2449

Established in 1947, Solve Your Problem supplies all types of domestic staff such as waiters and waitresses, cooks and cleaners, all personally interviewed at their offices in Oxford Street and references checked.

SOUTH OF THE RIVER 128c Northcote Road, SW11 6QZ
Tel: 071-228 5086 Fax: 071-228 6496

South of the River is a membership club which provides domestic and company members in South London with all day-to-day services including party help - waiting staff, butlers, washers-up and so on. They also operate a 'finding' service, so if you are looking for a baritone, for example, to sing at your party, they will find you one.

UNIVERSAL AUNTS P. O. Box 304, SW4 0NP
Tel: 071-738 8937

Britains original personal service bureau was established in 1921. Universal Aunts will supply all domestic staff, caterers, butlers, waitresses and cooks.

Toastmasters

The important roll of the professional toastmaster is explained by **Bernard Sullivan M.B.E.**

"The experienced toastmaster is a very much more valuable asset to banquet organisers than is generally realised. This man (or woman) is able to prevent things going wrong because he has very probably come across the most worrying of organisers' problems very many times before and has had the solutions at his fingertips.

With such a toastmaster, it is usually possible for organisers to say 'Here's the programme of what we want done' and then (settling back to enjoy the evening they have worked so hard for) confidently leave it to him.

The toastmaster will then, in liaison with the caterers, the band, the security staff and so on, keep things running to time, advise on matters of protocol and ceremonial, gently calm the President's lady, or the bride's mother, and provide many other little services, knowledge of which he has gathered from experience at thousands of previous functions, such as a suitable grace or a joke.

Briefly described, his duties 'on the night' will be to greet the guests and announce them to their hosts, counting them with a hand-clicker as he does so. Then, when all have arrived, and after consultation with the hosts, the head waiter and the band leader, he will proclaim that 'dinner (or luncheon) is served' and politely, tactfully, jokingly (whatever is required) get the guests to their tables on time ready for the processional entry of the host and principal guests. He will then announce Grace before the meal and the Loyal Toast, and the speeches and responses after it.

On the more formal occasions, he will, if required, announce all speakers with full honours - 'The Right Honourable Malcolm Rifkind, Her Majesty's Secretary of State for Transport and the Member of Parliament for Pentlands', but at the less formal wedding reception will probably prefer, if the client agrees, to use simpler forms of introduction - 'Your Bridegroom, John.'

At the conclusion of the formal proceedings, the toastmaster will announce the opening of the ball, or the departure of the principal guests, or that the bride and bridegroom will be taking their leave 'in thirty minutes time'."

CHRISTINE AKEHURST 74 Westfield Road, Dunstable, Beds LU6 1DH
Tel: 0582 666949

Christine's background of theatre, TV, radio, catering and Eight years as professional toastmaster working all over the country gives her a unique ability to contribute to the success of any function.

DAVID BEDFORD 49 Grovely Road, Sunbury-on-Thames, Surrey TW16 7LQ
Tel: 081-890 5577

A toastmaster and master of ceremonies with an up to date approach, David Bedford is definitely not the old fashioned sergeant major.

TOMMIE DRAPER 15 Thorney Hedge Road, Chiswick, W4 5SB
Tel: 081-994 7232

Tommie Draper is a past president of the Guild of Toastmasters and a member of The Grand Order of Water Rats.

KENNY ESSEX 152 Shaftesbury Avenue, West Harrow, Middx HA2 0AW
Tel: 081-422 8996

Not only is Kenny Essex a professional toastmaster, linkman, adviser and Town Crier to commerce and industry, but he is also a children's entertainer.

CHRISTINE GARNHAM Flat 3, Springfield Court, 21 Bawtry Road, Whetstone, N20 0SY
Tel: 081-361 4413

Christine Garnham is the only female toastmaster trained by the Guild of Professional Toastmasters. She is also an associate of the Institute of Linguists (French and German) and is available for weddings, barmitzvahs, parties, banquets, dinners and conferences anywhere in Great Britain or abroad.

PETER MOORE 18 College Gardens, SW17 7UG
Tel: 081-767 2103

With over 15 years of experience behind him, Peter Moore's duties have included weddings, luncheons, charity balls, masonic ladies' nights, civic dinners and functions attended by members of the Royal family, Heads of State and government ministers. He is also London's Town Crier and official toastmaster to the London Borough of Merton.

GORDON POLUCK 17 Grangecliffe Gardens, South Norwood, SE25
Tel: 081-653 1957

As toastmaster, master of ceremonies and auctioneer, Gordon Poluck can arrange all your function requirements.

IVOR SPENCER *(Right)*
12 Little Bornes,Dulwich, SE21 8SE
Tel: 081-670 5585 & 081-670 8424
Fax: 081-670 0055 & 081-776 7321

Life President of Guild of Professional Toastmasters, Ivor Spencer has officiated at over 950 Royal occasions in the U.K. and abroad. Many of those he has organised completely through his party planning service, Ivor Spencer Enterprises (see Party Organisers). He also runs a school for professional toastmasters and another for butlers.

Toastmasters

DEREK J SANDERS 50 Fairby Road, Lee, SE12 8JH
Tel: 081-318 0893

Derek Sanders is a past president of the Society of London Toastmasters (1988) and works regularly in the leading West End hotels and banqueting rooms. He has experience of City functions and is regularly employed at Jewish functions.

BERNARD SULLIVAN M.B.E.
77 Kingsway, Petts Wood, Kent BR5 1PN
Tel: 0689 830065

Secretary of Society of London Toastmasters, Bernard Sullivan has been a toastmaster for over 36 years. His vast experience over the years has covered 12 Lord Mayor's Banquets, 60 State Banquets (to foreign Sovereigns and Heads of State) and nearly 200 of the Semi-State Banquets given by the Lord Mayor. He has also had 24 years of experience as a boxing M.C. Such is his expertise that he is regularly consulted by other toastmasters on matters of procedure and protocol. His services were recently recognised by Her Majesty the Queen when she awarded him the MBE.

BRYN WILLIAMS Tanglewood, 50 The Ridgeway, Enfield, Middx EN2 8QS
Tel: 081-888 2398   Fax: 081-367 8248

Britain's longest practising toastmaster, Bryn Williams is the founder, past president and life vice president of the National Association of Toastmasters. Since he became a toastmaster at the age of 16, he has attended over 12,000 functions of every conceivable type, both here and abroad. In 1990, he celebrated his 40th year in the profession. He is an authority on public speaking and regularly runs seminars on the art of addressing an audience.

MELVYN ZEFF 22 Church Road, Newbury Park, Essex IG2 7ES
Tel: 081-597 3113

Melvyn Zeff is an international toastmaster and master of ceremonies. The functions he has officiated at include civic, masonic and Rotary occasions, banquets, dinners, luncheons, weddings, and barmitzvahs. He has also compared shows and variety evenings.

AGENCIES

TOASTMASTERS LIMITED 77 Kingsway, Petts Wood, Kent BR5 1PN
Tel: 0689 830065

Run by Bernard Sullivan and his wife Rosie, Toastmasters Limited is a specialist agency which supplies toastmasters, town criers, pipers, herald trumpeters and orchestras to banquet organisers.

Insurance

WEDDINGSURANCE
Cornhill Insurance, P.O. Box 10, 57 Ladymead,
Guildford, Surrey GU1 1DB
Tel: 0483 68161 Fax: 0483 300952

Cornhill Insurance provide a wedding insurance policy of comprehensive benefits covering almost any catastrophe which could spoil the big day. The £35 standard package gives up to £2,000 of cover against the wedding being cancelled for reasons beyond the policy holder's control such as through death, injury or illness, unforseen occupational posting of the bride or groom, being unable to hold the ceremony or the reception at the booked venue, loss or damage beyond repair to the brides dress or non-appearance of the booked transport. The policy also pays up to £1,000 for loss or damage to the wedding presents within 24 hours either side of the reception, or to the bridal attire including bridesmaids' dresses and hired menswear. There is also up to £1,000 cover to retake the photographs should the photographer fail to turn up or for loss or damage to the negatives. The policy also gives up to £1 million of public liability cover for accidental injury or damage to property. Most unforseen problems are covered, the only major exception is "disinclination to marry" if either the bride or groom decide not to turn up. Alternative policies can be drawn up to cover any type of function, not just weddings.

Security

The following associations will be able to guide you towards a security firm that best suits your needs. The duties of security staff would normally include checking invitations at the door and dealing with unruly guests and potential gatecrashers.

BRITISH SECURITY INDUSTRY ASSOCIATION (BSIA)
Security House, Barbourne, Worcester, WR1 1RS
Tel: 071-630 5183 Fax: 0905 613625

BSIA will supply a list of their members on request.

INTERNATIONAL PROFESSIONAL SECURITY ASSOCIATION (IPSA)
292a Torquay Road, Paignton, Devon TQ3 2ET
Tel: 0803 554849 Fax: 0803 529203

They will recommend a suitable security company for your needs from their membership list.

See also: Countrywide Parking Ltd (Valet Parking)

DRESS HIRE

Dress Hire

Obviously you want to look your best at the party and at the same time feel confident that you are dressed suitably for the occasion. It is a tribute to your hosts to show that you have taken the care to dress up in acknowledgement of the occasion.

There are very few rules regarding the correct style of dress for parties, it largely depends on fashion and preference. If your invitation stipulates 'lounge suit' for gentlemen, smart day or cocktail wear (depending on the time of the function) would be correct. A silky suit or little black dress would be appropriate. 'Black tie' means long or short evening dresses or dressy trousers. Knowing the venue might help you decide which length to wear - a full length ballgown might not be quite right at a party in a restaurant, for example. You could, perhaps, take your lead from the hostess, but you should never try to upstage her, unless you are the guest of honour. 'White tie' is reserved for very formal occasions, such as State functions, and the ballgown would be quite correct here.

Louise Eyre and Sarah Marques, who run 20th Century Frox, explain the advantages of hiring for the occasion...

"Ladies dress hire is now considered a smart and sensible option by most women. Gone are the days of extravagant spending for that one-off occasion. Hiring not only makes economical sense but can be fun. There is a certain freedom in hiring a dress, knowing that it costs only a fraction of it's purchase price it permits indulgence and gives you the opportunity to explore a new look every time.

A good hire shop should be able to offer you anything from a full-blown ballgown to little black numbers and Ascot or wedding outfits with co-ordinating accessories. Sizes usually range from 8 to 18 and prices, which include dry cleaning, can vary from £35 to £200 according to the original value of the dress, with accessories usually between £5 and £15.

All shops will require a cheque or credit card deposit which is fully refundable providing the dress is returned un-damaged; some now offer optional insurance cover. Should you fall in love with your dress, some shops will allow you to purchase it or have it made up for you in your choice of colours etc., or alternatively, you can wait for the bargains in their end of season sales."

Ladies Dress Hire

A CHANCE TO DANCE 57a Latchmere Road, Battersea, SW11 2DS
Tel: 071-350 1579

Ball gowns and cocktail dresses are for hire as well as sequined jackets, suits and wedding dresses. Accessories include evening gloves and costume jewellery. A Chance to Dance will also make and design dresses to order.

AFTER DARK 6 Ashbourne Parade, Finchley Road, Temple Fortune, NW11 0AD
Tel: 081-209 0195

Over 500 items of ladies evening wear are stocked at After Dark, catering for ages from teenagers to grandmothers with sizes ranging from 6 to 20. The entire stock changes each season so only current season designer ranges are used for hire. Ex-hire and new dresses are always available for sale. They also stock a range of accessories and offer a shoe and bag dyeing service.

CHIFFON 17 Station Parade, Whitchurch Lane, Canons Park, Edgware, Middx HA8 6RW
Tel: 081-952 7491

Chiffon have exclusive, one-off evening wear sizes 8 to 28 or altered to fit. First time hire is a possibility. A range of accessories is available which includes a concession of shoes which you can buy and have dyed to match any outfit in 72 hours. Chiffon also sells ready-to-wear and will design and make dresses to order.

168

FROCK AROUND THE CLOCK 42 Vardens Road, Battersea, SW11 1RH
Tel: 071-924 1669

You'll find a large selection of designer evening gowns, party dresses, cocktail dresses, jewellery, bags and gloves at Frock Around The Clock. The stock is constantly changing so there is always something new and up to the minute to choose. You will need to make an appointment but the hours are very flexible and you will receive individual attention.

FROCKS 29 Mount Ararat Road, Richmond, Surrey TW10 6PQ
Tel: 081-940 5391

High quality evening dresses, ball gowns, party frocks, cocktail dresses and dinner dresses are available in sizes 8 to 16. This fast expanding business is run from home, so visits are by appointment only, six mornings and evenings (until 10pm) a week.

NUIT ET JOUR 163 Manor Road, Chigwell, Essex JG7 52A
Tel: 081-500 0228

Elegant designer ball gowns, cocktail dresses, Ascot and wedding outfits are available for hire in sizes from 8 to 22 and styles suitable for all ages. They also offer a range of outfits designed and made exclusively for Nuit et Jour. Accessories include hats, jewellery, gloves and matching shoes and bags.

P.M. BALL GOWNS 158 Munster Road, Fulham, SW6
Tel: 071-371 7211

Contemporary evening gowns and cocktail wear can be hired or made to order for hire with one month's notice. Appointments are advisable.

PUTTIN' ON THE GLITZ Low Level Walkway, Hay's Galleria, Tooley Street, SE1 2HN
Tel: 071-403 8107
and at Galen Place, Pied Bull Court, Holborn, WC1 A 2JR
Tel: 071-404 5067

A sumptuous collection of ball gowns, cocktail and party dresses with matching gloves, bags, and jewellery can be found at each of their branches.

RITZY NIGHTS 41 St Quintin Avenue, W10 6NZ
Tel: 081-968 7371

The designer dresses for hire at Ritzy Nights range from short, young cocktail dresses to glamorous ball gowns in sizes from 6 to 20. There is even a selection of evening maternity wear - a very sensible idea. Accessories include jewellery, jackets and capes.

SCARLET RIBBONS 159 Dawes Road, Fulham, SW6 7EE
Tel: 071-381 5744

Scarlet Ribbons offers individually designed cocktail and evening dresses, jewellery, bags and gloves for hire. Wedding dresses are designed and made to order. Shoes and jewellery are for sale and they will also dye your shoes to match.

20th CENTURY FROX 614 Fulham Road, SW6 5RP
Tel: 071-731 3242

There is a wonderful selection of designer cocktail dresses, ball gowns, tops, skirts and jackets, day wear, hats, handbags and jewellery in sizes 6 to 16. They have an end of season sale every March and September so that there is new stock twice a year.

Dress Hire

Mens Formal Wear

A. KRITZ 19 Melcombe Street, NW1 6AG
Tel: 071-935 0304

Established in 1904, the company stocks evening and morning wear, white tie, white jackets and all accessories to hire or buy. They always have a selection of ex-hire stock for sale and offer a very personal service.

MOSS BROS H/O 8 St John's Hill, SW11 1SA
Tel: 071-924 1717 Fax: 071-350 0112

Moss Bros has exemplified the traditional image of formal wear hire for more than a century. With over 70 branches in the U.K., they offer morning, evening and Highland wear and page boy outfits with a wide range of accessories. Special rates are offered for corporate events and private parties. Phone or fax for a list of stockists.

NEAD 7 Ealing Broadway Station, Ealing, W5 2NU
Tel: 081-567 5039

Morning, day and evening suits with accessories and Highland wear are for hire or sale. Nead has been in the business for more than 35 years.

TUX 'N' TAILS BY LOSNERS 22 The Broadway, Stanmore, Middx
Tel: 081-954 4603

A good selection of morning and evening wear, tuxedos and accessories for men and boys can be found here. There is also a full range of ladies designer evening dresses for hire.

YOUNG AFTER DARK *(Right)*
Young Bride & Groom, 98 The Parade,
Watford, Herts WD1 2AW
Tel: 0923 249955

and

YOUNG BRIDE & GROOM, 7 Park Lane,
Wembley, Middx HA9 7RH
Tel: 081-902 6999

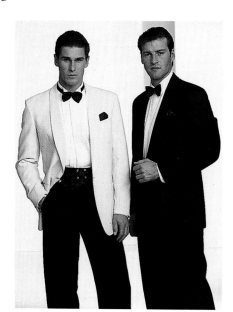

The company is owned by Victor Young who was originally managing director and menswear buyer of Youngs Formal Wear. He stocks a wide range of up-to-the-minute mens styling in evening wear, morning wear and accessories for men and boys.

YOUNGS FORMAL WEAR H/O Westminster Towers, 3
Albert Embankment, SE1 7SP
Tel: 071-587 3666

Youngs Formal Wear is the largest formal wear hire group in Britain with 115 branches nationwide - 11 of them in London. They stock high class, top style and quality designer ranges of evening, morning Highland and boys wear.

170

Period Costume and Fancy Dress Hire _____

AARDVARK FANCY DRESS HIRE 4 Ravey Street, EC2A 4QP
Tel: 071-739 3026

An extensive range of fancy dress, original 20th century period costume (20's, 30's. 40's, 50's, 60's and 70's) and historical costume available for hire.

ACT ONE HIRE 2a Scampston Mews, Cambridge Gardens, W10 6HX
Tel: 081-960 1456 Fax: 081-968 7843

A stunning collection of original authentic Victorian to 1950's clothes and accessories for women can be hired from this specialist company. They will dress you from top to toe in evening or day wear and everything from lingerie and shoes to jewellery and furs. To help you re-create an authentic atmosphere, Act One offer a consultation service on set decoration, special effects and lighting for the era or theme of your choice.

BERMANS 40 Camden Street, NW1 0EN
Tel: 071-387 0999 Fax: 071-383 5603

The world's premier costumier has over a million costumes which have actually been used on stage and screen. Some items still have the performer's name on the label.

CONTEMPORARY WARDROBE COLLECTION
Carlton House, 66-69 Great Queen Street, WC2B 5BZ
Tel: 071-242 4024 Fax: 071-430 2075

Over 10,000 original post-1950 fashion garments are stocked here and supplied to all over the world. They specialise in rock and pop fashion, such as outrageous Gary Glitter suits and film costumes. You can keep the complete outfits for three days.

COSTUME CALL 158 Munster Road, Fulham, SW6
Tel: 071-371 7211 Fax: 071-385 8526

At Costume Call you can hire period costumes, especially 18th century, Dickensian, Edwardian and Tudor, as well as traditional fancy dress costumes. The company will make any costume to order for hire, given one month's notice. Appointments are advisable.

COSTUME STUDIO 6 Penton Grove, off White Lion Street, N1 9HS
Tel: 071-388 4481 Fax: 071-837 5326

Historical and period costumes make up the bulk of the stock of over 3000 outfits at the Costume Studio. They also have animal and national costumes, uniforms and famous characters up to the 1970's, with corresponding accessories. Children's costumes are also available.

ESCAPADE 150 Camden High Street, NW1 0NE
Tel: 071-485 7384 Fax: 071-485 0950

Escapade has thousands of costumes for hire from giant bananas and gorillas to Louis XVI and Marie Antoinette for adults and children. They also sell hats, masks, make-up, wigs, disguises and party novelties.

LAURENCE CORNER 126-130 Drummond Street, NW1 2NV
Tel: 071-388 6811 Fax: 071-383 0334

There is a massive range of fancy dress and props (see Decorations), encompassing period,

171

Dress Hire

theatrical, topical, military, and themes for individual or group hire requirements. There are costumes for couples, characters from cult movies, fairy tales and musicals, personalities, animals, and objects ranging from Christmas trees to burgers.

MARDI GRAS 54 Browning Road, Manor Park, E12 6QZ
Tel: 081-472 2012 Fax: 081-472 5324

There are over 4000 hire costumes at Mardi Gras covering fancy dress (including animals and vegetables), military uniforms, period uniforms and costumes, chain mail with armour and weapons, spacewear, American sportswear, and national costumes. Outfits can be especially designed and made up for special promotions. They also stock a large selection of make-ups and hand-made beards and moustaches.

THEME TRADERS 16 North Square, NW11 7AD
Tel: 081-458 3253 Fax: 081-458 2462

Theme Traders specialise in providing theatrical costume and fancy dress in quantity - for staff at a theme party or for guests when costumes are being provided by the host for example. They use a mobile unit which includes facilities for make-up and styling. They also stock theme decorations and props (see Decorations). Viewing is by appointment only.

LOCATION
Venue
Marquee

FOOD & DRINK
Caterer
Wines, Spirits, Soft drinks
Cakes
Chocolates, Petits fours

HIRE
Tables, Chairs
Cutlery, Crockery, Glasses
Table linen
Catering equipment

DECORATION
Flowers
Balloons
Props
Lighting, special effects
Party decorations

ENTERTAINMENT
Agency
Band
Discotheque
Magician, Novelty act
Cabaret
Participation event
After-dinner speaker
Casino, Amusements
Fireworks

TOASTMASTER

PHOTOGRAPHY
Photographer
Video maker

STATIONERY
Invitations
Calligrapher
Menus
Place cards
Table plan
Other

TRANSPORT
Car
Carriage
Coach, Mini bus
Other

STAFF
Waiters, Waitresses
Bar staff
Cloakroom staff
Butler
Security
Cleaning
Valet Parking

TABLE GIFTS
Ladies' gifts
Gentlemen's gifts
Bonboniere, Chocolates
Crackers
Novelties

DRESS HIRE
Ladies' dress hire
Men's formal wear
Costumes, Fancy dress
Staff uniforms

INSURANCE

Index

Index